Edited on behalf
of the German Association
for American Studies by
REINHARD R. DOERRIES
GERHARD HOFFMANN
ALFRED HORNUNG

WILFRIED RAUSSERT

Negotiating Temporal Differences

Blues, Jazz and Narrativity in African American Culture

Universitätsverlag
C. WINTER
Heidelberg

Die Deutsche Bibliothek – CIP-Einheitsaufnahme

Raussert, Wilfried:
Negotiating temporal differences: blues, jazz and narrativity
in African American culture /
Wilfried Raussert. – Heidelberg: Winter, 2000

(American studies: Vol. 87)
Zugl.: Oxford (Miss.), Univ., Diss., 1995

ISBN 3-8253-1113-9

COVER PICTURE
Wilfried Raussert: Playing the Changes

ISBN 3-8253-1113-9

Contents

Acknowledgments...VII

Introduction.. 1

I. Concepts of Musical Time and Narrativity: Blues, Jazz and the
   African American Novel... 3

II. Discovering Musical Time for the Representation of History:
   Langston Hughes and the Harlem Renaissance... 17

III. Learning How to Play the Changes: Ralph Ellison and
   Temporary Patterns against the Flux of History.. 47

IV. Crossing Temporal Boundaries: Toni Morrison—Individual and
   Communal Concepts of History 75

V. Musical Time and Multicultural Aesthetics: Ishmael Reed and a
   Denial of Closure 105

VI. Blues, Jazz and Women's Time: Ntozake Shange and Feminine
   Visions of History 131

Afterword 161

Bibliography.. 165

Acknowledgments

Several friends inside and outside the academic world were essential to the creation and completion of the book at hand. Since this work started its life as a dissertation, the members of my committee at the University of Mississippi—Ann Fisher-Wirth, William Ferris, Jay Watson, and Deborah Barker—deserve my first thanks, for their encouragement, insight and criticism. Moreover, I want to thank Maryemma Graham and Jerry Ward, Jr., for their initial encouragement of this interdisciplinary study. Thanks also to John Lowe whose suggestions for revision and extension helped me complete the book.

I am grateful to all the people at the Center for the Study of Southern Culture that provided me with insightful suggestions about African American folklore and music. Their generous advice guided me on my academic journey through the rich diversity of African American lore that I found in libraries, the blues archive, the Delta Blues museum, and numerous exhibitions of African American folk art such as sculpture and quilt-making in the South.

Finally, I want to thank Alfred Hornung for his editorial help, André Roggan for helping me print the various drafts of this manuscript, and my wife and daughter, Susanne and Friederike, who tolerated my frequent disappearances into my study as well as my occasional trips back to Mississippi. And, in the end, I want to express my deep gratitude to Colby Kullman who always made me feel at home whenever I returned to the University of Mississippi.

Introduction

"It don't mean a thing if it ain't got that swing."
(Duke Ellington)

As an art form within time music responds to changes of outer time more immediately than other artistic modes of expression within the spectrum of African American culture. Of course, music engages a very close relationship with time across cultural boundaries. African American music, though, gives voice to a particularly complex understanding of individual and collective temporal experience. As an intercultural artistic expression African American music has developed and expressed time conceptions which unfold within an aesthetic space in between fixed cultural entities. Hence, blues and jazz, two of the most prominent features of African American music, stand at the crossroads of various temporal levels and conceptions.

The study at hand will examine the complexity of these musical modes in their relation to African American ways of rendering time. Due to music's pivotal role within African American culture, temporal conceptions expressed through various modes of rhythm and performance have turned into "models of time" on a larger cultural scale. Therefore, the music's complex rhythmic progression shapes the ways in which temporal experience is perceived and artistically represented in other African American art forms. This is especially true on the level of narrativity, as we find it in the African American novel.

Most approaches to African American fiction which draw on blues and/or jazz as critical tropes fail to acknowledge that blues and jazz are first of all musical modes of expression. When critics claim that the literary text "swings" or creates a "blues mood," they hardly ever legitimize their point of view by referring to musical criteria derived from blues or jazz directly. However, it is the musical quality of these forms which reveals the complex understanding of time within African American culture. Hence, in many instances, there remains a gap in the critical methodology which draws on jazz and blues as critical tools for literary and cultural studies. The terminology often appears vague and the choice of tropes arbitrary. Naturally, boundaries between media can become cutting edges and an intermedial approach to the study of African American culture always runs the risk of "not to be able to bridge the gap." It is moreover true that common cultural roots of oral, musical, and written discourse do not necessarily imply equivalence.

A criticial approach, however, that preserves the epistemological status of both media promises new insights as concerns the interaction of music and literature. Hence, my study differs from those forms of African American criticism that draw on musical tropes as cultural signs primarily. Of course, the blues becomes a striking cultural trope in Houston A. Baker's ideological reflections on his blues-inflected theory of black culture. Henry L. Gates, Jr., too, resorts to jazz when he develops his theory of signifying within the black cultural discourse. Both, yet, neglect to see that blues and jazz are primarily forms of musical expression. The impact of blues and jazz, on a temporal level in particular, is more pervasive—thematically and structurally—than the critical configuration of blues and jazz as merely abstract cultural tropes is able to suggest. Only in the context of musical form and performance do blues and jazz unfold their true potential as critical tropes. Starting out from this point of view, my study pursues a systematic approach to a so far unexplored temporal dimension which emerges from the influence of music on literature. As a result, a double reading strategy underlies the progression of this study.

While the first chapter analyzes the temporal dimension of blues and jazz in its relation to musical and cultural concepts of time, the subsequent chapters shift back and forth between music and literature. Two narrative strategies emerge accordingly. The first deals with the temporal dimension of music— time in music and music in time. Historically, this dimension undergoes metamorphoses, as diverse styles of blues and jazz emerge from early to postmodern forms of African American music. On a textual level, the reader will encounter the musical experiments with time and rhythm of various blues and jazz musicians such as Louis Armstrong, Bessie Smith, Ma Rainey, Count Basie, Charlie Parker, John Coltrane, Ornette Coleman, and James 'Son' Thomas among others. The second narrative strategy tells the story of the continuous yet changing impact of blues and jazz on time conceptions in the African American novel. As concerns the development of the literary genre, the scope of my analysis stretches from the Harlem Renaissance to the contemporary period. The reader will face the analysis of five key texts of the African American novel tradition of the 20th century in relation to musical experimentation with time. As the choice of five novelists underscores, my study does not aspire to give an all-inclusive history of the musical impact on the black novel. Rather, I am interested in the continuity and changes of the musical influence on the narrative discourse.

Whereas the temporal dimension of this intermedial process is the major concern of this study, other elements are closely linked to questions of time within the interrelation of music and literature: the impact of musical form on literary form, the use of music as paradigm for the understanding of historical time, the significance of memory as related to the music's cultural roots, and, finally, the interaction between musical time and visionary aspects of the texts. These temporal aspects represent my chosen strategic possibilities in discussing the interrelation of musical and literary conceptions of time within the African American cultural discourse.

Berlin
Wilfried Raussert

I. Concepts of Musical Time and Narrativity: Blues, Jazz and the African American Novel

The experience of time and the way it is rendered in jazz's handling of musical time reveal significant aspects of African American cultural contributions to the multicultural spectrum of the United States.[1] It is in the dimension of time that the process of cultural hybridization stands forth the strongest. And it is music which has responded to the experience of time in the most immediate and intense way throughout African American history.[2] Hence, I will focus on the relation of African American music to different conceptions of time—musical and cultural. Starting from the thesis that African American music—jazz in particular—created a complex sense of musical time, I will explore the ways in which this musical time adopts various time levels and mediates between them. Jazz represents an intercultural art form which was developed by African Americans within American culture. As a hybrid mode of expression, it reflects not only a diversity of musical traditions but also an awareness of diverging concepts of time. Indeed, jazz negotiates between musically and culturally different conceptions of time in an innovative manner. It is characterized by a fusion of temporal continuity and discontinuity. Breaks in jazz interact with progressive and recurrent elements of musical time. Through its emphasis on the moment—there time levels intersect and gain new significance—jazz exposes the significance of the "now" for conceptions of time within African American culture. As a "musical creole," to borrow a term from Berndt Ostendorf, it brought about a unique African American rendering of time which unfolds itself as the result of the encounter of Western and African time conceptions in the United States. This becomes most audible in jazz's swinging progression.

As an African American idiom jazz expresses a specifically modernist concern with the present as well as an avant-garde impulse. Each style in jazz

---

1   Numerous cultural studies publications in recent years document a reawakened interest in questions concerning time and memory within academia. I want to refer here to a few important texts. My selection is by no means comprehensive: John Bender and David E. Wellbery, eds., *Chronotypes: The Construction of Time* (Stanford: Stanford UP, 1991), Homi K. Bhabha, "'Race,' Time and the Revision of Modernity," *Oxford Literary Review* 13.1-2 (1991): 193-219, Michael Kammen, *Meadows of Memory: Images of Time and Tradition in American Art and Culture* (Austin: U of Texas P, 1992), Richard Terdiman, *Present Past: Modernity and the Memory Crisis* (Ithaca, NY: Cornell UP, 1993), Homi K. Bhabha, *The Location of Culture* (London: Routledge, 1994), and Hannah Möckel-Rieke, "Introduction: Media and Cultural Memory," *Amerikastudien / American Studies* 43.1 (1998): 5-17.

2   See Robert Walser, ed. *Keeping Time: Readings in Jazz History* (New York: Oxford UP, 1999) vii. As Walser explains in his preface, jazz musicians organize the flow of experience in keeping time.

embraced new rhythmic vitality resulting from changes in melody and harmony. Every renewal brought about harmonic and rhythmic expansions as the music retained "its immediacy and its emotional concurrency with contemporary life."[3] Through a series of fast-paced changes in style—New Orleans jazz, swing, bebop, cool jazz, free jazz—jazz embodied the spirit of the avant-garde with its yearning for constant renewal.[4] And it has remained an inspiration for the avant-garde arts throughout the 20th century.

Jazz, however, also experiments with a sense of time prevalent in African cultures such as Yoruba and Bantu. African cultures generally view time from a holistic perspective. Accordingly, past, present, and future exist simultaneously. Historically, Egyptian culture did not even provide an abstract term for time. An understanding of time has always been directly related to specific events or actions. Time, thus, remains neutral until an incident marks its significance.[5] Accordingly, concepts of simultaneity and intensity characterize an African experience of time. The notion of an abstract temporal sequence is absent from African thinking.[6]

---

[3]   Martin Williams, *The Jazz Tradition* (New York: Oxford UP, 1993) 49. Through its immediate response to historical changes, jazz draws on the tradition of African American folk music. Referring to the Delta region of Mississippi in particular, Alan Lomax points out that the changing presence of technology has had a tremendous and immediate impact on the development of folk music and work songs. Three major modes of transport and communication established a link between the Delta and the outside world; while the steamboat inspired the content of work songs in the early plantation era, the railroad informed the songs about sharecropping and black migration. Finally, the highway provided the background against which songs about rural displacement and solitary travelling could emerge. As Lomax puts it, "Coahoma County musical history had three periods, each signaled by a typical sound—a steamboat blowing for a landing, a locomotive whistling on a three-mile grade, and a Greyhound bus blaring down Highway 61." Alan Lomax, *The Land Where the Blues Began* (London: Minerva, 1995) 143-44.

[4]   Berndt Ostendorf points out that jazz mediates a cultural contradiction: "Though socially a subculture, it has been an aesthetic avant-garde since the time of Armstrong's Hot Five." See Berndt Ostendorf, "Ralph Waldo Ellison: Anthropolgy, Modernism, and Jazz," *New Essays on Invisible Man*, ed. Robert O'Meally (Cambridge: Cambridge UP, 1988) 95-121; 117.

[5]   See also Houston A. Baker, Jr., *The Workings of the Spirit: The Poetics of Afro-American Women's Writing* (Chicago: U of Chicago P, 1991) 199. Baker points out that time is here closely related to the specific place where the event occurs. In modern aesthetics this connection of time and place gains important momentum within Western culture, too. As Gerhard Hoffmann elucidates, the interrelatedness of time and space finds its artistic expression in modern novels by James Joyce, Marcel Proust, and William Faulkner as well as in the futurist experiments among the visual artists. Cf. Gerhard Hoffmann, *Raum, Situation, erzählte Wirklichkeit: Poetologische und historische Studien zum englischen und amerikanischen Roman* (Stuttgart: Metzler, 1978) 8.

[6]   See Wolfgang Achtner, Stefan Kuntz and Thomas Walter, *Dimensionen der Zeit: Die Zeitstrukturen Gottes, der Welt und des Menschen* (Darmstadt: Primus Verlag, 1998) 31.

Obviously such a conception marks a clear difference to its counterpart in Western cultures. Due to the impact of technology which has supported a mechanical sense of temporal progression, a rational time model predominates in Western cultures. Teleology and progress are its major characteristics. Accordingly, past, present, and future form a temporal sequence which follows a linear pattern.[7] And the avant-gardes—in their aesthetic and technological manifestations—have demonstrated that a future-oriented thinking has prevailed in modern Western societies since the 19th-century. As a blending of European march rhythms—a linear, progressive rhythmic pattern underlies them—with rhythmic elements of African American call-and-response patterns, jazz represents an African American musical creation out of hybrid cultural influences.[8]

Both musical and cultural notions of time clash in the development of jazz.[9] As an intercultural art form jazz translates the tensions between an African and

---

7   See Achtner 76-77.

8   During slavery Africans could not continue their musical traditions as they wished. Black codes such as the banning of drums in many parts of the United States left them culturally uprooted and economically repressed. Therefore, a process of assimilation to and reinterpretation of European musical forms characterizes the beginnings of African American music. While the process of acculturation was forced upon African Americans during their early history, aesthetic and commercial interests have spurred cultural exchange in the field of African American music in recent decades. See Helmut Rösing, "Interkultureller Musikaustausch," eds. Herbert Bruhn and Helmut Rösing, *Musikwissenschaft: Ein Grundkurs* (Reinbek: rowohlts enzyklopädie, 1998) 289-310; 291-92. Only in rather isolated areas of the United States could African elements persist for a longer period of time. The people of the sea islands of Georgia and the Carolinas as well as the black families living in the Talladega Forest of Alabama were separated from white influence. Therefore they could keep fragments of African speech, for instance. The black field hands in the Mississippi Delta were more isolated from white influence than most other groups of black population in the South. Hence the music they developed remained closer to African roots, the impact of white folk music almost absent. See Samuel Charters, *The Bluesmen: The Story and the Music of the Men who Made the Blues* (New York: Oak Publications, 1967) 27.

9   Music in contrast to sculpture and painting is seen as an art form within time. Musicologists and composers differentiate between two major time frames in which music evolves. They distinguish between lived and measured time, between personal and ontological time. Different epochs in musical history have produced diverging preferences for either one. The music of the romantic period is generally regarded as having emerged from a lived sense of time. The subjective experience of time for the act of composition is most important here. A lived sense of time becomes essential especially for the late romantics. Bach's music, on the other hand, has been interpreted as a musical expression of an ontological time concept. His music, according to critics, represents an expression of cosmic time, lived time remains subordinate. See for this distinction Joachim-Ernst Berendt, *Das Jazzbuch: Von New Orleans bis in die achtziger Jahre* (1991; Frankfurt/Main: Fischer Taschenbuch Verlag, 1993) 258-59. In my reading of musical time, a lived sense of time refers to the individual expression, a measured sense of time to basic rhythmic patterns or a form of group consensus. While this differentiation of time relates to musical style, the difference between African and European time concepts underlying musical progression is first of all cultural.

a Western sense of time rhythmically. The emerging dynamic movement which expresses jazz's unique sense of time is called swing. Here the rhythmic stiffness of European march appears softened; already early forms of jazz transformed the rigid rhythm into a flexible progression. Hence, polyrhythmic effects result from a shift of the rhythmical feel; strict bar patterns, for instance, give way to a rhythm of 12/8 superimposed over a basic 4/5 time.[10] As "changing same" critics like Carlo Bohländer describe the feeling of tension-release emerging from jazz's swinging movement.[11] The paradox behind this terminology well captures a complex African sense of time in which recurrent and progressive elements intersect. Swing, accordingly, subverts the idea of time as a linear, teleological process. Although it postulates a regularity of temporal progression—the influence of European marches becomes audible here—it continuously disrupts and even negates such a regular movement. A polyrhythmic effect—African sources manifest themselves—results from a flexible change of beat sequences.

A closer look at black dance helps extend our understanding of temporal differences between Western and African rhythms. Rhythmic elements in African music are multidimensional in space and time, as can be seen in the dances they evoke. Different from European dances which signify a bodily movement through space, African rhythms call forth a dance movement which is bound to a certain place. Kinetic energy in European dances tends to lead to a forward movement; in African dances it translates a polycentric movement on the spot. Whereas the dancer's body exerts movements in various dimensions, the dancer hardly ever leaves the place where she began to dance. Anthropological studies have pointed out, that the African dancer uses various body centers for the dance movements whereas the European dancer's body represents "a stiff linear unit in space."[12] Diverse body centers within the African dance performance create kinetic transformations; several physical movements take place simultaneously. Furthermore, the body movements can be seen as an expression of a polyrhythmic feeling since they have their own sense of pace and accent and are not necessarily coincidental with the rhythms played by the drums or marked by hand clappings. African American jazz dance fuses polycentric movements with spatial movements. In jazz dance motion and locomotion are differentiated. While the first category refers to the polycentric movement of the body—head, shoulders, arms, legs, chest, and pelvis form

---

10   For a more extensive definition of swing see Peter Wicke and Wieland Ziegenrücker, *Sachlexikon Populärmusik* (Leipzig: Deutsche Verlagsgesellschaft, 1987) 233. See also Alan Dawson and Don Demichael, *A Manual for the Modern Drummer* (Boston: Berklee Press, 1962) 86.

11   Cf. Carlo Bohländer, *Die Anatomie des swing* (1985; Frankfurt/Main: Jas Publikation, 1986) 12.

12   John Lovell, Jr., *Black Song: The Forge and the Flame: The Story of How the Afro-American Spiritual Was Hammered Out* (New York: The Macmillan Company, 1972) 44.

independent centers of motion—the second category—jazzwalks, for instance—signifies a movement from one point to another.[13] The presence of a multidimensional movement displays that the "now" is essential for African American time conceptions. The latter is an important temporal and spatial crossroad. Horizontal, vertical, diagonal movements express a complex spatial movement. And it is the single moment in which the dancer acts out diverse movements simultaneously.[14] She adds her own expression of experienced time and rhythm to the basic rhythmic pattern guiding her dance movements.

The multidimensional dance movements find their musical equivalent in the jazz musicians' handling of the beat. Jazz musicians aspire to a specific interpretation of the beat in order to avoid monotony of progression. Every beat has to be seen as an upward and downward movement. It comes into being, gains momentum, and reaches its climax of intensity; then it fades and, finally, vanishes.[15] Its point of beginning overlaps with the vanishing point of the preceding beat. While the intensity of the first beat loses its momentum, the next one is approaching its climax. The latter is not only the final point of a growing movement; it also represents the starting point of a falling movement. The fact that both movements can be experienced simultaneously demonstrates why the rhythmic quality of jazz has come to be seen as a musical expression of time conceptions which create the impression that past and future coexist at the same time. The present emerges from a simultaneous experience of past and future, the experience of the vanishing and rising beat.[16]

Crossing boundaries between temporal dimensions gains cultural significance, too. Jazz burials in New Orleans, for instance, take up the concept of simultaneity.[17] Ever since the earliest manifestations of jazz in New Orleans, black jazz musicians frequently have been honored by a musical ritual accompanying the burial ceremonies. While the jazz band usually plays a slow

13   See Christina Rosenberg, *Handbuch für Jazz Dance* (Aachen: Meyer und Meyer, 1995) 36-60.

14   The impact of American popular culture—strongly influenced by African American musical expressions—brought elements of African American rhythms to Europe and other continents. Rock and pop music translated African American rhythms into a popular idiom. Similarly, African American dance has continued to exert its influence on other cultures. While differences remain, an absolute separation of African American dance from European dance, then, can no longer be upheld nowadays.

15   See also Stephan Richter, *Zu einer Ästhetik des Jazz* (Frankfurt/Main: Peter Lang Europäische Hochschulschriften, 1995) 123-24. As Richter points out, jazz rhythmically confronts the audience with the ever-present process of creation following a process of fading.

16   Cf. Erich Ferstl, *Die Schule des Jazz mit 104 Notenbeispielen* (München: Nymphenburger Verlagshandlung, 1963) 44. See also Joe Viera, *Jazz: Musik unserer Zeit* (Schaftlach: Oreos Collection Jazz, 1992) 60. Viera points out that the beat should not be mistaken as a means to order or control time in a strict sense; instead, it represents a musical event—easy, light, flexible. Jazz develops a technique of changing beats which, in contrast to Western music, is more open and flexible.

17   See also Joachim-Ernst Berendt, *Das Jazzbuch* 26.

rhythm on the way to the graveyard, a sudden shift to an intensified beat due to playing double time characterizes the music performed when the band accompanies the mourning community on its way back. Double time leads to an intensification of the beat. The sad and melancholy music that initiated the burial ceremony is replaced by a joyful music inspiring the mourners to dance.[18] In their rendering of rhythm, jazz musicians in New Orleans symbolically cross the line not only between past and present but also between life and death.

Rhythm, in general, reflects the way in which music is organized within the temporal dimension. In terms of musical progression, rhythm signifies a sequence of unaccented and accented beats and their relation to one another. Western music—European art music in particular—tends to follow a regular pattern according to which pulses are divided into equal subgroups. African American music, on the contrary, embraces cross-rhythms, offbeat-phrasing, and polymeter.[19] African American musicians, then, welcome the act of manipulating the basic pulse while improvising rhythmically. Put briefly, the musicians play around the beat. These changes of the pulse open up numerous possibilities for individual improvisations. Thus the musician is able to express his time experience rhythmically. Dwight D. Andrews points out two jazz pieces in which the pulse is manipulated individually. Louis Armstrong's solo on *Big Butter and Egg Man* (1926) and his duet with Earl "Fatha" Hines in *Weather Bird* (1928) illustrate these individual changes.[20] Through his ability to obscure the beat by either speeding up or slowing down the tempo of his improvisations, Armstrong, according to Andrews, succeeds in mastering time "by playing against it."[21]

The technique of changing the beat which characterizes much of rhythmic progression within African American music finds a melodic parallel in the way black musicians change the sound. Hammering, pulling, or sliding the strings of the guitar, for instance, many blues musicians detach the sound of the instrument from that of the performance and notation of regular European art music. Blues musicians such as Robert Johnson and Elmore James developed

---

18   The crowd following the band after burial ceremonies has a fixed place in the New Orleans jazz tradition as "the second line." Many a jazz musician started his musical career as "second-liner," as did Louis Armstrong following the jazz bands in the poorer black quarters of New Orleans in the early twentieth century.

19   This rhythmic distinction between cultures tends to blur when we listen to rock music. See also my footnote 12 on jazz dance.

20   Dwight D. Andrews, "From Black to Blues," *Sacred Music of the Secular City*, ed. Jon M. Spencer (Duke UP: A Special Issue of *Black Sacred Music: A Journal of Theomusicology*, Spring 1992) 45-54; 52-53.

21   Andrews, "From Black to Blues" 53.

these techniques into sophisticated guitar performances.[22] Moreover, there seems a special preference for muddying clear sounds in the African American music tradition. This is true for both intrumental and singing techniques. The gutbucket sounds of jazz trumpeters who played into brass spitoons during the early years of New Orleans jazz and the singing techniques of Mahalia Jackson and James Brown provide striking examples.[23] In blues and jazz sound and regular time patterns are distorted or disrupted.

This phenomenon in regard to vocal techniques can be illustrated by a closer look at the singing styles of the classical blues singers. The modes of performance, for instance, shape Alberta Hunter's rendering of musical time in *Nobody Knows the Way I Feel This Mornin'*. Following the lead of Bessie Smith and Clara Smith, her singing style is "open, unembellished, focused on feeling rather than pulse or tempo, deeply simpatico and emotionally expressive."[24] Harrison's description emphasizes Hunter's concern with expressiveness and intensity. Pulse or tempo are only secondary forms of guidance for her way of singing *Nobody Knows the Way I Feel This Mornin'*. Techniques like antiphonic breaks give every word or line its full expressive potential. Hence, the single word as semantic equivalent to the moment in time assumes a particular significance. Thus the women of the classical blues period introduced and refined vocal techniques which added expressive power to the lyrics of the blues songs. Through their experiments with aspects of musical time they created a process of building up tension and then releasing it. Such sort of movement occurs at various points in the vocal performance:

> Some of these were instrumentality, voices growling and sliding like trombones, or wailing and piercing like clarinets; unexpected word stress; vocal breaks in antiphony with the accompaniment; syncopated phrasing; unlimited improvisation on repetitions, refrains or phrases. These innovations, in tandem with the talented instrumentalists who accompanied the blues women, advanced the development of vocal and instrumental jazz.[25]

Not only did these techniques support experiments in vocal and instrumental jazz, they also demonstrate an individualized form of handling musical time. Especially when the voice departs from the basic accompaniment or changes the word stress spontaneously, it expresses a radically individual sense of musical time. The steady progression of the rhythm is subverted when blues singers

---

22 Important contributions to various blues styles as developed by blues guitarists can be found in Jas Obrecht, ed. *Blues Guitar: The Men Who Made the Music*, 2nd edition (San Francisco: Miller Freeman Books, 1993).

23 See Robert Palmer, *Deep Blues* (New York: Penguin Books, 1981) 30.

24 Daphne Duval Harrison, Black Pearls: Blues Queens of the 1920s (Brunswick: Rutgers UP, 1988) 209.

25 Harrison 221.

such as Bessie Smith resort to antiphonic breaks. Disrupting the flow of the basic pulse, the singer emphasizes the moment of performance which then gains temporal significance. According to Bernd Ostendorf, "the true jazz moment could be defined as ecstatic creativity in transience. The jazz session is an ephemeral happening in which creation, reception, composition, and performance become one."[26] The act of performance, then, enables the singer to add a new experience of time to the performance, as she can turn away from the basic pattern to enter a new time level. Hence, the notion of syncopation—a regular pattern of beat change in Western music—does not describe the changes of beat in jazz sufficiently. Rather, the jazz musician sets the beat according to his own sense of musical time. His experience of time interacts with a regular rhythmic design. A lived sense of time, accordingly, superimposes itself upon the measured sense of time represented by the basic rhythmic pattern.

A complex interaction of various time levels can be found in New Orleans jazz. Different melodic lines—primarily played by cornet, tuba (or trumpet), and clarinet—express a diverse spectrum of individual time. This variety encounters the regular pulse—in later days its swinging variation—of the underlying rhythmic progression. Most recordings of New Orleans jazz that were made in Chicago document such temporal complexity. Here the polyphonic and swinging style of New Orleans jazz reached its most fully developed stage. At the end of the 1920s, however, the collective improvisational style got under commercial pressure. Mainstream culture called for a homophonic style with a distinct differentiation between solo and accompaniment and, in the music business, these new arrangements were generally considered more suitable for raising record sales. Therefore a reduction of temporal and rhythmic complexity resulted from this tendency toward homophonic sound and effective arrangement.[27]

While the separation between soloist and accompanying group marked the heydays of the swing era, a more intense interaction between various musical expressions of time accompanies a renewed emphasis on group improvisations in free jazz. As a result, ametrical progressions emerge which do not swing in the conventional way. A relaxed structuring of time evolves, however, as high tempi merge with a pulsating basic rhythm.[28] It forms the flexible basis for group and solo improvisations. Within this loose structure the moment of experienced time becomes the matrix for improvising motives or runs. A duo improvisation by Charlie Haden on trumpet and Ornette Coleman on alto sax provides a good example:

---

26   Berndt Ostendorf, "Ralph Waldo Ellison: Anthropology, Modernism, and Jazz" 113.

27   Herbert Hellhund, "Jazz: Traditionslinien zwischen Folklore, Kommerz und Kunst," *Amerikanische Musik seit Charles Ives: Interpretationen, Quellentexte, Komponistenmonographien*, eds. Herman Danuser, Dietrich Kämper and Paul Terse (Laaber: Laaber-Verlag, 1987) 39-49; 43.

28   Hellhund 48.

> After the theme of *Free*, trumpet and alto engage in a brief duo improvisation during which Coleman discovers a solo-generating cell in a rising phrase. But that initiating motive is abandoned a half minute later, when he finds a three-note motive, which then becomes a trill phrase, a long zigzag phrase, repeated rising phrases, a longer snaking phrase—and so on, in multiple disguises throughout the rest of the solo. . . . Coleman's motivic evolution is a matter of continually reshaping the initiating cell. Even if specific intervals become approximate, the rhythmic shape remains, intact, compressed, or extended; far less commonly, the intervallic shape remains while the rhythmic shape is distorted; the cell motive is heard at the beginning, within, or at the end of phrases; it is upended, turned on its side, and viewed from different perspectives again and again; its meaning is altered and renewed.[29]

In free jazz the motives are developed through the interaction of the group. Musical ideas of the soloist are paraphrased and transformed and then given back to their originator. Hence, various expressions of lived time mold the progression of a jazz piece and shape its fundamental repetition-variation pattern, as the process of "reshaping the initiating cell" demonstrates. The juxtaposition and merging of different shades of experienced time brings forth an intense interaction between musicians and a constant exchange of musical ideas out of the moment emerges from this process.

According to Ostendorf's definition of the 'jazz moment,' performance and reception become an inseparable temporal unit in the intensity of the instant. Hence, both signal the idea of shared time. This is true for jazz and blues, perhaps the former's most important musical backbone. A level of spontaneous communication between the musicians and audience we can detect in the blues house parties, as they occur in the Mississippi Delta.[30] During these blues sessions the lyrics are made up collectively. Various members of a band or listeners join in and actively participate in the progression of the blues pieces. Narrative and music intertwine, especially when the blues is played in very intimate situations. The blues musician opens the blues with spoken narration and sometimes adds narrative parts during the performance. William Ferris describes the interaction of blues talk and blues playing when he depicts a blues gathering in the Mississippi Delta:

---

[29] John Litweiler, *The Freedom Principle: Jazz After 1958* (New York: William Morrow and Company, Inc., 1984) 37-38.

[30] This communicative aspect have their aesthetic matrix in the blues' basic pattern which emerges from a call-and-response structure. According to Keil, "a blues chorus or verse usually falls into a 4/4 twelve bar pattern, divided into three call-and-response sections with the over-all rhyme scheme of A A B. . . . There is something like a double dialectic to be found in many blues renditions: on one level every sung phrase is balanced or commented upon by an instrumental response that often carries as important a message as the preceding words. Following this interaction the blues chorus can be divided into six parts of overlapping vocal calls and instrumental responses." Charles Keil, *Urban Blues* (Chicago: U of Chicago P, 1991) 51-52.

> Bluesmen 'talk the blues' with the power and eloquence of their music, for
> both spoken and sung performances describe the same emotional core. Blues
> speech comments on the black man's condition and shows how the artist
> studies his people and voices their experiences. As in the music, his
> audience responds to the impact of blues narrative with comments like
> "Yeah," "That's right," and "Tell it like it is."[31]

The flexibility of the performance reflects a continuous pattern interspersed
with discontinuous elements. The actual performance turns into a perpetual
change between production and reception.

As the cited above example illustrates, jazz's negotiation between time
levels characterizes the act of reception, too. Two levels of lived time interact
when musicians and listeners communicate during the performance. On the one
hand there is the sense of relative time experienced by the musician; on the
other hand there is the experience of the performance by the audience. Both
time levels overlap when shouts from the audience or calls from the musicians
open a direct form of communication. Frequently the performance takes a new
direction thus. The listener leaves his passive role of reception and takes part in
the act of performance. The musicians in turn respond to the audience
immediately and directly.

This communal experience of time in the present finds its roots musically
and historically in the call-and-response pattern. Especially group activities
among African Americans in the New World provided the basis for African
American adaptations of the this musical technique. Apart from the church
services—the overlapping of leader and chorus were distinctive traits of sacred
music, too—, the working world brought forth musical forms based on
polyphonic progression.[32] Work songs, field songs, boat songs and levee songs

---

31   William Ferris, *Blues from the Delta* (New York: Anchor Books, 1979) 41. For the communal
      experience of blues talk and blues performance see the chapter on "The House Party" 115-
      130. Within very private settings, make-ups shape the progression of a blues tune. At a dance,
      for instance, the blues musician includes comments on people on the dance floor in his lyrics
      while performing. During a private dance party in the Mississippi Delta, folk blues singer
      James "Son" Thomas composed a make-up in which he dedicated four out of six stanzas to
      Poppa Jazz, at whose home the dance took place. Jazz's name was inserted in the lyrics various
      times with specific reference to his abilities with women. For the complete text of the lyrics see
      Blues from the Delta 64-65.

32   See Marshall W. Stearns, *The Story of Jazz* (1956; New York: Oxford UP 1970) 123-39.
      Stearns discusses the call-and-response pattern at length. Dance performances were closely
      linked to praise meetings in the 19th century. As an expression and outburst of their religious
      fervor, African Americans performed ring-shouts as an immediate follow-up to praise meetings.
      Clapping hands and beating time with their feet, they created the rhythmic accompaniment to
      their singing and shouting physically. Other members of the congregation joined the rhythm
      and singing group in the form of a dance circle. At times they participated with the singing
      activities. Not seldom, these dance performances lasted up to an hour. Along with the ring-
      shouts, the song-sermon and the spiritual resulted from the blending of African, African
      American, and European music, all manifesting the communal and collective significance of

represent the diverse musical material which emerged from musical patterns of call-and-response. They all suggest an individual as well as a group response to the experience of time. Through the interaction between individual and community within these musical forms, the barrier between personal and collective time experience collapses at least for the moment of performance. A shared sense of time evolves which demonstrates that distinctions between performers and audience have tended to blur in African and African American forms of music.[33]

Musical time, as rendered in jazz's swinging and polyrhythmic movement, bears cultural meaning beyond the musical discourse.[34] Jazz's negotiations between various time levels brought forth a rhythmic complexity which has shaped aspects of narrativity in particular. Since the Harlem Renaissance African American musical forms have had an impact on the development of the written expression—primarily within African American culture but also outside of it, think of writers such as Robert Creeley and Jack Kerouac. The Harlem Renaissance marks the point from which folklore/oral tradition is no longer looked down upon as simplistic or inferior. Rather, folklore—black music in particular—shapes the literary imagination of authors such as Langston Hughes, Sterling Brown, Zora Neale Hurston, and Claude McKay who make use of the vernacular resorting to its various cultural, social and linguistic functions. The intellectual climate of the time was characterized by an increasing interest in jazz and the study of African arts and cultures. The emergence of an African "craze" at the time was the result of both popular and intellectual effort. Against this cultural background music steadily established its presence in the literary text. Many novelists selected a musician for protagonist: Claude McKay in his novel Banjo (1929), for instance. Many poets resorted to blues as theme and

---

black musical performances. With an intensified emphasis on harmony and melody, the concert spiritual bore more European traits than any other form of African American music. But even then, the call-and-response pattern shaped the musical progression decisively. A combination of voices produced a heterophonic sound, the result of a complex interaction of the leading voice and those who backed it up. Ever since plantation times, this style of performance has endured in the tradition of African American church singing. The call-and-response pattern took on economic meaning, too, as the performances of spasm bands in New Orleans at the turn from the 19th to the 20th century illustrate. The musicians' immediate contact with the audience on street corners signified an essential source for the way they improvised collectively. Shouts and comments from the audience were often responsible for the direction an improvisation would take. The fact that spasm bands like most other jazz bands depended upon tips underlines the significant influence of the audience upon the music. Not only did they have to play specific blues, jazz or popular tunes, they also had to adjust the mode of playing to the listeners' taste. Hence, they had to play "hot" or "sweet" upon the audiences' request.

[33] See Robert Palmer, *Deep Blues* 28.

[34] For a most recent collection of essays and texts dealing with the omnipresent effect of jazz on diverse aspects of American culture see Robert O'Meally, ed., *The Jazz Cadence of American Culture* (New York: Columbia UP, 1998).

form in developing African American verse; Sterling A. Brown's "Ma Rainey" (1932) and Frank Marshall Davis' "Cabaret" (1935) are significant examples.

Discussing the impact of African American music on literature and culture, Craig Hansen Werner speaks of three basic musical impulses which manifest themselves in the written discourse: the gospel, the blues, and the jazz impulse. In the gospel he sees the source for both blues and jazz as musical form and cultural mode of expression. To him gospel opens up "an entry into the fullness of life that provides the energy for all moral and political action." It nourishes both "the secular idealism of the blues impulse as well as "the synthetic multiculturalism of the jazz impulse."[35] Emerging from the black church, an institutional space relatively far away from the mediation and control of the white system, the gospel has the power to articulate black experience with relative autonomy. Less influenced by the strategies of the music market—if compared with blues and jazz—, the gospel has expressed a black perspective less ambivalent and ambiguous than that propagated by blues or soul music. Due to the demands of the music business, secular and popular forms had to make adjustments. More than any other expression or institution, the gospel and the black church keep on connecting the music of African Americans with a more holistic conception of time:

> Extending the values of African—and other oral—cultures, gospel focuses insistently on the now, apprehended as a rhythm connecting past with future. To participate fully in the moment—to feel the presence of the Lord, the gospel spirit, soul—demands a consciousness transcending the divisions of intellect, emotion, and body, of self and other.[36]

According to Werner, the focus on the moment so prevalent in jazz's improvisations relates to the gospel impulse. Moreover the gospel impulse carries with it a sense of presence which is complex and synthesizes various time levels. As we have seen, it is jazz in particular that translates the gospel impulse rhythmically. Polyrhythms emerge from the aesthetic tensions between different conceptions of time juxtaposed and superimposed in jazz. These temporal aspects are also essential for the presence of musical elements in African American writing. Gayl Jones provides a comprehensive survey of the presence of jazz in written forms. Her account emphasizes that narrative voice, syntax, and form, especially, are shaped by literary adaptations of jazz music:

> In literature jazz can affect the subject matter—the conceptual and symbolic functions of a text, translate directly into the jazz hero, or have stylistic implications. The writer's attempt to imply or reproduce musical rhythms can take the form of jazz—like flexibility and fluidity in prose rhythms (words, lines, paragraphs, the whole text), such as nonchronological

---

[35]   Craig H. Werner, *Playing the Changes: From Afro-Modernism to the Jazz Impulse* (Urbana: U of Illinois P, 1994) 221.

[36]   Werner 220.

syncopated order, pacing, or tempo. A sense of jazz—the jam session—can also emerge from the interplay of voices improvising on basic themes or motifs of the text, in key words and phrases. Often seemingly nonlogical and associational, the jazz text is generally more complex and sophisticated than the blues text in its harmonies, rhythms, and surface structures.[37]

Jones traces these jazz elements in poetry, short fiction, and the African American novel. At length she discusses the influence of jazz on prose and poetic structures in authors such as Ann Petry, Amiri Baraka, Toni Morrison, and Ralph Ellison in her study. Although she hints to temporal aspects of jazz in the above summary she does not address specific aspects of musical time in her reading of the texts. Jazz, however, plays an important role for the rendering of time on a narrative level as well. More intensely than any other aesthetic mode, jazz and its backbone the blues have informed the historical imagination of African American novelists in the 20th century.

Various reasons account for the novelists' attraction to musical time patterns. Historically, musical models are particularly desirable for the black novelist because music and the oral tradition have played a very important role in the process of recording and expressing historical experience in African American culture. Critics have repeatedly pointed toward the history-making function which music has occupied in the African American cultural spectrum. Culturally, African American music has been the dominant force in the process of "blackening" the United States of America. And it keeps on doing so, as the recent impact of rap music illustrates. In terms of form, finally, the musical time levels can be adopted by the novelist because, as a modern literary genre, the novel in particular is open to incorporate influences from other genres and art forms.[38] To critics such as M. M. Bakhtin, the novel even represents the only still developing genre in the field of literature. "Therefore it reflects more deeply, more essentially, more sensitively and rapidly reality itself in the process of its unfolding." As he continues, "only that which itself is developing can comprehend development as a process."[39] Through its openedness, as Bakhtin makes clear, the novel bears a very intense relationship to flux and time. And more than other genres, it has developed subgenres directly related to temporal categories—the historical novel, the utopian novel, the science fiction novel. Hence, as a type of time-art, the novel shares blues' and jazz's serious concern with the temporal dimension, especially when it unfolds a narrative

---

[37] Gayl Jones, *Liberating Voices: Oral Tradition in African-American Literature* (Cambridge, Mass.: Harvard UP, 1991) 200.

[38] See also Karl Migner, *Theorie des modernen Romans* (Stuttgart: Kröner, 1970) 27.

[39] M.M. Bakhtin, *The Dialogic Imagination: Four Essays by M.M Bakhtin*, ed. Michael Holquist, trans. Caryl Emerson and M. Holquist (Austin: U of Texas P, 1994) 7.

pattern—expressing progress, describing development, telling a story.[40] This affinity on the level of time between the different artistic modes makes the musical borrowings of African American novelists all the more comprehensible. While blues and jazz have had a thematic and formal impact on African American poetry and drama as well, the influence of musical time is most visible in the African American novel. In the following chapters I will analyze the development of this pattern of influence and its cultural significance. While the musical impact is a continuous one, it has brought forth numerous and—due to the differing shades of race, class, and gender—different concepts of culture and history in the African American cultural discourse.

---

[40]   For an extensive analysis of the novel and its relation to the representation of time and history see René Wellek and Austin Warren, *A Theory of Literature* (New York: Harcourt, Brace & World, 1956) 212-15.

II. Discovering Musical Time for the Representation of History: Langston Hughes and the Harlem Renaissance

Langston Hughes' first novel *Not Without Laughter* (1930) appeared at the end of the Harlem Renaissance, the first modern movement of the African American. As such the Harlem Renaissance also represented an era in which black conceptions of time became clearly visible and audible in the United States for the first time. Literature, the visual arts, and most of all music expressed African American views of temporal intensity and progression. Langston Hughes' name and work are irrevocably connected with Harlem and the Harlem Renaissance. Drawing upon both the male and female traditions of African American music, he provides in *Not Without Laughter* the most comprehensive literary rendering of clashing views of time and history in African American culture during the early decades of the 20th century. Thus he also lays the matrix for future generations of novelists to resort to musical time for literary versions of history.[1]

Historically, the first African American arts movement marks the point from which African American folklore/oral tradition is no longer stigmatized as simplistic, quaint, or restrictive. Rather, folklore turns into a matrix for complex literary influence, for authors such as Sterling Brown, Zora Neale Hurston, Claude McKay, and Countee Cullen make use of the vernacular cognizant of its various cultural, social, and linguistic functions. Arna Bontemps describes the Harlem Renaissance, as follows:

> The cult of primitivism which gripped many American intellectuals during the 1920s manifested itself in a number of ways. The rising interest in jazz, the study of African art forms, and the examination of tribal cultures were all variations on the theme of the primitive.[2]

Various social factors influenced and shaped Harlem's unique role in the development of African American art in the 1920s. After a short period of postwar decline, the American economy soared because of the tremendous

---

1 Many of the artistic and cultural themes of postmodernism are thematized and anticipated by Harlem Renaissance writers such as Langston Hughes and Zora N. Hurston. Critics point to criteria like, the privileging of pluralism, the discovery of the discourse of the other, a critique of dualism and binarism, eclectic mixings of codes and styles among others to illustrate the link between Harlem modernism and postmodernist culture. See Ropo Sekoni, "Africanisms and Postmodernist Imagination in the Popular Fiction of Langston Hughes," *Langston Hughes: The Man, His Art, and His Continuing Influence*, ed. C. James Trotman (New York: Garland Publishing, 1995) 63-73; 63-65. Sekoni refers to Langston Hughes' Jesse B. Semple stories in particular.

2 Arna Bontemps, *The Harlem Renaissance Remembered* (New York: Dodd, Mead & Company, 1972) 127.

profits earned from World War I. African Americans in the Northern cities also profited from this economic boom. In years of general prosperity, African American artists found a way into the cultural business industry. Wealthy patrons would sponsor black artists, inviting the latter to regular salon gatherings of artists and patrons. Harlem was a place where optimism developed in the black community. In general African Americans seemed to consider Harlem the ideal place for the life of a liberated black community. James De Jongh points out that Harlem provided the matrix for the growth of new ideas and new concepts of race: "new kinds of Negroes, with new ways of thinking could flourish."[3]

At a time when ritual lynchings in the South and race riots against African Americans in the North were still popular, Harlem was taken to be an enclave of change. Whereas colonial policy continued the worldwide suppression of black people, Harlem profited from the cult of primitivism accompanying the modernist period. Many white writers and intellectuals experienced the period after World War I as a phase of stagnation; the Harlem Renaissance, on the contrary, witnessed the break of dawn for black art in America for the first time in the twentieth century. Especially African sculpture had a tremendous impact on modern art forms such as cubism. This rise of primitivism opened the market for black art sponsored and propagated by white capital. In spite of the overall racial and economic oppression of African Americans in the United States, a new sense of black culture could develop.

Essential to the artistic creativity of the Harlem Renaissance was a reevaluation of the rich oral tradition within African American culture. During the years of the Civil War and Reconstruction the emphasis among black educators, activists, and ministers had been on integration. They focused largely on "asserting the capability of the African-American to achieve within the boundaries of the dominant white culture."[4] In their writings they explored antislavery issues and emphasized the popular image of the tragic mulatto caught between the expectations of the white and black worlds. Hence, black folklore scarcely appeared as a positive force in African American writing until the beginning of the Harlem Renaissance. A new awareness of race and tradition paved the way for black folklore into the world of African American literature since many poets and writers resorted to folk elements for thematic and formal inspiration.

This awareness came into being after a period of tremendous social and geographical change within the black community. The years of the protagonist's growing up in *Not Without Laughter* clearly point to the years of the big migration between 1914 and 1918, and to World War I. Both events are

---

3   James D. Jongh, *Vicious Modernism: Black Harlem and the Literary Imagination* (New York: Cambridge UP, 1990) 9.

4   Stephen C. Tracy, *Langston Hughes & the Blues* (Urbana: U of Illinois P, 1988) 16.

interrelated in their significance for black people.[5] The outbreak of World War I launched a reversal of European migration. At the beginning of the war immigration actually reached a stand-still. Many a foreign-born man returned to his home country in Europe to join the troops in combat. While American industry experienced increasing production during the war years, it had to confront a lack of labor force, too. Many recruiting agents travelled south to attract black people to the urban centers up North. Cotton farming had repeatedly been set back through flood, famine, and the boll weevil epidemic. Due to harsh social and economic conditions—not to speak of the local racial problems—many African Americans moved to Chicago; family members and distant relatives often followed them later.

While industrial centers up North faced a steadily increasing wave of black migrants from the South, Harlem witnessed the arrival of many black artists of different national descent. They arrived from the Caribbean, Africa, and Latin America. Despite their individual differences most of the writers at the time pursued the goal of establishing an alternative aesthetic to the modernist forms of Euro-American art. This aesthetic was "tied to a sense of myth, geography, history, and culture that was truly indigenous to their countries, rather than merely reflective of European trends, whether conservative or avant-garde."[6] As the international set-up of the Harlem scene shows, multiple views on history gained access to the cultural discourse.

The use of blues and jazz became commonplace in the writings of the young Harlem Renaissance poets and novelists. In many instances, it was more or less casual, but some of the young writers went beyond a conventionalized use of music as background to their poems and novels. As Kathy J. Ogren mentions, Claude McKay, Langston Hughes, and Zora Neale Hurston were the foremost writers of the Harlem Renaissance resorting to blues and jazz performance to give voice to a black aesthetic. "In addition to exploring the communicative and historical meaning of jazz, Harlem Renaissance writers pointed to jazz and blues as evidence of the Afro-American creative potential crucial to the developing renaissance."[7]

As a pioneer in adapting African American music to literary form, Hughes occupies a rather unique position within the various polarizations among black

---

5   See St. Clair Drake and Horace R. Cayton, *Black Metropolis: A Study of Negro Life in a Modern Community* (New York: Harcourt, Brace & World, Inc. 1945) 55-64. As concerns the drafting of African Americans in war times, see Emmett J. Scott, "The Participation of Negroes in World War I" in Henry N. Drewry and Cecilia H. Drewry, eds., *Afro-American History: Past to Present* (New York: Charles Scribner's Sons, 1971) 308-317.

6   Arnold Rampersad, "Langston Hughes and Approaches to Modernism in the Harlem Renaissance," *The Harlem Renaissance: Revaluations*, eds. Amritjit Singh, William S. Shiver, Stanley Brodwin (New York: Garland, 1989) 49-72; 67.

7   Kathy J. Ogren, "Controversial Sounds: Jazz Performance as Theme and Language in the Harlem Renaissance," *The Harlem Renaissance: Revaluations* (New York: Garland, 1989) 159-184; 162.

artists and intellectuals during the 1920s. He had personal as well as professional contact with both the traditionalists and the innovative thinkers and artists.[8] In general, two major poles crystallized in the African American community.[9] The advocators of cultural assimilation accepted white standards while propagating the view that black artists were equally capable of fulfilling these standards. As far as black tradition was concerned, they required a thematic concern with the problems within the community on the part of the black artist. The second major group rejected these assimilationist tendencies. Instead they embraced a romanticized view of the ancient world of Africa. They indulged in a sort of "African craze." Together with a group of white intellectuals and artists they saw in precolonial Africa a vital alternative to the technological sterility of industrial America. Pan-Africanism culminated in the figure of Marcus Garvey, who urged the return of all blacks to Africa. Rejecting general miscegenation and racial amalgamation, Garvey advocated an all-out black racist response to the yoke of white dominion.[10]

Both these groups, however, ignored the significance of blues and jazz as authentic African American art forms. They also neglected the social conditions for colored people in the United States. Hughes corrects both omissions in *Not Without Laughter*, where he relates culture to economy explicitly.[11] Primarily he focuses on the artistic achievements of the black community in his novel. Within this communal vision Hughes thoroughly embeds the female contributions to early blues and jazz in the African American cultural discourse.

---

[8]   From those who fostered traditional values Hughes inherited a legacy of higher education, a belief in the significance of cultural heritage, and a sense of racial pride. Although Hughes had problems with the middle-class thinking of leading figures such as W.E.B. DuBois he respected the latter's importance for the New Negro movement in the United States. Accordingly, DuBois, Alain Locke as well as James Weldon Johnson exerted a significant influence on Hughes' writings. Among the three it was Locke, though, who most directly encouraged the new generation of black writers to draw upon African American folklore and folk music. Despite his middle-class leanings he saw the need to transfer the essence of the folk experience into the artistic and critical discourse of African Americans. Writers such as Sterling A. Brown, Zora N. Hurston, and Langston Hughes then formed a new generation of writers enthusiastically embracing African American folk material as well as the values of rural and working-class people. See Steven Tracy, *Langston Hughes & the Blues* 17-29.

[9]   See Ekkehart Jost, *Sozialgeschichte des Jazz in den USA* (Frankfurt/Main: Fischer Verlag, 1982) 58-61.

[10] See Harold R. Isaacs, *The New World of Negro Americans* (New York: The John Day Company, Inc., 1963) 132-46.

[11] Indeed few writers were willing to consider seriously the contributions of blues musicians to African American culture and its politics. As Davis points out, Hughes represents a notable exception. See Angela Y. Davis, *Blues Legacies and Black Feminism: Gertrude Ma Rainey, Bessie Smith, and Billie Holiday* (New York: Pantheon Books, 1998) xiii.

Indeed, Hughes is the first writer to create a female blues figure in fiction.[12] White art is only marginally present on the shelves of Aunt Tempy. African art per se is absent from the content of the novel. David Levering Lewis may be right speculating that "it may have been because he was the only poet from Harlem ever to tack along the West coast [of Africa] . . . that Hughes avoided romanticizing Africa excessively." [13] Rather racial pride, in the hands of Hughes, takes root in a concept of blackness symbolizing diversity. Poetically, this concept is best expressed in his famous poem "The Negro Speaks of Rivers":

> I've known rivers: / I've known rivers ancient as the world and older / than the flow of human blood in human veins. / My soul has grown deep like the rivers. / I bathed in the Euphrates when dawns were young. / I built my hut near the Congo and it lulled me to/sleep. / I looked upon the Nile and raised the pyramids above / it. / I heard the singing of the Mississippi when Abe / Lincoln went down to New Orleans, and I've seen / its muddy bossom turn all golden in the sunset. / I've known rivers:/ Ancient, dusky rivers. / My soul has grown deep like the rivers.[14]

Hughes expresses here the poetics of a collective history of black cultures. Accordingly, the water imagery related to musical expression stands as a metaphor for a crosscontinental cosmology. Various time layers are thematically juxtaposed and imply a presence of multiple temporal dimensions related to different cultural backgrounds of black origin. Hughes' travels as well as his work continuously reveal that his vision is not restricted by cultural borderlines. Apart from his own writings Hughes is known for his translations of other black writers into English from Cuban Spanish, Haitian French, and Creole from New Orleans. Although he is deeply conscious of a black cultural heritage, Hughes never embraces Pan-African ideologies. Instead, he focuses mainly on the social conditions of African Americans within the United States, as in the novel at hand.

Hughes' *Not Without Laughter* tells the story of Sandy, a young black boy growing up in a small town in Kansas. The historical setting of the novel is the time period before and around World War I. Due to the harsh economic conditions in rural areas, Jimboy, Sandy's father, is frequently absent from the family. He roams the country, playing the blues and looking for temporary jobs. Hence, Sandy grows up in a primarily female environment. His mother Annjee and his grandmother Aunt Hager, both serving white households to make ends meet, provide social and emotional shelter for Sandy while he is growing up.

---

12 See Cheryl A. Wall, "Whose Sweet Angel Child? Blues Women, Langston Hughes, and Writing During the Harlem Renaissance," *Langston Hughes: The Man, His Art, and his Continuing Influence*, ed. C. James Trotman, 37-50; 39.

13 David L. Lewis, *When Harlem Was in Vogue* (New York: Alfred Knopf, 1981) 83.

14 Langston Hughes, "The Negro Speaks of Rivers," *The Norton Anthology of Modern Poetry*, eds. Richard Ellman and Robert O'Clair (New York: W. W. Norton & Company, 1973) 634-35.

His aunt Harriet, a blues singer and dancer, introduces him to the hedonistic side of black culture. Her way of life in the ambience of dance halls and vaudeville shows differs distinctly from the religious and work-ethic-oriented outlook of Annjee and Hager. Sandy's aunt Tempy, a member of the African American bourgeoisie, introduces him to the world of books. Overall, Hughes portrays six years of Sandy's life during which the latter completes school, takes odd jobs at barbershops and hotel lobbies, and finally decides to pursue higher education.

The strong presence of music on a thematic level in *Not Without Laughter* suggests that the author is very much concerned with making the richness and complexity of African American culture known, especially to a white public.[15] Indeed, Hughes gives large space in the novel to scenes describing music and dance performances which shows that blues and jazz in particular shape his literary vision of history.[16] These scenes are both descriptive and expressive. Naturally, Hughes' poems come to mind first when one explores the interrelation of oral and written code in his work. Poems such as "The Weary Blues" and "Dream Boogie" represent magnificent examples of his literary adaptations of musical form and rhythm. Correspondingly, most critics agree that Hughes keeps the oral material as authentic as possible when used in a literary context.[17] Besides rhythm and content in his poetry, African American music penetrates Hughes temporal vision as well. To a lesser extent, though,

---

[15]   Steven Tracy points out that the necessity to please both African American and white audiences during the Harlem Renaissance represented a dilemma for many black artists at the time. The white audience, for instance, primarily expected stereotypes: lazy, passionate, savage. The black audiences longed for and demanded characters that were educated and oriented toward middle-class values. Another complex issue emerged from the desire to create forms of black identity, considering both the African and the African American heritage. See Steven C. Tracy, *Langston Hughes & the Blues* 17-23.

[16]   Langston Hughes was more interested in blues and jazz than in gospel music. Most of his writings deal with the blues as major mode of African American cultural expression. For the first time he encountered the blues in Kansas City. Moreover he was familiar with the blues of Ma Rainey, the ragtime and boogie woogie of the Chicago scene, and the blues and jazz of Harlem from the 1920s on. See also Steven C. Tracy, "Langston Hughes: Poetry, Blues, and Gospel—Somewhere to Stand," *Langston Hughes: The Man, His Art and His Continuing Influence* 51-61; 55.

[17]   Hughes was aware of the problems involved in transferring folk material into a written and/or intellectual discourse; especially because he recognized that the folk material itself underwent changes due to the shift from rural to urban life. Hughes decided to include both the rural folk roots as well as their urban transformations into his writings. Hence, he also paid tribute to folk-based material—think of the blues recordings of the 1920s—because he saw in them the urban extension of African American folklore. For further discussion of Hughes relationship to folklore see Steven Tracy, *Langston Hughes & the Blues* 41-49. Tracy also points out that Hughes had his limitations as a commentator on the blues tradition. Especially early in his career Hughes' discussions of the roots of the blues were often unsystematic and broad. Cf. Steven Tracy, "Poetry, Blues, and Gospel - Somewhere to Stand" 51-61; 57.

blues and jazz inspire formal experimentation in Hughes's prose work. Primarily they function as carriers of race consciousness and pride which find their expression in Hughes' conception of time and history."

"The Weary Blues", a poem about a piano player performing at Lenox Avenue Nightclub, represents a song of utter dejection and despair and gives voice to Hughes' historical imagination:

> I got the Weary Blues / And I can't be satisfied. / Got the Weary Blues / And can't be satisfied— / I ain't happy no mo'/And I wish that I had died.[18]

Yet after the performance the blues has had a cathartic effect. The blues singer masters his own pain artistically:

> While the Weary Blues echoed through his head. / He slept like a rock or a man that's dead.[19]

In its embrace of suffering and catharsis "The Weary Blues" provides a basic understanding of Hughes' view of the blues in relation to history. In Hughes' imagination blues and jazz give expression to a view of history as absurd and grotesque. He regards with irony Tempy's belief that the loyalty of black soldiers in the American troops overseas will ameliorate the situation for blacks at home. Tempy says: "White folks will see that the Negro can be trusted in war as well as peace. Times will be better after this for all of us."[20] Hughes, instead, signals that fighting for democracy overseas and being denied democratic rights at home are not easily reconciled. The war situation exposes the double standards of white morality and the absurdity of historical circumstances refusing African Americans full citizenship. Hughes then repeatedly resorts to adjectives such as "grotesque" and "absurd" to comment on events in the novel. And in most instances they appear in contexts of music. Hughes describes Jimboy singing the blues with adverbial phrases such as "crying grotesquely" or "crying absurdly."[21] When Sandy catches a glimpse of the Gavitts' house destroyed by the storm, the view of the piano "flat on its back in the grass" disturbs him: "Its ivory keys gleamed in the moonlight like grinning teeth, and the strange sight made his little body shiver. . . ."[22] This grotesque imagery stands for history and nature alike.

Symbolically, the piano's "grinning teeth" express the power of cultural heritage, especially that of music. The musical instrument signifies endurance and survival. Not only does the black community survive the destructive natural forces, when a storm hits the small town of Kansas, it also has endured the yoke of slavery and that of racial discrimination in the decades that followed.

---

[18]   Langston Hughes, "The Weary Blues," *The Norton Anthology of Modern Poetry* 635.

[19]   Langston Hughes 635.

[20]   Langston Hughes, *Not Without Laughter* (New York: Collier Books, 1969) 257.

[21]   Langston Hughes 51.

[22]   Langston Hughes 8.

Cultural assertion via affirming rather than negating is at issue in the writings of the Harlem Renaissance. African American music in particular functioned as an affirmative platform for many writers. In *Not Without Laughter* historical change is intertwined with musical forms that are constantly associated with motion. As pulsating life-forces they signify African American affirmation in the face of racial discrimination. Playing with the historical and sociological implications of blues and jazz, Hughes resorts to manifold facets of African American music in developing his conception of history. Blues and jazz speak of their own history—the development from folk blues to classical blues—and accompany the story of Sandy's growing up. The various connotations of black music Hughes resorts to display why his adaptations of music in his first novel have had such profound impact on generations of African American writers to follow. The presence of blues and jazz goes beyond a purely musical-theoretical or sociological representation in *Not Without Laughter*. In his close association of music with the realm of nature and the idea of flux, Hughes touches on magic and mythic effects. Thus he breaks ground for the use of musical rhythm as a device for rendering different notions of time and history in subsequent African American fictions.

Blues and jazz represent the momentum behind historical changes within the black community. In Hughes' rendering musical modes express traditional time concepts—the ones linked with Christianity—and express new ones which transfer the gospel impulse with its emphasis on the now into the realm of secular art forms such as blues and jazz. In the latter musical forms, new temporal complexity and intensity rhythmically translate the various historical concepts present during the Harlem Renaissance. Not only does the novel portray economic conditions surrounding the black communities, it also displays class and gender differences between the various members of Sandy's family. Here personal and family history function as a gateway to history on a larger scale. And *Not Without Laughter* draws on the rich treasure of African American folk culture, especially blues and jazz, when it demonstrates the historical change from assimilation to black affirmation in the African American community during the early twentieth century.

Important for this shift is a tension at work within the African American community. It is the conflict between the secular and the sacred world that nourishes this unrest within. In terms of music, Hughes juxtaposes the world of the spirituals with the performance of blues and jazz. This juxtaposition indicates the diversity that Hughes discerns in the race's own communal set-up. Blues and jazz stand for the young and progressive stance while the spirituals preserve tradition and appeal to conservative values. The two major poles of Hughes's historical imagination become visible in this context. The communal spirit is primarily preserved through the church congregation's singing of the spiritual. Hager even sings with Jimboy when the latter plays a spiritual or hymn. Overall, her world view is bound up with values such as work, sacrifice, and mutual help. To Hughes, these values express the adaptation of the Protestant work ethic by African Americans following christianization during the days of slavery. Hence, the black Baptist church embodies strong assimilationist aspects. With their emphasis on duty and work these church ethics are twofold: on the one hand they strengthen the familial ties within the African American community; on the other hand they please and solidify the hierarchy of the white power structure.

Blues and jazz, in contrast, bear hedonistic aspects. Both signify entertainment and pleasure. They are associated with spiritual and physical ecstasy throughout *Not Without Laughter*. They also oppose a merely communal spirit with their embrace of individuality. Hughes links blues and jazz to the younger generations and celebrates these musical expressions as possibilities for cultural assertion and renewal. Generational and cultural conflicts coincide when Hughes develops an alternative aesthetic to the Protestant work ethic. Hence, the secular musical forms express a protest spirit.[23]

Blues and jazz are rejected by the traditional members of the older generation as well as by the rising members of the black middle class. To Hughes, the first group has given up cultural roots; the second group has exchanged spiritual values for material substitutes. Especially to folks like Aunt Hager, blues and jazz signify a devil's music.[24] Although Hughes portrays almost all parts of the black community with sympathy, it becomes obvious that the aesthetics of blues and jazz with their focus on individuality within a community are the sublime guidelines for asserting race consciousness in the future.

Blues and jazz represent both individual and communal assertion to Hughes since both negotiate between individual and historical time. Communication takes place on three levels. First, there is the interaction between man and woman while dancing or singing; this also corresponds to the communication between performer and audience.[25] Second, Hughes refers to moments of

---

23   While blues critics such as Paul Oliver and Samuel Charters deny or play down the element of protest in the blues, critics like Paul Garon and, most recently, Angela Davis emphasize the rebellious aspects of the blues tradition. The latter focuses on the protest material created and performed by female blues and jazz singers in particular. Discussing the recordings of Ma Rainey, Bessie Smith, and Billie Holiday, Davis stresses the fusion of the private and public, the personal and political in their blues and jazz songs. Davis reads most of the songs as part of the social protest genre and puts an emphasis on issues of female oppression and liberation. As she sees it, blues songs such as "Backwater Blues" and "Chain Gang Blues" can be interpreted as "historical preparation for political protest (119)." See Angela Y. Davis, *Blues Legacies and Black Feminism: Gertrude "Ma" Rainey, Bessie Smith, and Billie Holiday* 91-119.

24   See also Berthold Klostermann, *Blue Notes-Black Fiction: Schwarze Musik in der afroamerikanischen Erzählliteratur der zwanziger und dreißiger Jahre* (Trier: Wissenschaftlicher Verlag Trier, 1993) 145-74. As Klostermann stresses, the characters' social and religious attitudes are closely interwoven with each character's relationship to music, blues and spirituals in particular.

25   This aspect of communication was also important for Hughes' performances of poetry. The act of performance was seen as a dialogue between audience and poet, audience and musician and

ecstasy related to music. A communion between the individual and a spiritual world results from the exposure to blues and jazz. And, finally, Hughes establishes a communicative bond between music and nature. Quite often he resorts to nature imagery when he depicts musical performances: "The singing notes of the guitar became a plaintive hum, like a breeze in a grove of palmettos; became a low-moan, like the wind in a forest of live-oaks strung with long strands of hanging moss."[26] Nature, art, and human voices intertwine in many of the passages describing blues or jazz performances. Hughes, for instance, personifies instruments, equipping them with a scale of emotional vicissitudes. The cornet moans, the banjo cries, the piano sobs, and the drums laugh. Hughes uses onomatopoetic expressions—"Eu-o-oo-ooo-oooo - moaned the cornet"—to translate the vitality of music acoustically.[27] These sound-imitating expressions attempt the immediate translation of the musical expression to the written page. Read aloud, these onomatopoetic terms illustrate Hughes' belief in the high expressive quality of African American folk art. They furthermore point toward the urge of black artists—poets and musicians alike—to make themselves heard during the years of the Harlem Renaissance.

Even if Hughes celebrates the artistic achievement of African Americans in the United States, he never indulges in an art-for-art's sake attitude toward the black aesthetic expression. The interrelation between black art and history is causal to Hughes. "Dancers because of their poverty; singers because they suffered; laughing all the time because they must forget."[28] As he puts it, black artistic expression traces history back to the memory of slavery. He thus places social, psychological, and physical suffering at the roots of black artistic creation.[29] Hughes conceives the condition of the African American as ambiguous during the tumultuous period of the 1920s. On the one hand black artists have the potential to create the first black aesthetic celebrating African American culture. On the other hand they are still restricted through economic

---

active participation through foot-patting and handclapping was encouraged. Cf. Steven Tracy, "Langston Hughes: Poetry, Blues, and Gospel—Somewhere to Stand" 51-61; 57.

[26]   Langston Hughes, *Not Without Laughter* 51.

[27]   Hughes 88.

[28]   Hughes 293.

[29]   This also explains why Hughes resorts to the blues to comment upon the historical conditions of African Americans. The blues keeps the memory of slavery and suffering alive. Baker, for instance, stresses the historical development and social functioning of blues, as follows:"Originating in the field hollers and work-songs of the black agrarian South and becoming codified as stable forms by the second decade of the twentieth century, the blues offer a language that connotes a world of transience, instability, hard luck, brutalizing work, lost love, minimal security, and enduring human wit and resourcefulness in the face of such discouragement." Houston A. Baker, Jr., "To Move Without Moving: Creativity and Commerce in Ralph Ellison's Trueblood Episode," *Black Literature and Theory*, ed. Henry L. Gates, Jr. (New York: Methuen, 1984) 221-48; 236.

dependence on white capital; this is true in spite of the newly opening market for black art in the days of the Harlem Renaissance, as Harriet's life as blues singer illustrates. In spite of her success as an artist, she still depends on white agents and sponsors.

Harlem depended on the economic support of the white downtown. This awareness shapes Hughes' use of blues and jazz in developing his view of history in *Not Without Laughter*. He juxtaposes the creative potential of the African American community with its severe economic deprivation. Sandy's mother Annjee and his grandmother Aunt Hager can only survive as servants of white families. The picture Hughes draws of the African American condition is neither sinister nor naturalistic, though; rather he points toward African American music as a creative force capable of sustaining the black people culturally as well as economically.

Music, like laughter, assumes the function of emotional and psychic cleansing so desperately needed in the face of white supremacy and racial discrimination. Especially blues and jazz express a growing yearning among African Americans to establish an alternative value-system to the working aesthetic of the white world and black bourgeoisie. Jimboy and Harriet in particular look for a new spiritual dimension different from old time religion and daily work routine. This new form of spirituality is expressed through physical pleasures such as sexuality and dance. Their singing gives voice to a sense of emotional and sexual longing and a feeling of ecstasy alike. Hughes juxtaposes this desire with the monotony and sterility of the white world:

> Jazz to me is one of the inherent expressions of Negro life in America; the eternal tom-tom beating in the Negro Soul—the tom-tom of revolt against the weariness in a white world, a world of subway trains, and work, work, work; the tom-tom of joy and laughter, and pain swallowed in a smile. [30]

Here Hughes draws no waste land image of white society. Yet he associates the white life-style with a static and spiritless condition based upon the routine of work. He resorts to the rhythmic matrix of blues and jazz to juxtapose this lifeless shape with a hedonistic spirit leaving space for physical and sensual pleasure.

All the appearances of blues and jazz in the novel express a defiance of stasis. Metaphorically Hughes draws on images of nature related to music, as we have seen, to underscore the presence of flux. Verbally and structurally, moreover, Hughes creates an opposition of kinesis and stasis, of passion and sterility, which he discerns as ultimate differences between black and white approaches toward history. Those African Americans influenced by white ethics follow either a linear rational concept of time—Tempy—or remain in a static view of it; thus, Aunt Hager is fixed on the past and the cultural heritage involved. Characters that indulge in the new secular music or perform it break

---

[30] Langston Hughes, "The Negro Artist and the Racial Mountain," *Einführung in die schwarzamerikanische Literatur*, ed. Klaus Ensslen (Stuttgart: Kohlhammer, 1982) 105-06.

out of mechanically controlled time frames and pursue more flexible temporal conceptions, though, which is also expressed spatially and physically. Both the lyrics and the musical scenes imply spatial and erotic movement. Accordingly, Harriet's dance movements accompany Jimboy's blues songs: "But Harriet kept on, her hands picking imaginary cherries out of the stars, her hips speaking an earthy language quite their own."[31] In some of the dance scenes Hughes' language evokes sexuality explicitly. "Couples began to sway languidly, melting together like candy in the sun as hips rotated effortlessly to the music."[32] As the description suggests, the dance movement does not follow a straight linear pattern; instead, circularity and synthesis are implied by the motion of the dancers. The dance signals the presence of various temporal layers and movements. Thus it aesthetically reflects upon different temporal and spatial shiftings throughout the course of African American history.

In a similar way, the blues lyrics connote spatial movement as well as sexual longing, dealing with men departing from their wives and lovers. Spatial shift is also expressed through the novel's switching from the rural setting in Kansas to the urban environment of Chicago. Movement, then, becomes not only a consequence of economic necessity—as in the case of the great migration between 1914 and 1918—but also a sign of individual fulfillment and freedom. "People danced their own individual movements to the scream and the moan of the music."[33] Movement here has artistic as well as political meaning. It refers to the black arts movement in Harlem as well as to the individual departure from Southern communal life of those African Americans who moved North. Both "movements" signify social improvement for the black community as concerns the job market and the selling and distributing of art products. Overall, then, motion implies artistic and economic change in *Not Without Laughter*.

Hughes' idea of flux, so thoroughly associated with images of music and nature, bears direct relation to the historical period he chooses for the framework of his novel. During World War I, Jimboy, like many colored people from rural areas, moves to Chicago where he finds a job. Annjee finally follows him up there, and a minor family reunion takes place at Harriet's concert when Sandy and his mother visit Harriet in the dressing room. At one of her visits back home, Harriet expresses why so many African Americans left the South for the cities up North:

> I'm out of the South now. It's a hell - I mean it's an awful place if you don't know anybody! And more hungry niggers down there! I wonder who made up that song about Dear Old Southland. There's nothing dear about it that I can see. Good God! It's awful! . . . But I'm back. [34]

---

31   Langston Hughes, *Not Without Laughter* 48.

32   Hughes 88.

33   Hughes 89.

34   Hughes 162.

Harriet replaces "that song about Dear Old South" through her blues songs she performs so successfully in Chicago. The blues which expresses a difference in place also suggests a new historical phase. Hence, the idea of change and of new rhythms as an engine of change gives expression to a generally felt hope among African Americans for cultural renewal. What is historically important for the emergence of diverse jazz styles—new rhythmic patterns—Hughes adopts as a cultural model for new directions in history. Blues and jazz not only come alive in the personification of musical instruments; they also carry the hope for a new beginning. The instruments are further embedded in a larger context of nature. Their presence fuses with the existence of natural elements:

> To drum-beats barely audible, the tall boy in the tan suit walked his partner
> round and round after time, revolving at each corner with eyes uplifted,
> while the piano was the water flowing, and the high, thin chords of the banjo
> were the mountains floating in the clouds.[35]

Here music even transcends nature and stands for a larger cosmology in Hughes'conception of history: "The earth rolls relentlessly, and the sun blazes for ever on the earth, breeding, breeding. But why do you insist like the earth, music?"[36] The answer lies in Hughes' interpretation of blues and jazz as pulsating life-forces physically expressed through the dance movements, acoustically through the train whistle calling the blues man for a journey, and, finally, verbally through the appropriation of sound through language.

As Hughes' analogies underscore, blues and jazz embrace a spirituality of body and nature at the same time opposing and complementing the religious spirituality of the church hymns. This anti-Christian stance continues throughout the history of jazz. Jazz critic Berendt points out that jazz, especially from the 1960s onward, welcomed a new spirituality nourished by religions other than Christianity. Earlier, bebop had already witnessed a shift from Christian to Islamic faith among musicians and supporters alike. Two examples of this new spirituality in the free jazz era are John Coltrane's "Love Supreme" and Ornette Coleman's "Peace".[37] Referring to blues and jazz in Kansas in particular, Hughes links the expression of a new sense of spirituality of the young black generation during the early decades of this century with African American secular music.

During the 1920s the channels through which blues and jazz reached the public multiplied rapidly. The phonograph, the radio, and talking pictures took the market by storm and helped to spread various forms of African American music. Social factors such as black migration from rural to urban, Southern to Northern regions shaped the diversification of African American music, jazz in

---

[35]   Hughes 84.

[36]   Hughes 90.

[37]   Joachim-Ernst Berendt, *Ein Fenster aus Jazz* (Frankfurt/Main: Fischer Verlag, 1977) 27-31.

particular. Different styles emerged and four cities occupied spearhead positions in the development of blues and jazz: New Orleans, Chicago, New York, and Kansas City. Each of them formed its own unique scene of blues and jazz music before and during the 1920s. In *Not Without Laughter*, Kansas and Chicago figure as important places where new musical forms could emerge. Apparently Hughes picked Kansas because that is where he first encountered the blues. Moreover the region provided him with the musical material necessary for a historical vision which builds on the musical traditions of the working people as well as on more sophisticated forms of secular music. Historically, the Southwest opened up after the Civil War and represented the final reservoir of cheap black labor and "low-down" African American music. This source of African American folk heritage gained new impact on blues and jazz during the migration years after World War I. The number of migrants doubled and tripled as African Americans from Louisiana, Mississippi, and Texas arrived in Arkansas, Oklahoma, and Kansas where dance music flourished and meant big business.[38]

Hughes appears to have the Southwestern style in mind when he presents Bill Benbow's Famous Kansas City Band's performance in the novel.[39] The cultural clash in the region brought forth a new "hot" style of jazz which developed in direct response to the fusion of folk dance rhythms of the deep South and the rhythmic performances of the popular big bands. Count Basie and Benny Goodman developed this style to perfection so that even large ensembles were able to perform "hot" jazz by adopting the call-and-response pattern, developing riffs, and harmonizing the solo. Count Basie in particular shaped the Kansas City style, as Lewis Erenberg points out:

> Basie's demeanor—and his music—reflected the Kansas City milieu. Symbolized by the blues, Kansas City fostered and preserved more traditional elements of black industrial oral culture than did New York. Compared to those of New York and Chicago, its black middle class was small and its ideology of progress and assimiliation negligible. Instead, its black population drew its cultural employment in meat packing, the river trade, and construction.[40]

---

[38] Cf. Marshall W. Stearns, *The Story of Jazz* (New York: Oxford UP, 1970) 186-89.

[39] Steven Tracy points out that it was the early blues of the first two decades of the 20th century which influened Hughes in his Kansas days the most. These blues forms derived directly from slave and work songs. As concerns the depiction of Bill Benbow's Band, however, Hughes seems already to point toward the orchestral-type blues which flourished from 1925-42. See Steven C. Tracy, "To the Tune of Those Weary Blues," *Langston Hughes: Critical Perspectives Past and Present*, eds. Henry L. Gates, Jr. And K. A. Appiah (New York: Amistad, 1993) 69-93; 71.

[40] Lewis A. Erenberg, *Swingin' the Dream: Big Band Jazz and the Rebirth of American Culture* (Chicago: U of Chicago P, 1998) 102.

Kansas City's significance for music grew, as the depression caused the collapse of the blues and jazz scene in surrounding areas.[41] Since blues and jazz flourished in the city many jazz musicians from the entire region flooded the city to perform in numerous night spots. Stylistically, the regional blues forms gained more influence on the jazz in the city because Kansas City's jazz scene remained isolated from other national jazz currents. As a result a preference for a jam session mode turned into a key element for jazz performances in Kansas City.[42] And it kept alive jazz's extension of collective improvisation so prevalent in the African American musical heritage. When Count Basie brought his band to New York he preserved both the improvisational and the collective aspects of the Kansas City jam session. Rhythmically, too, Basie's band set itself apart from those playing on the East coast. Extended riffs and a strong 4/4 rhythm characterized Count Basie's big band style. Similar to Benbow's part in his band, Basie led his big band from the rhythm section. As a piano player he regarded himself as a member of the rhythm section. And rhythm was meant to propel the dancers.[43] Although Benbow's band is smaller in size the aesthetic affinity between his and that of Count Basie is striking.

Especially the close interaction of musicians and dancers associated with the Kansas City style turns the latter into an ideal medium for Hughes to express the yearning for a spiritual renewal through music which involves various

---

[41]   The blues endured as a vital cultural tradition even during the depression. While the economic clash may have caused the decline of the Harlem Renaissance, African American music continued to bring forth new styles based upon black folk traditions. The traditional country blues with its regional variations superseded the stylistically declining classical blues tradition. Recordings in the late 1920s and 1930s featured blues performers such as Big Bill Broonzy, Blind Boy Fuller, Memphis Minnie, and, certainly the most influential of them all, Robert Johnson. Cf. Robert H. Cataliotti, *The Music in African American Fiction* (New York: Garland Publishing, 1995) 118-19.

[42]   Ross Russell discusses the nature of the Kansas City style, as follows: "Kansas City style began as a grass roots movement and retained its earthy, proletarian character to the end. In the beginning it was plain, rather stiff and crude, but aggressively indigenious, and colloquial. It drew from two main sources, folksong and ragtime. From folksong—with its grab bag of country dances, field hollers, ballads and work songs—and from the blues— both the old country blues and the newer urban blues Kansas City extracted much of its material. In its early stages Kansas City jazz might have been described as folksy, raggy, blues-saturated dance music." Ross Russell, *Jazz Style in Kansas City and the Southwest* (Berkeley: U of California P, 1971) 321.

[43]   Erenberg discusses Count Basie' unique position in the big band era, as follows: "The riff structure allowed Basie to unite individual contributions to a collective sound with a minimum of formal planning, a process at the heart of African American improvisatory tradition. Ellington composed the talents of his musicians into miniature orchestral gems, while Henderson, Lunceford, and Webb relied on well-written arrangements. Basie, on the other hand, reduced the process to its essence, combining down-home blues with popular dance music and the arranged performance with the jam session. The simple riff structure gave soloists room to improvise that no formal arrangement could match." *Swinging' the Dream* 104.

emotional vicissitudes. The human emotions that Hughes associates with the audience-response to musical performance range from melancholy to anger, from sadness to joyful ecstasy. Within this broad range attributed to African American musical forms Hughes equips blues and jazz with a rich spectrum of emotions giving expression to the historical condition of the black community. "The scream and the moan of music" that the narrator discerns in the performance of Bill Benbow's Famous Kansas City Band suggest that suffering and catharsis are at the roots of the music at Chaver's Hall. Hughes, accordingly, finds more than entertainment in blues and jazz. They also bear the element of revolt, as the subsequent passage illustrates:

> Whaw! Whaw! Whaw! mocked the cornet—but the steady tomtom of the drums was no longer laughter now, no longer even pleasant: the drum beats had become sharp with surly sound, like heavy waves that beat angrily on a granite rock. And under the dissolute spell of its own rhythm the music had got quite beyond itself.[44]

Hughes draws no direct link between the revolutionary undertone of the music and social action in this scene. However, since art is viewed as being embedded within an economic context, Hughes connects African American music with the potential of economic change. Symbolically, the chapter "The Princess of Blues" presenting Harriet's triumphant success during a Chicago blues performance completes the novel. *Not Without Laughter* ends on an optimistic tone, then, for Harriet's triumph is artistic and economic as well. With the money she gains from her cabaret work she is even capable of paying Sandy's way through school.

The drum in particular becomes associated with revolt in *Not Without Laughter*. In the history of black music the drum stands as a symbol for oppression and rebellion alike. Interestingly enough for the development of jazz, it was the ban on drums in Protestant settings that paved the way for alternative ways of improvising rhythm. Whereas Latin-Catholic colonial systems were more willing to pursue a cultural laissez-faire, colonialists of Protestant descent have tended to impose cultural standards upon the colonized people.[45] Banning the drum, many a colonialist hoped to smother black cultural roots. Hughes, then, chooses the drum to illustrate the revolutionary side of black music. As instrument it represents a means of secret communication in black culture. Its absence due to colonialist ban urged black communities to improvise rhythm through other percussive modes. Discussing the interrelation of jazz and West African musical forms, Stearns, for instance, points toward the significance of the ring shout for the development of jazz. The ring-shout ceremonies were brought back to church services in the South to attract especially young people who wanted to combine spiritual with physical ecstasy.

---

[44]   Langston Hughes, *Not Without Laughter* 89.

[45]   See Marshall W. Stearns, *The Story of Jazz* 19.

Foot-stomping and hand-clapping created the rhythmic background to the shouting preacher during the singing of church hymns.[46] In *Not Without Laughter*, the rhythmic tomtom of the drums expresses a rebellious spirit that is directed against the cultural doctrines of Protestantism and their black manifestations in the Baptist church. The drum, symbol of the polyrhythmic complexity of African music in *Not Without Laughter*, mocks the mechanical course of history guided by subway trains and assembly lines. Ultimately, it defies the rigid order and discipline of the Protestant work ethic.

Hughes' description of Bill Benbow's gig with his famous Kansas City Band includes references to blues, ragtime as well as jazz. When Hughes depicts the movements of the dancers with an earthy and erotic imagery, he portrays a world distant from so-called white civilization. The world he creates appears wild and passionate. As far as musical reference is concerned Duke Ellington's jungle style of the 1920s—next to Count Basie's jam sessions—seems to have nourished Hughes' presentation of blues and jazz performances; for instance, during Harriet's concert in Chicago, Hughes describes her as "beautiful as a jungle princess."[47] Many of the popular tunes that the Duke Ellington orchestra performed at the Cotton Club in New York in the 1920s already evoke associations with jungle imagery in their titles. Jazz pieces such as "Jungle Jamboree", "Jungle Blues", "Jungle Nights in Harlem," and "Echoes of the Jungle" belonged to the standard program of Duke Ellington's floor show productions.[48] His "jungle style" expressed exuberant cheerfulness and optimism. "Black And Tan Fantasy" and "East St. Louis Toodle-Oo" are two more perfect examples of the vitality created through "jungle effects".[49] Thus he played with the popularity of the "African craze" when he colored his jazz arrangements with special sound effects calling forth images of an exotic jungle world in the minds of the audience and dancers. Jazz historian Marshall Stearns depicts the African cult performances at the Cotton Club as follows:

> The floor shows at the Cotton Club, which admitted only gangsters, whites, and Negro celebrities, were an incredible mishmash of talent and nonsense which might well fascinate both sociologists and psychiatrists. I recall one where a light-skinned and magnificently muscled Negro burst through a papier-mâché jungle onto the dance floor, clad in an aviator's helmet, goggles, and shorts. He had obviously been 'forced down in darkest Africa,' and in the center of the floor he came upon a white goddess clad in long golden tresses and being worshipped by a circle of cringing 'blacks.' Producing a bull whip from heaven knows where, the aviator rescued the blonde and they did an erotic dance. In the background, Bubber Miley,

---

[46]   Stearns 13.

[47]   Langston Hughes, *Not Without Laughter* 297.

[48]   Ekkehard Jost, *Sozialgeschichte des Jazz in den USA* 64.

[49]   Hans Ruland, *Duke Ellington* (Gauting-Buchendorf: Oreos Verlag, 1983) 66-68.

Tricky Sam Nanton, and other members of the Ellington band growled,
wheezed, and snorted obscenely.[50]

Such performances made rational time seem to tip over into an irrational
discourse. Ellington's jazz effects creating the famous jungle sound were chiefly
produced by the horn section of his orchestra; growling, glissando, and muting
effects played the most important parts thereby. These effects of the horn
section's mimicking human and animal sounds find a parallel in the folk blues
way of playing slide guitar. Hughes uses Jimboy's parody of a church hymn to
illustrate the effects of sliding a bottleneck up and down the strings of a guitar:

Then with rapid glides, groans, and shouts the instrument screamed of a
sudden in profane frenzy, and Harriet began to ball-the-jack, her arms
flopping like the wings of a headless pigeon, the guitar string whining in
ecstasy, the player rocking gaily to the urgent music, his happy mouth
crying: "Tack 'em down, gal! Tack 'em on down, Harrie!"[51]

Even if this passage reveals no direct reference to an "African craze" it
exposes the high degree of sensuality and spiritual ecstasy involved with
Jimboy's blues.

Hughes' presentation of blues and jazz performances is lyrical as well as
analytical. In a very detailed manner he also describes the sounds of the various
instruments and their interplay throughout the gig of Bill Benbow's band. The
ecstasy accompanying the passages of musical performance and reception is
both individual and communal. In the early days of jazz, as Hughes puts it,
inspiration works on a mutual level of interaction between musician and
audience. The blues and jazz musicians inspire the physical movements of the
dancers and their instrumental improvisations respond to the mood and motion
on the dance floor.

Underneath this implied community, there is a dialectical pattern running
like a thread through the novel. This pattern constitutes itself in the distinct
juxtaposition of male and female worlds. The blues songs of both Harriet and
Jimboy nourish and reflect this binary opposition. Most of the lyrics presented
in *Not Without Laughter* give expression to the emotional disturbance ensuing
on failed relationships between the two sexes. Hughes draws upon the blues
especially to display the huge gulf between the two sexes in the larger black
community. To him the blues becomes the primary medium to translate the
struggle between the sexes lyrically. In *Urban Blues* Charles Keil describes the
antagonism based on gender difference with the following words:

The female forces on one side of the battle line consist of units like mother
and daughter, sister and sister, niece and aunt, wife and mother-in-law, a
matriarch with her daughters and grandchildren. Facing this formidable

---

50   Marshall W. Stearns, *The Story of Jazz* 183-84.

51   Langston Hughes, *Not Without Laughter* 54.

> opposition is the independent Negro male who seeks allies where he can—in
> the gang, pool hall, blues bar, and barber shop.[52]

Keil refers to working-class blacks in particular when he makes the above distinction. Hughes, on his part, plays on this gender difference without yielding to simplistic reductivism. Although women have the most significant influence on Sandy's awareness of cultural tradition, Hughes does not shun the male contribution to African American lore. Accordingly, he contrasts the female blues tradition with the male folk blues tradition. His depiction of Jimboy's blues reveals important aspects of the history of blues and ways of composing and performing the blues:

> On and on the song complained, man-verses and woman-verses, to the
> evening air in stanzas that Jimboy had heard in the pine-woods of Arkansas
> from the lumber-camp workers; in other stanzas that were desperate and
> dirty like the weary roads where they were sung; and in still others that the
> singer created spontaneously in his own mouth then and there.[53]

The stanzas that Jimboy creates on the spot exemplify a blues tradition called "make-ups". Discussing this tradition while referring to Mississippi Delta blues as an important example, William Ferris points out that this flexible handling of the lyrics by a trained blues musician intensifies the interaction between singer and audience, musician and dancers. Not seldom, the blues singer includes personal names of people in the audience to make up stanzas spontaneously. [54]

Whereas the improvised stanzas indicate the urge for innovation and individuality with an emphasis on the here-and-now, "the man-verses and woman-verses" that Jimboy remembers from his work in lumber-camps illustrate the way of handing down tradition orally—a form of cultural continuity so prevalent within African American lore. Similarly, the juxtaposition of stanzas from a male and those from a female point of view points toward a cultural technique deeply rooted within the black artistic expression on American soil. As the preceding chapter on musical time has illustrated, the call-and-response technique penetrates both the secular and the sacred musical traditions of African Americans. When men and women perform together "a call and response session frequently develops, exposing clearly different sexual perspectives."[55]

The blues in *Not Without Laughter* repeatedly evokes the idea of male absence. The theme of male departure and absence refers especially to the folk blues period and is expressed in Jimboy's blues lyrics:

---

[52]   Charles Keil, *Urban Blues* (Chicago: U of Chicago P, 1991) 9.

[53]   Langston Hughes 52.

[54]   William Ferris, *Blues from the Delta* (New York: Anchor Books, 1979) 63-65.

[55]   Ferris 26.

> I got a mule to ride / I got a mule to ride / Down in the South somewhere/I
> got a mule to ride
>
> You say you goin' North / You say you goin' North / How 'bout yo' . . . lovin'
> gal? / You say you goin' North
>
> O, don't you leave me here / Babe, don't you leave me here / Dog-gone yo'
> comin back! / Said don't you leave me here.[56]

The first stanza suggests poverty but also mobility and a sense of freedom.
Yet the other two stanzas seem to express a feminine point of view. The female
voice moans that the opportunity up North means separation down South.
Especially in the last stanza, the voice assumes a begging as well as an angry
tone. Similarly, the solitary and wandering spirit of men is also essential to the
blues sung by Harriet:

> It's a mighty blue mornin' when yo' daddy leaves / yo' bed. / I says a blue,
> blue mornin' when yo' daddy leaves /yo' bed—t / 'Cause if you lose yo' man,
> you'd just as well be / dead! [57]

Apart from emotional and sexual longing these blues lyrics underline the
uprootedness of black families on American soil. Indeed the transition from
Africa to the New World marks a chain of disruptions for black family
structures. The imposed separation of family members during the period of
slavery was followed by economic and social causes driving a wedge between
male and female members of the African American community in the era of
reconstruction and during the process of urbanization. While it was relatively
easy for a black woman to get hired in a white household, black men faced
tremendous difficulties in finding jobs in a rural area.[58]

As Hughes presents black masculinity in *Not Without Laughter*, growing up
for a black boy means maturing in a matrifocal system. Although Sandy makes
progress in handling the rough sense of humor as part of male companionship,
there is no male role model physically present in the novel that he could identify
with.[59] Protected and guided by the various women in the family, Sandy has to
create a positive male ego figuratively. It is only in the world of books that

---

[56]   Langston Hughes, *Not Without Laughter* 51-52.

[57]   Hughes 298.

[58]   These historical circumstances have nourished the theme of male departure from the early blues
       tradition up to contemporary African American literature, especially by black women. Alice
       Walker's *Color Purple* (1982) and Bebe Moore Campbell's *Your Blues Ain't Like Mine* (1992)
       are just two examples of more recent feminine treatments of the subject.

[59]   Smaller male communities are found in the novel's chapters "Barber-shop" and "Pool Hall."
       Beneath the level of local gossip, smoking, and playing the dozens there is certainly an anti-
       female stance discernible in the talk of men in the barbershop:"Aw, all de womens in de world
       ain't worth two cents to me," one of the waiters comments while being shaved. He continues: "I
       don't respect no woman but my mother" (189). As this excerpt illustrates, even in a exclusively
       male environment the mother plays a central role.

Sandy encounters examples of male guidance, such as in the writings of Frederick Douglass, Booker T. Washington, and W. E. B. DuBois. Unlike his father Jimboy, who embodies the irresponsible and shiftless African American male in Aunt Hager's eyes, these intellectual leaders signify male social achievement. While Jimboy signifies the absence of male time patterns, the three provide him with a theoretical matrix for an orientation in time. Sandy's aspirations, propagated by all the women in the family, are to follow in the footsteps of these famous black leaders. Not surprisingly, the three above fuse as role models in Sandy's imagination when he decides to return to the world of education.

Different from the abstract presence of men in the novel, the appearance of women is connected with strong will and action. It is women who want Sandy to attend college and it is women who are willing to support him financially. On a temporal level, they provide Sandy with a sense of time where past, present, and future are intertwined. In Hughes' rendering, 'woman' comes to represent the ever-present. Baxter Miller concentrates upon the epic dimension of women in Hughes' work when he maintains:

> What Hughes sensed in the folk source of woman was the dynamic will to epic heroism in both the physical and spiritual dimensions, and while the compulsion revealed itself in varying forms—the disciplined application to labor, the folk trickery that allows comic wit to circumvent defeat, the direct act of social defiance—Black woman incarnated the complex imagination and the masks through which it appeared.[60]

The female family ties assume an almost mythic dimension in the figure of Sandy's grandmother Aunt Hager. She teaches him the gospel and makes him acquainted with the African American tradition of storytelling. It is especially she who takes on epic stature when she helps black and white folks after the storm hits the little town in Kansas. The cyclone that hits Kansas leaves large parts of the small town destroyed. Consequently, black neighborhoods are damaged as well as the houses of the white folks in this area. A pattern of mutual dependence becomes visible when Aunt Hager consoles and takes care of the injured and horrified whites after the storm. She embodies African American strength and power having white folks rely on her. In order to strenghten the image of her being closely linked with the past Hughes lets her sing spirituals and emphasizes how well she is versed in African American lore. Hence, telling Sandy stories about the times of slavery and folk tales, Aunt Hager gives the young boy access to the past. When the black washwoman narrates tales about the Rabbit she not only initiates Sandy into folk myths

---

60   R. Baxter Miller, *The Art and the Imagination of Langston Hughes* (Lexington: The UP of Kentucky, 1989) 33.

created in times of slavery, but also makes him aware of black wit and cunning.[61]

Accordingly, the folkloric belief in a cunning black superiority informs Sandy's growing sense of racial pride. Together with the impact of African American music the folk tales help him compensate for the painful experiences of racism during childhood days. Throughout the six years of Sandy's growing up that the reader witnesses, Sandy lives primarily in the company of women. His growing consciousness of self and historical circumstances is consequently shaped by female ethics which Hughes presents indeed in a surprisingly complex and diverse way for the period of the late 1920s. The four women in Sandy's early life signify the diversity that Hughes discerns within the black community. He resorts to color imagery to emphasize the complexity of blackness, visually and verbally, when he describes the sweating dancers on the floor of Cavet's Hall: "Faces gleaming like circus balloons—lemon-yellow, coal-black, powder-grey, ebony-black, blue-black faces; chocolate, brown, orange, tan, creamy-gold faces."[62] Just as the various degrees of color differ from one another, the four women show distinctly different traits. Sandy sympathizes with all except for Tempy, whose bourgeois values he rejects. Although the closeness with the four family members at times causes emotional conflicts—the clash between Hager's and Harriet's life-styles, for instance— Sandy profits from all their experience and guidance.

As becomes obvious, Hughes divides the attributes pointed out by Baxter Miller above among the different women of the family. While Harriet incarnates social defiance, Aunt Hager and Annjee personify the disciplined and hard-

---

61   Brer Rabbit represents an extension of Jack or John, a great human culture hero in African American folklore who "nevertheless, or in spite of laughter, usually defeats Ole Massa, God and the Devil." No matter how superior Ole Massa may appear Brer Rabbit generally ends up winning out by a trick. Zora Neale Hurston, *Mules and Men* (Bloomington: Indiana UP, 1963) 253. A. M. H. Christensen reminds us that Brer Rabbit does not possess the wisdom, intelligence, strength, or beauty of the fox , the elephant, the alligator, or the serpent. Only by means of cunning can he gain success. " So the negro, without education or wealth, could only hope to succeed by stratagem." A. M. H. Christensen, *Afro-American Folk Lore* (New York: Negro UP, 1969) xi-xii. Since Hughes focuses more explicitly on African American music than other sources of the African American folk heritage I want to add here that even within the storytelling tradition music played a central role. Lawrence W. Levine, for instance, explains that many African American tales featured music as a device to trick and deceive the whites. In this context he refers to a black tale from Indianapolis. "In one such story a master dropped in on his slave on a rainy day to hear him play the fiddle. The slave had just stolen a shoat and hidden it under his bed. Afraid that his master would notice the pig's leg sticking out, he sang as he played the fiddle: 'Ding-Ding a Dingy—Old lady put the pig's foot further on the bed.' His wife walked to the bed while harmonizing, 'Ummmmmmmmmmm,' and jerked the cover down over the pig's foot. 'Yessir, that's a new one,' the master said, delighting in the improvised song. 'Yessir, that's a new one.' Lawrence W. Levine, *Black Culture and Consciousness* (New York: Oxford UP, 1977) 11.

62   Langston Hughes, *Not Without Laughter* 91.

working hands of the family. Hughes picks the blues princess Harriet as an artistic role model for Sandy rather than Sandy's father Jimboy, who represents the folk blues tradition. One reason may be that Hughes wants to complete the picture of female guidance for Sandy. Another reason may be that Hughes intends to put more emphasis on the female blues tradition since it was mainly female blues singers who dominated the early recordings of jazz and the jazz scene in vaudeville shows and cabaret.[63] While the male singers dominated the rural folk blues recordings, the women held the upper hand in urban classical blues recordings.[64] Most convincing, however, the assumption appears that Hughes selected a female blues performer because—more than the blues songs by the wandering blues guitarists—the female classical blues tradition stressed the communal aspect of African American music. Usually, artists like Ida Cox, Bessie Smith, and Ma Rainey performed with a jazz band. And the shows that took place in the cities up North set up an atmosphere recalling the communal strength of the days down South. For many migrating African Americans these vaudeville shows created a new sense of place in a strange urban environment.

Shifting in emphasis from Jimboy to Harriet, Hughes traces the transition from folk blues to classical blues as well as the northward migration. When Sandy meets Harriet again she performs successfully in Chicago—the home of the classical blues. Like all the other female members of her family Harriet never loses touch with familial or communal interests. She continues to cultivate both her career as blues singer and her responsibility for the family when she offers Sandy financial support for his education.

Harriet's breakthrough in the world of blues and jazz is not a simple success story, though. In spite of Hughes' celebration of African American folklore, he never denies the harsh socio-economic conditions surrounding the black community. For many women during the early years of jazz, the world of music was irrevocably tied to prostitution and sexual amusement. The promiscuity attributed to Harriet in the small town of Kansas is audible in the man-talk at the barber and in the pool hall. One day she gets arrested for street-walking—an event that upsets her Baptist mother Hager terribly. While Hager gathers strength from the spiritual source of the church, Harriet turns to the dance hall for entertainment and inspiration. Naturally, Harriet's gaiety sharply contrasts with her mother's seriousness; Harriet's way of life not only calls forth images of blues-singing prostitutes in the Tenderloin district but also evokes memories of the emotionally and sexually turbulent life of Bessie Smith and her style of performance.

While Louis Armstrong turned instrumental jazz into a commercial art form, Bessie Smith did the same for the blues in the 1920s.[65] Bessie Smith's shows

---

63   For a very comprehensive view of the female contributions to the classical blues read Daphne
     Duval Harrison, *Black Pearls: Blues Queens of the 1920s* (Brunswick: Rutgers UP, 1988).

64   William Ferris, *Blues from the Delta* 27.

65   Arrigo Polillo, *Jazz*, trans. Egino Biagioni (München: Piper/Schott, 1991) 300-08.

took place partly in tents, partly in theaters. Obviously, the parallels between her shows and Harriet's in *Not Without Laughter* are striking. The former's shows were modern variations of minstrel and carnival shows and, in general, they consisted of a variety of vaudeville presentations. Most of the time, Bessie Smith and her band members travelled by train, and signs like "Bessie Smith And Her Gang Are Here" announced their performances. Even in small Southern towns Bessie Smith managed to fill the tent for several evenings. As a sign of black and female pride hair decoration and jewelry belonged to her regular stage outfit. Although she had a rough side to her character this did not prevent her from establishing the blues in the black as well as the white world artistically and commercially. More than 160 recordings, including such masterpieces as "St. Louis Blues" and "Nobody knows you when you're down and out," illustrate her tremendous artistic productivity.

Harriet's life-style encapsulates part of the social history accompanying the marketing of African American music. Her shift from the folk blues to the classical blues parallels the change from folk art to commercialised art. Moreover, Harriet's career takes on symbolical meaning. Similar to Harriet's life-style her artistic appearance calls forth images of female blues singers such as Bessie Smith and Ida Cox, flamboyantly dressed and decorated with plenty of jewelry for each performance. In the 1920s the female blues performers' fashion articulated female and black affirmation as well as their songs did.[66] To intensify the symbolical meaning of Harriet's career, Hughes draws on a significant clothes metaphor in *Not Without Laughter* which shows that a subtle act of liberation takes place between the beginning and the end of Hughes' panoramic view of African American communal life. Aunt Hager makes both ends meet washing clothes for the white folks. Like Sandy's mother Annjee, who cooks and cleans for the white Rice family, Hager lives on her services for white people and is rather poorly dressed. Harriet complains once that her mother would always walk in the streets with an apron on. In this context it is especially significant that during Harriet's Chicago performance, the blues princess changes dresses twice. First, "stepping out from among the blue curtains, Harriet entered in a dress of glowing orange, flame-like against the ebony of the skin. . . ."[67] She returns to the stage in a new outfit. "When she appeared again, in an apron of blue calico, with a bandanna handkerchief knotted about her head, she walked very slowly. . . ."[68] For her final appearance

---

[66]   See Cheryl A. Wall, "Whose Sweet Angel Child? Blues Women, Langston Hughes, and Writing During the Harlem Renaissance," *Langston Hughes: The Man, His Art and His Continuing Influence* 37-50; 38. Wall points out that the female performers reckless behavior as well as their way of dressing embarrased many members of the African American middle-class. This may also be one of the reason why intellectuals such as W.E.B. DuBois and Alain Locke neglected the classical blues scene almost totally.

[67]   Langston Hughes, *Not Without Laughter* 297.

[68]   Hughes 297.

on stage she again changes her dress. "Her final number was a dance-song which she sang in a sparkling dress of white sequins. . . ."[69]

To complete the clothes metaphor Hughes makes her let her furs slip to the ground after the performance. Clearly Hughes suggests that Harriet reveals the blackness underneath the artist's outfit. Symbolically she drops the furs to expose the African American heritage of her music. Hence she translates in the act of performance an awareness of the past. Her appearance on stage in Chicago not only manifests a sign of cultural assertion, but also marks an act of racial rebellion claiming a better socio-economic status for African Americans.[70] Thus she also points toward a better future for African Americans, as her music calls for historical change.[71] From her mother's work as servant for the white people Harriet, indeed, has come a long way in establishing herself as a successful artist. Naturally, she is still dependent on the white and Jewish proprietors controlling the theaters, but she is confident enough to express her achievement through music and fashion.

Harriet's rebellion is directed against whites in particular but also against those African Americans who deny their own heritage. Hence, she becomes a spokeswoman for Hughes' critique of the African American middle-class. Assimiliationist tendencies, particularly visible in the life-style of black bourgeoisie, are under harsh attack in the novel. Hughes' portrayal of Tempy, for example, pictures the general tendency among the black middle-class to succumb to white standards of art, education, and ethics. Tempy is heavily criticized by her younger sister Harriet:

> Just because she's married a mail-clerk with a little property, she won't even
> see her own family any more. When niggers get up in the world, they act just
> like white folks—don't pay you no mind. And Tempy's that kind of a
> nigger—she's up in the world now![72]

Hughes uses African American music as commentary on the class differences within the family, as the divergent attitudes of Harriet and Tempy toward these musical forms show. Not only does Tempy ignore her own family; she generally rejects the folk culture derived from African American lore. Her

---

69   Hughes 298.

70   See Kristin Hunter-Lattany, "The Girl with the Red Dress On," *Langston Hughes: The Man, His Art and His Continuing Influence* 141-148; Lattany claims that Harriet's dress shows best Hughes' challenge of Christianity and Christian ethics. Indeed Harriet uses both performance and fashion to create a counterworld. Her view of life embraces change, movement, and pleasure whereas she characterizes Jesus as stiff and without meaning for an African American community. Harriet's rhetoric also anticipates the tone of Hughes class-struggling writings of later decades.

71   Hughes' presentation of the rebellious blues woman thus precedes contemporary images of powerful and autonomous blues performers in writings by African American women such as Toni Cade Bambara, Sherley Ann Williams, Ntozake Shange, and Toni Morrison.

72   Langston Hughes, *Not Without Laughter* 41.

social status keeps her within the circle of well-to-do African Americans—
"doctors, schoolteachers, a dentist, a lawyer, a hairdresser."[73] To make his point
Hughes refers to music in particular: "Blues and spirituals Tempy and her
husband hated because they were too Negro."[74] Since Tempy's taste in art is
clearly bourgeois she dismisses folk art as inferior and low-class. Thus she
tolerates the black poet Paul Dunbar on account of his fame, while at the same
time rejecting his use of dialect and his concern with the troubles of lower-class
blacks.[75] It is a matter of good taste for her, though, to subscribe to the black
magazine *The Crisis* whose editorials are written by the intellectually brilliant
W. E. B. DuBois.

Aunt Hager's admiration for the pragmatic philosophy of Booker T.
Washington sharply contrasts with Tempy's embrace of the bookish DuBois and
bourgeois tradition. Obviously, Booker T. Washington and W. E. B. DuBois
function as opposite poles for Hughes' dialectical framework. Washington's
pragmatic approach expresses an accommodationist attitude. The harmonizing
tendencies of Washington's appeals shine through in Hager's balanced world
view. Telling Sandy about love, she explains:

> These young ones what's comin' up now, they calls us ole fogies, an'
> handkerchief heads, an' white folks' niggers 'cause we don't get mad an rar'
> up in arms like they does 'cause things is kinder hard, but, honey, when you
> gets old, you knows they ain't no sense in gettin' mad an' sourin' yo' soul
> with hatin' peoples. White folks is white folks, an' colored folks is colored,
> an neither one of 'em is bad as other make out.[76]

Hager shares Washington's belief when she favors the virtues of patience,
obedience, and hard work for the social improvement of the black race. In the
long run, Washington believed, these virtues will lead to equality in social and
political terms.[77] DuBois' emphasis, on the other hand, lies on black affirmation
and pride when he advocates higher learning for talented African Americans.
He rejects the traits of submission and flattery toward whites present in
Washington's ideology. To him the right to vote, civic equality, and education
represent touchstones for racial improvement.[78] Sandy, then, is caught up in a
generational conflict and a period of historical transition. He, finally, embraces

---

[73] Hughes 240.

[74] Hughes 240.

[75] Hughes 244.

[76] Hughes 177.

[77] See Booker T. Washington, *Up from Slavery: An Autobiography* (New York: Doubleday & Company, Inc., 1933) 151-71.

[78] See W. E. B. DuBois, *Souls of Black Folk* (New York: Fawcett Premier Books, 1916) 42-54.

the blackness of both traditions, though. Having read books by both black leaders, he concludes: "I guess they are both great men."[79]

When Sandy embraces the contrary outlooks, he expresses the idea of cultural synthesis at the same time acknowlegding the diversity within the African American cultural spectrum. In the beginning of the novel sacred and secular music are juxtaposed as two opposite ways of looking at life. In the final chapter, "The Blues Princess", Hughes fuses both traditions, demonstrating a reconciliation of the old and the new, though. The songs of the old-time religion filling the quiet night outside a Chicago Southern Baptist church reach Sandy's ears right after Harriet's blues performance. Sandy's embrace of both traditions signifies cultural identity and historical awareness on his part. This form of cultural fusion signals Sandy's acknowledgement of the common roots of sacred and secular music in times of slavery and their importance for the survival of African Americans in the United States. It becomes clear here that African American music does not only function as negotiating factor on the level of time—between the now and progressing time. Hughes also uses African American music as a platform from which to mediate between differing cultural and historical models within the African American discourse. He does not ignore the fissures within African American social and cultural life in *Not Without Laughter*; yet, while the various rhythms underlying blues and jazz mark for him a force setting black culture apart from its white counterpart they also represent a synthesizing element shaping his historical imagination decisively. In the course of the novel Hughes stresses the music's potential for bringing together colliding forces in history.

When Hager tells Sandy about love and Christian ethics, she not only refers to a generational shift in religious and moral attitude, but obviously suggests a change of paradigm as concerns the relationship between black and white when she criticizes the younger generation for restlessness and aggression. Though Hughes portrays her with sympathy, he shares Harriet's belief in the necessity to change the course of history. Within this context he also makes clear that changes have to precede cultural synthesis, as the generational shift from peaceful accommodation to open critique of white culture reveals. Similar to Harriet, Sandy's consciousness registers the racial barrier resulting in class and caste differentiations, too: "Being colored is like being born in the basement of life, with the door to the light locked and barred—and the white folks live upstairs."[80]

His growing racial pride takes an aggressive turn in the lobby of the Drummer's Hotel. Humiliated by a white southerner who considers colored folks dumb, Sandy throws his boot-black box at the drunken southerner and a group of laughing white men.[81] This is the only instant of immediate revolt

---

79   Hughes 245.

80   Langston Hughes, *Not Without Laughter* 262.

81   Hughes 234.

against white racist behavior within the novel. Interestingly enough, Hughes selects a specific name for the hotel—"Drummer's Hotel"—implying the associative connection between rhythm and rebellion. Historically, the hotel's name refers to "the drummers", a professional group of traveling salesmen who "drummed up" business. But in Hughes's novel the drumming clearly suggests temporal and cultural change. Again music appears in a context where authority is challenged, and the drum occupies a central function.

Overall Sandy's act of rebellion results from a long repressed anger at white supremacy. His childhood experiences of racial segregation, for instance, show that there is a silent rage accompanying his developing sense of racial pride. The angry tears in Sandy's eyes, when he witnesses Mrs. Rice scold his mother for her supposedly careless services in the Rice household, express the helplessness the young boy feels in the face of white dominion. Again and again he has to confront the color line while he is growing up.

Throughout the novel, the panoramic structure of the novel underscores that Hughes' concern transcends the story of just one black boy. He aims at a comprehensive view of the African American community and the historical processes involved with its social conditions. As a novelist Hughes is not concerned with developing economic models, yet tradition and education seem to coincide as complementary concepts in his portrayal of the black community and its potential economic future. Hughes, then, stresses the significance of education without succumbing to elitist thinking. Not surprisingly, he concludes the novel with a scene that resorts to folk music one more time. To him, the music carries the spirit of survival, affirmation, and continuity. At the end of the novel, Sandy and his mother witness "a stream of faith" evoked by the singing of old black worshippers in a Chicago Southern church.[82] This musical scene documents the continuous presence of African American folk music in a new urban context. Hence, the music keeps on providing an orientation in time. It is an open-ended story when the reader leaves Sandy listening to the old women at church. Yet it becomes obvious that Sandy has immersed himself in African American tradition wholeheartedly. And Sandy's implied return to the world of education displays his ambition to play an active role in history and within the black community whose values and cultural tradition he has thoroughly absorbed. While the spirituals express continuity, blues and jazz, implying motion and change, stand forth as artistic models for a deepened black consciousness and self-determined future.

As we have seen, due to the strong presence of black music on the level of content and character, Hughes' novel provides profound insight into the history and sociology of African American musical forms. Hughes' pivotal contribution to the tradition of African American fiction writing lies in his literary adaptations of female and male versions of the blues in their relevance for the representation of time and history on a narrative level. As a work of early

---

82   Hughes 304.

African American modernism *Not Without Laughter* provides the matrix for new experimental uses of musical time as concerns the rendering of history and culture in fiction. Ellison's *Invisible Man* (1952)—the novel which I will discuss in the following chapter—represents the high modernism of African American fiction and functions as a bridge from Hughes' early modernist experiments with blues and jazz to the increasingly more abstract and innovative uses of music and musical time in postmodern fictions.

III. Learning How to Play the Changes: Ralph Ellison and Temporary Patterns against the Flux of History

Recent cultural studies dealing with the problematics of race have pointed out that from the New Deal programs in the 1930s on forms of race-neutrality or color-blindness have characterized racial ideology and public policy in the United States.[1] The new discourses on interracial connections emerging then emphasized that culture was the specific product of a group's sociohistorical experience. Thus new assertions about culture disengaged themselves from the previously dominant "scientific racism" which had focused on inherited differences. Instead, cultural differences were now seen as the outcome of historical development. Temporal progression was regarded as having had a decisive impact on the distribution of material wealth and economic power within a social system. As a result, the new dominant racial paradigm in the postwar era fostered a paradoxical approach toward race. While sociologists exposed racist attitudes among white Americans, they still preserved the historically established racial hierarchy. Accordingly, assimilation was considered inevitable as well as desirable for ethnic minorities. In a similar way color-blindness helped obscure the distinctiveness of jazz as an African American aesthetic mode. Frequent connections between jazz musicians and classical composers made within the cultural discourse placed the innovations of bebop in the orbit of European American culture.

Despite his overall integrationist outlook, Ralph Ellison counteracts the dominant racial ideology at the time emphasizing a unique African American understanding of time. Drawing on the heritage of African American folk culture—blues and jazz in particular—, the protagonist of Ellison's *Invisible Man* (1952) shapes his own account of black history in the United States from an underground perspective. Describing how he wrote the novel, Ellison elucidates:

> I knew that I was composing a work of fiction, a work of literary art and one that would allow me to take advantage of the novel's capacity for telling the truth while actually telling a "lie," which is the Afro-American term for an improvised story. Having worked in barbershops where that form of oral art flourished, I knew that I could draw upon the rich culture of the folk tale as well as that of the novel, and that being uncertain of my skill I would have

---

[1] My argumentation in the opening paragraphs refers to two texts in particular: Jon Panish, *The Color of Jazz: Race and Representation in Postwar American Culture* (Jackson: UP of Mississippi, 1997) 6-10 and Ruth Frankenberg, *White Women, Racial Matters: The Social Construction of Whiteness* (Minneapolis: U of Minnesota P, 1993) 13-14.

>to improvise upon my materials in the manner of a jazz-musician putting a
>musical theme through a wild star-burst metamorphosis.[2]

Frequent references to African American music in its cultural and economic meaning link *Invisible Man* to the descriptive presence of blues and jazz in *Not Without Laughter*. Yet, while Hughes develops his temporal vision in the context of a rather stable panoramic frame of narrativity, Ellison, structurally and thematically, experiments with time within the dialectics of order and chaos. Thus his narrative progression pays tribute both to the complexities of historical developments at the time and the temporal innovations of newly emerging jazz styles in the 1940s.[3]

Between publications of Hughes' novel in 1930 and Ellison's in 1952, historical circumstances such as the Great Depression, the dissatisfactory political alignment of African Americans with the communist party, and the growing ghettoization in the cities up North seemed to have silenced the black community politically and aesthetically. The NAACP only slowly reacted to the social and racial consequences of the desperate economic situation. The Scottsboro case was symbolic of the deep racial hatred separating black from white during Depression. In 1931 nine black youths were accused of raping two white girls of bad reputation while travelling in an open freight car in Alabama. In spite of their protestations of innocence and missing links in the chain of testimony, eight of them were sentenced to death. The NAACP saw itself confronted with violent actions by white Southerners and communist propaganda exploiting the Scottsboro case for ideological purposes. Leftist political organizations such as the International Labor Defense set out to subvert the capitalist hold on black people. They emphasized class, color, and social differences within the black community to win over blacks for communist ideology. However, only a few black intellectuals, discontented with the moderate politics of the NAACP, and minor parts of the working-class African Americans lined up with the communist party. Due to the lack of racial and cultural awareness—many leftists ignored the importance of church and religion

---

2   Ralph Ellison, "Introduction," *Invisible Man* (New York: Vintage Books, 1972) xix.

3   Thematically Ellison signifies upon Hughes's view of the blues as an artistic mode expressing cathartic transcendence of human suffering. Structurally, however, Ellison's adaptation of the blues pattern and the polyphonic set-up of jazz anticipates the more abstract and formal influence of African American musical modes on more recent novels by Toni Morrison, Ishmael Reed, and Ntozake Shange. Hence, this chapter is both forward- and backward-looking, aspiring simultaneously to the historical depth of the Hughes chapter and the more performative textual interpretations of the chapters to come. In my view, Ellison's use of music functions as a gateway from Hughes to contemporary African American novelists as concerns literary adaptations of musical expressions. Necessarily textual and contextual details coincide in my endeavor to exemplify Ellison's central position within the African American narrative tradition.

in the black community—the communist party failed to win over the majority of African Americans.[4]

In the mid-forties, however, political stasis gave way to new hope and action in the African American community. Adopting some of the social awareness of leftist groups, the NAACP turned into a better organized agency of racial protest toward the end of the Depression. The "Double V Campaign—meaning double victory—expressed the political hope of many African Americans during World War II that equality could be established at home as well as abroad. In terms of culture a new black confidence found its musical and religious expression. Musically, bebop expressed the African American difference from the white mainstream; it represented an artistic renewal, a turning away from old patterns, and a resurrection of African rhythmical elements.[5] Thus bebop marked a revolt against the newly popularized swing and implied social and cultural change since many bebop musicians and their

---

[4]   See for further historical information Wilson Record, "The NAACP and the Communist Party," *Afro-American History: Past to Present*, eds. Henry N. Drewry and Cecelia H. Drewry (New York: Charles Scribner's Sons, 1971) 414-20.

[5]   See also Scott DeVeaux, *The Birth of Bebop: A Social and Musical History* (Berkeley: U of California P, 1997) 17-24. Even if bebop represented a revival of African American elements in jazz and expressed a new black consciousness, musicians such as Charlie Parker and Dizzy Gillespie affirmed music "to be a meritocracy rather than a racial privilege" (19), as DeVeaux points out. Both innovators hired white musicians for some of the earliest bebop bands. DeVeaux shares the common assumptions about the ethnic sensibility at the roots of bebop. Yet, to him, the revolutionary potential of bebop has to be seen in the context of musical style and music industry, since "swing was more than a constellation of techniques and procedures to be altered at will by strong-minded artists. It was an integral part of the burgeoning entertainment industry, a genre of dance music embedded within an elaborate framework linking musicians within an elaborate network linking musicians with booking agents, dance-hall and theater operators, songwriters, publishers, journalists, radio broadcasters, record companies—and of course, the public" (29). The bebop musicians revolted from within that system. Amiri Baraka, on the other hand, stresses the ethnicity of jazz and detects in bebop a matrix for social and cultural revolution. See Amiri Baraka and Amina Baraka, *The Music: Reflections on Jazz and Blues* (New York: William Morrow, 1987) 331. It is interesting that Ellison chooses Louis Armstrong as musical model for literary experiments. Obviously he rates the latter's contributions to jazz higher than the innovations brought about by the bebop bands. As various comments by Ellison in *Shadow and Act* (New York: Random House, 1964) underscore, he sees no political vision in bebop. Instead, he locates in bebop a search for new opportunities in the music industry. Preferring Armstrong's contribution to that of bebop musicians, Ellison pays tribute to the former's groundbreaking innovations in jazz. As Eric Nisenson claims,"jazz probably would have faded away by the end of the 1920s if it had retained its ensemble form, a form that restrained much development and in which individualism was eschewed in favor of the ensemble. Radical ideas had to be discouraged when one was playing mostly within an ensemble. And an art form that did not allow for fierce individualism (albeit within the context of a group) really can roughshed against the American grain. So Armstrong's innovations did more than change the jazz of his time; it made possible all jazz innovations to come." Eric Nisenson, *Blue: The Murder of Jazz* (New York: St. Martin's Press, 1997) 64.

followers converted to the Islamic faith. Parallel to these innovations in music, this religious orientation toward Islam expressed a rebellious stance against the white power structure. And a violent dimension, too, gained access to African American politics. In 1943 militant activists resorted to race riots to protest against lynchings and other acts of discrimination in black ghettoes in Harlem, Philadelphia, and Detroit.[6]

Against this turbulent historical background, Ellison set out to write the story of an invisible black man's search for his place in history. In *Invisible Man*, Ellison's artistic representation of constant flux and his view of history as something absurd and grotesque give voice to the radical change, the quest for new orientations in the black community, and the growing sense of a new African American consciousness at the time. Overall, the main plot of the novel signifies a modern black rite of passage. The invisible protagonist's South-to-North journey recalls the movement of African Americans from the postbellum South to the urban centers up North. Metaphorically the protagonist's journey exhibits major periods of African American history—from Reconstruction to the Harlem riots in the 1940s. Spiritually his geographical movement marks a search for cultural roots. Historically, finally, his wanderings reflect his search for a social and political role. While his cultural heritage has been diluted during the years of college education down South, his role modelling undergoes numerous metamorphoses on his journey up North. The journey leads him to Harlem, an anchor of black artistic creativity, but also a scenery for existential chaos as well as political and racial warfare.

Connecting questions of temporality with aspects of disorder, Ellison aesthetically precedes contemporary chaos theories in science and other discourses on a narrative level. According to current assumptions about chaos, each system bears a time frame intrinisic to its own structure. Hence, a rather stable temporal condition persists within a given framework. If a disorder occurs inside the system, the latter's degree of temporal plasticity allows for a rebalancing of temporary disruptions. However, if disruptive elements function outside those oscillations which are tolerated by the system, the frame runs the risk of falling apart. These two poles of chaotic intrusion form the matrix for theories which deal with temporal borderlines determining whether a system dissolves because it cannot preserve its own intrinsic time conception or if it continues to develop by adapting its temporality to outside influences.[7]

Ellison addresses questions of temporal stability and disorder juxtaposing a black sense of time located in the underground with a Western concept

---

6   Cf. Iron Werther, *Bebop: Geschichte einer musikalischen Revolution und ihrer Interpreten* (Frankfurt/Main: Fischer, 1988) 49.

7   For a more extended discussion of time and chaos theories see Wolfgang Achtner, Stefan Kunz and Thomas Walter, *Dimensionen der Zeit: Die Zeitstrukturen Gottes, der Welt und des Menschen* (Darmstadt: Primus Verlag, 1998) 131-39.

dominating mainstream culture.[8] The clash of different experiences of time leads to a series of variations on the theme of alienation throughout the novel in which the invisible man encounters various time zones which are related to African American history as well as to specific categories of social stratification. Starting off from African American bourgeois education, an institution supporting the time system of mainstream culture, Ellison's protagonist enters the temporal experience of the black working class. Besides this vertical shift from upper class to lower class, Ellison makes him move from the center to the margins when the latter gets aligned with the communist party. The underground, finally, marks a time zone in which African American culture manages to articulate its own sense of history.[9]

A closer look at the various stages of the protagonist's journey displays the sense of alienation resulting from the continuous encounter with differing notions of time. And music repeatedly functions as a commentary on the protagonist's relation to past and flux while the plot progresses.[10] Accordingly, Ellison's approach to history resembles a blues or jazz musician's approach to the musical sheet. History—or better, the quest for the nature of history— signifies the central theme of *Invisible Man*. Ellison plays variations upon this theme, confronting the reader with various references to historical events or periods. Yet, he chooses the artist's indirect approach to history in that he rather evokes than names actual events. As regards the history of African Americans in the United States, the invisible man's story signifies significant periods such as Reconstruction, Great Migration, Great Depression, and Harlem riots.[11]

---

8   Ellison's creation of a specific African American conception of time underscores the growing ethnic awareness among minority writers in the 1950s and 60s. Cf. Alfred Hornung, "Postmoderne bis zur Gegenwart," *Amerikanische Literaturgeschichte*, ed. Hubert Zapf (Stuttgart: J.B. Metzler, 1997) 257-304; 317.

9   Ellison chooses the underground as a space for cultural affirmation. As concerns the relationship between the races, the factory episode—"Optic White" in particular—stands as a symbol for the process of acculturation in America. Ironically, African Americans are still invisible while blackness continues to blacken the white world. The batches of paint for the national monuments are still of the purest white; even the campus buildings and the Golden Day were once painted white. And the ten drops of dead black paint almost disappear in the bucket of white paint. What remains is "Optic White"(196).

10   Various folk art forms (the blues, jazz, folk rhymes, and folk tales), folk figures based in oral traditions (B'rer Rabbit and Stakolee), and verbal games function as guidelines for the invisible man to come closer to the roots of his African American heritage. At the same time they reveal his distorted relationship to the past and his problems with flux and change. See also Lawrence R. Rodgers, *Canaan Bound: The African-American Great migration Novel* (Urbana: U of Illinois P, 1997). Rodgers emphasizes that folk art forms provide Ellison's protagonist with numerous authentic models for reconstituting the Harlem environment "within the context of a usable southern cultural and communal tradition" (158).

11   Susan L. Blake, "Ritual and Rationalization: Black Folklore in the Works of Ralph Ellison," *Ralph Ellison*, ed. Harold Bloom (New York: Chelsea House Publishers, 1986) 77-99; 86.

The college, for instance, which the invisible man attends, bears the traits of the philosophy of Booker T. Washington that emerged in the years of reconstruction. Dr. Bledsoe embodies the integrationist, if not submissive, aspect of Washington's social outlook. To be humble, to study and work hard, to live up to the standards of white culture represent touchstones of Washington's advice for black people.[12]

When the invisible man heads North with Dr. Bledsoe's fake letters of recommendation, he undergoes a journey that parallels the migration of thousands of black families at the turn of the century to the urban areas in the North. Many left the South because of a lack of economic and social opportunity. Similarly, the invisible man has to leave the South since he is expelled from college. His arrival in New York implies the calamities involved in this change of place and milieu. It is difficult for him to find housing and a job. When he finally gets hired in a paint factory, his contact with the trade unions gets him into a fight with a black foreman, who is afraid to lose his job. While fighting, the two man fail to watch one of the boilers, which overheats and causes an explosion in the factory basement

The invisible man's expulsion from his position in the paint factory, along with the eviction of the old black couple in Harlem, call forth the social dilemma of the Great Depression of the 1930s. The same time period is evoked when the invisible man joins the communist organization of the Brotherhood, since various groups of the African American population felt attracted to communist ideology at the time. The riot lead by Ras the Destroyer, finally, evokes a series of upheavals in the streets of Harlem and other American cities during the 1940s, when African Americans turned to violent action. Overall, Ellison uses the period from the invisible man's adolescence to manhood to portray more than fifty years of African American history.

The invisible man's journey is accompanied by a series of collapsing value systems and ideologies. First, the protagonist receives a scholarship to a black college down South after a "battle royal," a brawl in which several blindfolded black boys fight for the entertainment of an all-white audience. At the college he cultivates an image of himself based upon the assimilative values of the black bourgeoisie. Losing direction on his trip with Mr. Norton, a financier and college benefactor from New England, he faces the poorer black quarters for the first time. He encounters the incestuous Trueblood and the world of prostitution in The Golden Day, a black brothel for army vets. Trueblood shatters the protagonist's innocent outlook, telling him and Mr. Norton all about his incestuous act with his daughter, his wife's attack on him with an axe, and his final decision to return and take care of his wife and daughter, who are both pregnant. The ideal world of black bourgeois education collapses further in The Golden Day where the invisible protagonist and Mr Norton stop, since the latter

---

12   See Booker T. Washington, *Up from Slavery: An Autobiography* (New York: Doubleday & Company, Inc. 1933) 151-71.

has suffered a nervous breakdown after the encounter with Trueblood. Ironically the invisible protagonist encounters primarily caricatures of black bourgeoisie there, such as doctors and lawyers.

After his release from the factory hospital he joins the Brotherhood, an organization modelled on the communist party, to become a political activist. Caught between diverse factions, he experiences the denial of individuality within the political group. A similar experience characterizes his encounter with manifestations of black nationalism. During a Harlem race riot Ras the Destroyer, a militant black nationalist, chases him into a panic-driven crowd that pushes the invisible man underground. To the invisible man, neither the communist utopia of Brother Jack nor the black utopia of Ras the Destroyer bears potential for social fulfillment.[13] Beneath the surface of public history he burns all the documents and signs of his former identities.

Overall the protagonist's journey suggests an up-and-down movement between the above ground and the underground, between the white and the black world. Repeatedly he disappears underground—in the factory scene, in the New York subway, and into the lighted hole—to return again to the above world throughout the main plot. Dismissing the projection of an African American utopia, the invisible man narrates various time experiences in a way which is comic and tragic at the same time, thus reminiscent of the blues.

Throughout the novel blues and jazz function as guidance for cultural orientation.[14] Ellison sets up a series of situations in which the protagonist confronts his own cultural background, after having become gradually defamiliarized with it in his college setting. While the college faculty teaches history to be a linear, teleological progression based upon the Protestant work ethic, the blues exposes the ambiguity of historical reality for African Americans. It is difficult for the invisible man, though, to comprehend ambivalence. He rejects Trueblood's "talkin' the blues;" moreover the protagonist is embarrassed and shocked at Mr. Norton's interest in Trueblood's story. Trueblood hits the nail on the head when he points out the class difference between the protagonist and himself: "The nigguhs up at school don't

---

13   For a discussion of utopia in 19th and 20th century art and literature see Italo Calvino, *Kybernetik und Gespenster: Überlegungen zu Literatur und Gesellschaft*, trans. Susanne Schoop (München: Carl Hanser Verlag, 1984) 78-86. As Calvino puts it, utopia as a literary genre is superseded by utopian energies in the field of art and literature in the course of the 20th century. In the literary tradition utopian and anti-utopian elements often stand side-by-side. In Invisible Man, too, both aspects of the utopian tradition are juxtaposed in a dialectical manner. For an extensive analysis of utopian and anti-utopian aspects in English literature see Willi Erzgräber, *Utopie und Antiutopie in der englischen Literatur* (München:Wilhelm Fink Verlag, 1980).

14   As Cataliotti points out, African American music functions as a touchstone for racial and cultural identity in Invisible Man. Cf. Robert H. Cataliotti. *The Music in African American Fiction* (New York: Garland Publishing, 1995) 160.

like me."[15] Later the narrator smashes the grinning African sculpture in Mary
Rambo's apartment and burns one of the Sambo dolls sold by his former friend
and colleague in the Brotherhood, Tod Clifton. The protagonist's encounter with
the blues sung by Pete Wheatstraw finally leaves him in a state of confusion and
repulsion. Pete Wheatstraw is obviously modelled on a living blues musician
who was often referred to as the devil. As Polillo mentions, Peetie Wheatstraw
used the epithet "the devil's son-in-law" for his performances after the repeal
had ended prohibition in 1933.[16]

In the novel, Pete Wheatstraw's blues evokes in the protagonist a sense of
ambivalence:

> She's got feet like a monkey / Legs like a frog—Lawd, Lawd! But when she
> starts to loving me / I holler Whoooo, God-dog! Cause I loves my baabay /
> Better than I do myself. . . .[17]

The blues lyrics uttered by the blues singing pushcart man play on the
discrepancy between being and appearance. The attitude of the blues singer
toward the woman wooed is characterized by ambiguity. The sexual pleasure
expressed by Wheatstraw sharply contrasts with the description of the woman's
body. A sense of humor—"Whoooo, God-dog"—accompanies the obvious
contradiction. Ellison draws on the tremendous treasure of humor in blues lyrics
setting up the Wheatstraw episode. The blues singer responds with a sense of
humor to the uncertainty implied by the ambivalent content of the lyrics. The
invisible protagonist, however, still lacks the insight and humor necessary to
comprehend and endure the complexity of life. "And why describe anyone in
such contradictory words? . . . . What kind of a woman could love a dirty fellow
like that, anyway? And how could he even love her if she were as repulsive as
the song described."[18] The invisible man's attitude toward his folk roots has not
changed since his reaction to Trueblood's story. By and large, he continues to
feel repelled by the folk heritage and cannot comprehend the coexistence of
comic and tragic aspects in Wheatstraw's blues. Still the innocent protagonist
does not realize the interrelation between folklore and economics, between
cultural heritage and personal grounding, as long as he moves above ground. As
his positive response to Mary Rambo's singing of Bessie Smith's *Back Water
Blues* indicates, though, the invisible protagonist begins to recognize the
significance of his cultural past step by step. He even detects the potential for

---

[15]   Ralph Ellison, *Invisible Man* 67.

[16]   Arrigo Polillo, *Jazz: Geschichte und Persönlichkeiten*, trans. Egino Biagioni (München:
       Piper/Schott, 1991) 134. Frequently in the history of blues the music has been labelled "the
       devil's music," primarily because of its bawdy, sensuous lyrics. See also Giles Oakley, *The
       Devil's Music: A History of the Blues* (New York: Harcourt Brace Jovanovich Inc., 1976) 186-
       88.

[17]   Ralph Ellison, *Invisible Man* 170.

[18]   Ellison 173-74.

survival in his folk heritage and he learns how to use it, as the Sybil episode—full of blues humor— underscores.[19] His final descent from the ivory tower of college life to the depth of the blues signifies a reunion of the individual with his cultural heritage. "Old Bad Air is still around with his music and his dancing and his diversity, and I'll be up and around with mine," the invisible man announces from the underground.[20] Writing his story, the black modern artist has found his roots. Trueblood and the invisible man merge into a common cultural tradition, finally.

This synthesis may be modelled upon Ellison's own carrer as a writer and his fusion of modernist writing with African American folklore. Indeed, the connection of Ellison with blues and jazz is a well-established one in the world of literary criticism. While Kerry McSweeney argues that blues and jazz are not "the predominant artistic influences on the novel"—he favors the literary influence of Dostoyevski, Eliot, and Joyce—I suggest, with a nod to critics like Baker, Bone, and Ostendorf, that blues and jazz in particular have shaped Ellison's historical imagination.[21] Ellison's novel, his essays, and his biographical background reflect his close affiliation with the treasure of African American music and that of classical music as well. Already at Douglass High School in Oklahoma City, Ellison entered the musical stage as first chair trumpeter in the school band. As Dorothea Fischer-Hornung points out, "the school which Ellison attended placed a strong emphasis upon classical music. Classical music and jazz were in no way contradictory for Ellison, and both styles gave him a sense of both the Western and the Afro-American tradition, including the interaction of both."[22] Before he decided to become a writer he studied music and music theory at Tuskegee Institute.[23] Despite the presence

---

[19] Here Ellison signifies on white stereotyping in the erotic parody with Sybil. His irony is at its best when he reverses attributes generally given to black males by whites. The classical images of the black entertainer and the black rapist are undermined and projected upon Sybil, the white woman. In this episode the invisible man becomes aware of the threat of white supremacy and knows how to play it. Sybil asks him to rape her. Whereas he is supposed to live up to her expectations, he gets her drunk and puts her to sleep instead. Quickly he writes on her belly: "SYBIL, YOU WERE RAPED BY SANTA CLAUS SURPRISE" (511). Although he erases the letters immediately he indulges in make-believe when Sybil wakes up from her inebriation: "I leaped straight out of the wall. I overpowered you in the empty lobby—remember? I smothered your terrified dreams" (512). Indeed this scene embodies the comic aspects of the blues. And the invisible man has embraced a sort of blues humor: "Poor Sybil, she picked a boy for a man's job and nothing was as it was supposed to be. Even the black bruiser fell down on the job" (512). Learning the art of signifying, he comes a lot closer to his cultural roots. And folk culture, to Ellison, becomes a firm stand from which to explore art as well as life.

[20] Ellison, *Invisible Man* 568.

[21] Kerry McSweeney, *Invisible Man: Race and Identity* (Boston: Twayne Publishers, 1988) 7.

[22] Dorothea Fischer-Hornung, *Folklore and Myth in Ralph Ellison's Early Works*, diss., U Heidelberg, 1979 (Stuttgart: Hochschulverlag, 1979) 12.

[23] Kerry McSweeney, *Invisible Man: Race and Identity* xi.

of classical music in *Invisible Man*, blues and jazz stand forth as the chief musical influences on Ellison's novel, for most references to music are related to African American music. His interest in African American music finds further expression in *Shadow and Act* (1964), a collection of essays, interviews, and reviews. There Ellison explicitly focuses on the African American musical expression and the interrelation of African American and American mainstream culture.

In *Invisible Man*, Ellison explores the literary possibilities of musical form and its temporal dimension. Hence, blues and jazz shape the novel in terms of structure, too. The overall set-up of the novel—prologue, main plot, and epilogue—recalls the statement-repetition-resolution pattern underlying the three vocal stanzas of the classical blues form. While the general statement is repeated in the second stanza, the third stanza signifies a sort of resolution, as regards the first two stanzas.[24] Ellison introduces the trope of invisibility, implying a sense of spatial and temporal displacement already in the prologue: "I am an invisible man."[25] He then signifies upon this trope throughout the main plot of the invisible man's journey.[26] Accordingly, a sense of disturbance accompanies the scenes at college, in the paint factory, in the hospital, and in the political setting of Harlem. The epilogue, finally, returns to the trope of invisibility, commenting on both the prologue and the main plot. The voice of the epilogue expresses a sort of resolution since it states the narrator's loss of innocence and announces the possibility of his return to public history.

Jazz, too, shapes the artistic form that Ellison develops around his view of history. He translates the polyrhythmic progression of jazz into a variety of

---

[24]   Cf. Charles Keil, *Urban Blues* (Chicago: U of Chicago P, 1991) 51-52. As concerns structure, Keil describes the blues, its basic pattern, and improvisations, as follows: "A blues chorus or verse usually falls into a 4/4 twelve bar pattern, divided into three call-and-response sections with the over-all rhyme scheme of A A B. Occasionally this basic verse unit is contracted to eight bars or expanded to sixteen or twenty-four, but most recorded blues renditions are based upon this twelve bar sequence. Typically the singer delivers a line or two in iambic pentameter over the first eight or nine beats, filling the remainder of the four-bar melodic phrase with complementary instrumental figures that usually lead into a word-for-word repetition of the first stanza, sometimes punctuated at the beginning or end with an exclamation like "yeah," "Lord have mercy," "I said"; the third stanza resolves in some way the thought reiterated in the first two stanzas. There is something like a double dialectic to be found in many blues renditions: on the one level every sung phrase is balanced or commented upon by an instrumental response that often carries as important a message as the preceding words. Following this interaction the blues chorus can be divided into six parts of overlapping vocal calls and instrumental responses." As Keil's definition persuasively illustrates, the blues form represents both a formal and a temporal model for Ellison, as he plays with the interaction of various time experiences in *Invisible Man*.

[25]   Ralph Ellison, *Invisible Man* 3.

[26]   In a similar way Cataliotti regards the prologue as matrix for further improvisations throughout the main plot. Cf. Robert H. Cataliotti, *The Music in African American Fiction* (New York: Garland Publishing, 1995) 158.

literary styles, giving voice to the constant change underlying history. The changes, however, follow a certain cyclical pattern reminiscent of the theme and variation sequences in jazz. And the tropes of invisibility and alienation are presented by a narrative voice adopting various modes of expression. These different modes play on the above tropes, illuminating the invisibility of blackness in various geographical and historical settings. Like the different solo voices of a collective jazz improvisation, these modes comment upon the historical invisibility of blackness. In traditional jazz such as New Orleans jazz, for instance, polyphony occurs when the cornet, clarinet, and trombone are each improvising on their own simultaneously. The three melodic lines complement one another, thus building up group improvisation. The novel's movement then resembles that of a jazz improvisation superimposing various themes, rhythms, and instrumental or singing solo voices on one another.

In his literary conception of history Ellison relates blues to metaphysics. Ellison defines the blues as a comic-tragic expression of the human condition in a well-known passage in *Shadow and Act*:

> The blues is an impulse to keep the painful details and episodes of a brutal experience alive in one's aching consciousness, to finger its jagged grain, and to transcend it, not by consolation of philosophy but squeezing from it a near-tragic, near-comic lyricism. As a form, the blues is an autobiographical chronicle of personal catastrophe expressed lyrically.[27]

The novel draws on the blues as an autobiographical form developing the protagonist's growth from innocence to experience. On a temporal level, the individual existence functions as a comment on history in general and African American history in particular. Likewise, the individual growth is accompanied by a series of personal catastrophes that reflect Ellison's larger view of history. The sense of uncertainty in many blues lyrics underlies the overall human condition, as Ellison would put it. History cannot be projected or controlled by a design. When the invisible man expresses his belief that life should be lived according to a plan, the blues-singing push-cart man Pete Wheatstraw reveals the former's immaturity: "Folks is always making plans and changing 'em. . . . You kinda young daddy-O."[28] Wheatstraw's reply not only represents a piece of advice for his younger opposite; it also foreshadows the invisible man's destiny in the future course of the novel. As Wheatstraw's comment on the ever-changing plans of folks suggests, kinesis represents the force behind history. As an artistic reaction to flux, the blues performance provides a cathartic effect enabling the blues singer to pattern a sense of self against the turmoil of historical change. Even if the blues musician is still invisible, the blues has rendered black culture audible. Finally, Ellison resorts to blues and jazz to achieve a fusion of African American folklore and modernist art. As Berndt

---

27   Ralph Ellison, *Shadow and Act* (New York: Random House, 1964) 78-79.

28   Ralph Ellison, *Invisible Man* 172.

Ostendorf points out, jazz represents the ideal paradigm for Ellison to bridge the gap between these two artistic modes:

> Jazz is indeed a squaring of the circle: it is deeply rooted in the black folk and its music (Charlie Parker and Ornette Coleman played in jump bands) and it has repeatedly been revitalized by black folk energy such as the blues and the gospel. At the same time it is a global, Modernist idiom.[29]

Ostendorf, thus, underscores the integrationist aspect that jazz plays in Ellison's writings. Jazz represents the supreme African American art form that paves the way for black folklore into the American mainstream.

In Ellison's view of history, white culture has driven black culture into the underground. Symbolically his use of music suggests racial hierarchy and a cultural rebellion from underneath. The traumatic experience of the invisible man's awakening in the hospital, for instance, is accompanied by the sounds of Beethoven's Fifth Symphony: "the Fifth Symphony rhythm racked me."[30] The scene portrays an all-powerful team of white doctors and nurses attempting to brainwash the invisible man. In Ellison's rendering, the white power system becomes associated with the dramatic progression of classical music. Armstrong's blues, in contrast, signifies a subversive tune from the black world in the underground. When we encounter the protagonist listening to Armstrong's blues we enter a new time dimension evoking history as well as a sense of unreal time; for the protagonist is stoned when he approaches the depth of the blues.

Ellison, thus, builds on the association of jazz with the world of drugs and brothels so prevalent in the early decades of this century. Particularly Ellison seems to have in mind the Storyville quarter in New Orleans where, according to the jazz legend, one of jazz's birthplaces can be located. His choice of Armstrong for the underground musical experience becomes almost self-evident for Louis Armstrong's "Basin Street Blues" signifies an homage to all the honky tonks around Basin Street in the Storyville district which became the red-light-district of New Orleans in 1897. The city administration brought this restricted area into being in order to fight the rapidly expanding prostitution with all its consequences of violence and deceit. As numerous historical documents illustrate, the atmosphere in Storyville was characterized by a mixture of game and crime, pleasure and intoxication, music, drugs, and business.[31]

In *Invisible Man* the underworld is part of a subculture and the lighted cellar signifies the removed place of the artist. Interestingly enough, Ellison chooses no tower—ivory tower—as many white modernist writers would have; on the contrary, he selects the underground for his evolving artist. The hint is clearly

---

[29]   Berndt Ostendorf, "Ralph Waldo Ellison: Anthropology, Modernism, and Jazz" *New Essays on Invisible Man*, ed. Robert O'Meally (New York: Cambridge UP, 1988) 95-121; 117.

[30]   Ralph Ellison, *Invisible Man* 228.

[31]   Cf. Anne Faber, *Louis Armstrong* (Hamburg: Cecilie Dressler Verlag, 1977) 58-61.

social and racial. Only from the underground can black culture modify its white mainstream counterpart. Jazz and blues, too, have often been performed in places different from the sunny side of the street. Even during the heydays of jazz in the 1920s traits such as sleazy and low-class were attributed to the clubs where blues and jazz were performed. The atmosphere in The Golden Day symbolizes the "hot" atmosphere associated with these clubs at the turn of the century and during the Harlem Renaissance. Most significant, yet, life in the underground, according to Ellison, is accompanied by a different sense of time: "Invisibility, let me explain, gives one a slightly different sense of time, you're never quite on the beat."[32] Describing the different conception of time, Ellison continues: "Sometimes you're ahead and sometimes behind. Instead of the swift and imperceptible flowing of time, you are aware of its nodes, those points where time stands still or from which it leaps ahead."[33] Ellison emphasizes the smallest perceptible time unit, the moment. Relating it to breaks in jazz, he makes clear that a regular flow of time is not part of the world outside mainstream culture. As we know by now, the accentuation in jazz is more flexible and subtle as compared to its counterpart in European music. The jazz musician can place the accentuation at any place between two beats, thus playing off beat.[34] The break, too, marks a rhythmic quality that sets blues and jazz apart from the European tradition. As a musical technique, it causes a melodic and rhythmic effect ensuing from the sudden interruption of all instruments. What emerges is a moment where music and audience alike are taken out of a rhythmic movement to enter it again or to enter a new one afterward. In the protagonist's black hole where a new sense of time leads him to a new state of cultural awareness, breaks imply discontinuity. Hence, changing tempos characterize the temporal experience in the underground.

Analyzing Louis Armstrong's "What Did I Do to Be So Black and Blue," the invisible man realizes the meaning of blackness within a dominant white society. Interestingly enough, Ellison resorts to the call-and-response pattern to develop the invisible man's descent into the world of Armstrong's music. This pattern is embedded in a scene of a church service and it moves from the call-and-response ceremony of the servive to a question-and-answer conversation between the invisible man and an old black woman. Throughout this descent, Ellison's protagonist moves through various dimensions of time, indicated by the changing tempos of Armstrong's performance:

> And beneath the swiftness of the hot tempo there was a slower tempo and a cave and I entered it and looked around and heard an old woman singing a spiritual as full of Weltschmerz as flamenco, and beneath that lay a still lower level on which I saw a beautiful girl the color of ivory pleading in a

---

[32]   Ralph Ellison, *Invisible Man* 8.

[33]   Ellison 8.

[34]   Joachim E. Berendt, *Das Jazzbuch* (Frankfurt/Main: Fischer Verlag, 1991) 257.

voice like my mother's as she stood before a group of slaveowners who bid for her naked body, and below that I found a lower level and a more rapid tempo and I heard someone shout: "Brothers and sisters, my text this morning is the 'Blackness of Blackness'.[35]

As Ellison suggests, jazz's complex rendering of musical time provides a paradigm for the protagonist to come to terms with the complexities of history. The latter cannot be understood as a one-dimensional category of time. Instead, as the changes of rhythm demonstrate, one needs to be aware of diverse time levels to comprehend the historical process. Jazz enables the invisible man to anchor his life in a time pattern intrinsic to his own intercultural background. With its negotiations between different cultural time conceptions jazz is essential for an African American to assert at least a temporary cultural identity. Therefore jazz turns into an aesthetic model which functions as a balancing element within the dialectics of chaos and order.

Roughly, Ellison divides history into a static and a kinetic dimension. History as dialectical pattern also nourishes the ideas of critics such as Keith E. Byerman and C.W.E. Bigsby. They describe Ellison's conception of history as a juxtaposition of order and disorder. Byerman, for instance, contrasts the ideological, abstract view of history with the particularly individual, emotional experience of historical circumstances.[36] Bigsby follows a similar path opposing chaos and order as crucial poles of human experience.[37] In *Invisible Man* the fixed pattern that society urges on the perpetual flux of time is represented through the various social roles such as Dr. Bledsoe, the director; Reverend Barbee, the preacher, and Tod Clifton, the political speaker and activist, all of whom the invisible man faces while searching for a role in history. Ellison then dialectically contrasts the history of fixed social roles with the ultimate disorder and chaos embodied in the protean figure of Rinehart: "Rine the runner and Rine the gambler and Rine the briber and Rine the lover and Rinehart the Reverend. . . ."[38] Rinehart's metamorphoses suggest chaos as well as possibility. The lack of form describing his personality links him to the other worlds of disorder in Invisible Man—the Golden Day, the factory, and Harlem. Rinehart symbolizes "infinite possibilities" but lacks any clue as to what form these possibilities might take. In musical terms, he remains a soloist who cannot fit in a group framework. Although Rinehart is never present, as a historical manifestation of chaos, he represents a constant reminder that flux is

35   Ralph Ellison, *Invisible Man* 9.

36   Keith E. Byerman, *Fingering the Jagged Grain: Form and Tradition in Recent Black Fiction* (Athens: The U of Georgia P, 1985) 12.

37   C. W. E. Bigsby, "Improvising America: Ralph Ellison and the Paradox of Form" *Speaking For You: The Vision of Ellison*, ed. Kimberly W. Benston (Washington D.C.: Howard UP, 1987) 173-83; 175.

38   Ralph Ellison *Invisible Man* 486-87.

ever–present; form can only be patterned against the always already there—chaos.

The invisible protagonist then finds himself in a similar situation as the jazz musician during the bebop period. As Stearns describes it, the effort of the individual for the sake of group improvisation always required new adjustment to new open forms. In adopting the traits and procedures of the jam session and turning them into the central focus of performance, bebop radically revised the definition of jazz prevalent in the swing era. Characterized by rhythmic flexibility, displays of virtuosity, and an absence of closure, the jam seession provided the ideal matrix for a frameless performance practice.[39] Constant improvisation then was/is required for both the bebop musician and the invisible protagonist on the way to form temporary patterns against the constant flux.[40]

As a balancing and negotiating medium, improvisation clearly contrasts with rigid scientific method. Rinehart, the historical chameleon, dismantles the delusive ideology of the Brotherhood. The latter, a political organization modelled on the communist party, advocates belief in the possibility of controlling historical process: "Still it was a world that could be controlled by science, and the Brotherhood had both science and history under control."[41] The invisible protagonist's encounter with Rinehart's manifold facets opens the borderline between chaos and static social role playing and lets him enter a new dimension on his way to define his self and his place in history. At first he appears trapped between social control and complete chaos, between the documents and certificates of social order and the confusion in a world of mere signs as created by Rinehart. To the protagonist's understanding of self—only slowly evolving in a process of belief and delusion—the limitless freedom of Rinehart seems as smothering as the narrow cage of social history and its destined professional roles. To the naive protagonist, halfway through the novel, established social roles bear heavy attraction since they promise solid and static order.

Recalling the belief in a life-design of Melville's Captain Ahab and Faulkner's Colonel Sutpen, Ellison equips his protagonist with a deep loyalty to a form once it is adopted. As Ellison makes clear, this form is always controlled by the white power structure. African Americans who aspire to take their share in this ruling system have to wear masks. Hence, they have to succumb to

---

[39]   The repertory of the jam session is limited to the blues, Gershwin's *I Got Rhythm*, and a number of popular tunes. As DeVeaux points out, "the only fixed personnel is a rhythm section of piano, bass, guitar, drums. . . . The Format is a string of solos—each instrumentalist playing for as many cycles or choruses, as desired. The other 'horns' either wait their turn or improvise background figures behind the soloist." Scott DeVeaux, *The Birth of Bebop: A Social and Musical History* (Berkeley: U of California P, 1997) 202-04.

[40]   Cf. Marshall W. Stearns, *The Story of Jazz* (New York: Oxford UP, 1970) 221-22.

[41]   Ralph Ellison, *Invisible Man* 373.

telling lies and manipulating. At first the invisible protagonist sees nothing but honesty and integrity in the lives of the college director Dr. Bledsoe, the Northern trustee Mr. Norton, and the young liberal Mr. Emerson during his age of innocence. Only gradually does he disclose the trickery and fakery behind their lives. He has to learn that, in this border area between stasis and kinesis, ambiguity reigns. Ellison's social and artistic vision takes shape against this background of uncertainty. Here the significant role of improvisation comes into play again. In moments of uncertainty improvisation becomes a means of survival. Explicitly, Ellison comments on the flux of time and the ordering pattern of music in "The World and the Jug":

> Perhaps in the swift change of American society in which the meanings of one's origin are so quickly lost, one of the chief values of living with music lies in its power to give us an orientation in time. . . . In the swift whirl of time music is a constant reminding us of what we were and of that toward which we aspired. 'Art thou troubled? Music will not only calm, it will ennoble thee.'[42]

Ellison sees not only a link to the past in blues and jazz. To him these musical forms nourish memory as well as vision. Many critics of African American music share Ellison's belief that jazz in particular responds to time shifts. To them jazz represents an ideal paradigm for the individual and the artist to give shape to the flux of modern times. And the history of jazz documents it, since each style in jazz embraced a new rhythmic vitality bringing forth changes in melody and harmony. Every renewal brought about harmonic and rhythmic expansions as the music retained "its immediacy and its emotional concurrency with contemporary life."[43]

Ellison plays on various notions of time in *Invisible Man*. Drawing upon jazz's multiple layers of time, he subverts a rigidly linear and teleological pattern of temporal progression. The jazz structure of the novel reflects the protagonist's final conception of history, as expressed in the prologue: "That (by contradiction, I mean) is how the world moves: Not like an arrow, but a boomerang."[44] The image of the boomerang suggests a forward as well as a backward, an upward as well as a downward movement. Departure and return imply future and past and their interdependence. Likewise Ellison moves back and forth between lived and measured time and his rendering of temporality establishes personal experience as a gateway to history on a larger scale. What emerges is not a chronological pattern in the conventional sense. Although the invisible man's shift from rural to an urban area recalls African American migration and presents time as a continuous process, Ellison adds elements of discontinuity. The invisible man's encounter with Trueblood in the poor black

---

42   Ralph Ellison, *Shadow and Act* 198.

43   Martin Williams, *The Jazz Tradition* (New York: Oxford UP, 1993) 49.

44   Ralph Ellison, *Invisible Man* 6.

quarters near the college or his stay with Mary Rambo in New York suggest a return to earlier stages in African American history. Progression then is interrupted by a temporal countermovement. Recursive elements disrupt the progressive flow. For African Americans especially, the historical process represents a constant wandering between the world above ground and its counterpart in the underground. As concerns Ellison's literary vision of history, jazz serves as artistic model for a dialogical art without closure. It shall suffice here to point to Louis Armstrong and Charlie "Bird" Parker as just two examples of jazz musicians who always looked for new harmonies and rhythmical progression within a respect for tradition. Although they kept on referring to traditional material they never accepted any set musical boundaries.

Artistically, Ellison improvises upon black history by translating the different time stages into a movement from an idyllic state to the state of violence and confusion. Life on campus, in the eyes of the narrator, still signifies an idyllic view of history. Gradually, though, history begins to display signs of eruption and turbulence. Trueblood's narration hints at the darker forces at work in history. Inside the walls of the Golden Day, chaos reigns. History breaks out of a controllable pattern and exposes the idea of progress as illusion. The education on campus meant to uplift the race has driven African Americans into a state of madness, so it seems. Most of the patients seem to be caricatures of the self-same black middle-class the invisible man hopes to join—lawyers, doctors, and businessmen. In the course of the novel history loses its cover of innocence; it gives way to absurd and grotesque manifestations. Accordingly, narrow conceptions of history like those of Dr. Bledsoe, Mr. Emerson, or Brother Jack break down in the narrator's consciousness. History becomes more and more fragmentary and manifold. Accordingly, numerous facets of history leave an imprint on the mind of the narrator.

In terms of literary technique, Ellison translates various conceptions of time into a continuously changing narrative voice. When the protagonist listens to Armstrong's recording the four musical tempos are conceived of as temporal layers. And they signal four levels of consciousness expressed by the changing voice of the narrator. As Ellison draws on polyphony, the voice assumes four major modes of expression, shifting back and forth. In its early stage it is omniscient, recording and expressing events in a realistic/mimetic manner; so, for instance, when the protagonist recalls the last words of his grandfather on the latter's deathbed, he renders his memories from a seemingly omniscient point of view:

> But my folks were more alarmed over his last words than over his dying. It was as though he had not died at all, his words caused so much anxiety. I was warned emphatically to forget what he had said and, indeed, this was the first time it has been mentioned outside the family circle. It had a tremendous effect upon me, however. I could never be sure of what he meant. Grandfather had been a quiet old man who never made any trouble, yet on his deathbed he had called himself a traitor and a spy, and he had

> spoken of his meekness as dangerous activity. It became a constant puzzle
> which lay unanswered in the back of my mind.[45]

The voice in this passage is apparently giving an objective account of the
narrator's past. It reflects the idea of linear time, for adjectives such as "first"
and "constant" suggest a temporal pattern consisting of successive units –past,
present, and future. Yet, the more the novel progresses the more the narrator's
voice loses its predominantly realistic tone. It shifts to an impressionistic mode
of expression. Accordingly, the outer world—people, objects, and events—is
perceived through the eyes of the narrator. The description, then, relies heavily
upon the narrator's lived sense of time. On a narrative level, Ellison gives
minute expression to the protagonist's momentary physical and sensory
responses. And these are emotionally colored, as in the following passage:

> I couldn't open my eyes. I seemed to exist in some other dimension, utterly
> alone; until after a while a nurse bent down and forced a warm fluid between
> my lips. I gagged, swallowed, feeling the fluid course slowly to my vague
> middle. A huge iridescent bubble seemed to enfold me. Gentle hands moved
> over me, bringing vague impressions of memory. I was laved with warm
> liquids, felt gentle hands move through the indefinite limits of my flesh. . . .
> I heard a friendly voice, uttering familiar words to which I could assign no
> meaning. I listened intensely, aware of the form and movement of sentences
> and grasping the now subtle rhythmical differences between progressions of
> sound that questioned and those that made a statement. But still their
> meanings were lost in the vast whiteness in which I myself was lost.[46]

In this excerpt a highly subjective mode of expression supersedes the
omniscient-objective mode of the earlier passage. The voice records and
expresses the narrator's personal state of mind while he is undergoing a
brainwashing in the hospital of the paint factory. Within this state the narrator
gains a more complex perception of time. In order to mark the invisible man's
awareness of different rhythms and time levels, Ellison draws on the call-and-
response pattern. Although the protagonist is not yet able to read the cultural
significance of these temporal differences, he has accomplished a first step on
his way to comprehend the movements of time and history.

The protagonist's journey into the complex structure of time reaches
another, deeper level in the scene of the Harlem race riot. Here the process of
subjectifying time reaches a more intense stage and the outer world appears
abstract, grotesque, and absurd. This is due to the fact that the narrator distorts
descriptions of reality consciously. Events are constantly compared with
impressions related to earlier experiences of the protagonist. Hence, his sense of
lived time functions as a comment upon incidents taking place in the world
around him. On a narrative level Ellison resorts to analogy as structural device:

---

[45]   Ellison 16.

[46]   Ellison 233.

> And I could see the great forward lunge of the horses and the crowd
> breaking and rolling back *like a wave* . . . as the horses . . .went over the
> curb to land stiff-legged and slide over the cleared *walk as upon ice skates*
> and past. . . . And my heart tightened as the first crowd swung imperturbably
> back . . . *like sandpipers* swinging around to glean the shore after a furious
> wave's recession.[47]

Linking various events during the Harlem race riot, the narrator attempts to
express his newly gained temporal awareness verbally. He resorts to long
sentences—clauses and subordinate clauses—which are repeatedly connected
by the word "and." Therefore, his narration is based upon accumulation rather
than differentiation. Events and impressions are listed in long sequences but the
syntax does not translate differences in time rhythmically.

A fourth level of consciousness—the narrator creates his own sense of
time—appears in the surreal, dream-like moments in which the reader
encounters the narrator's free-wheeling mind in an oracular mode. At this stage
the voice reaches a "more rapid tempo:"

> Hey! Old connoisseur of voice sounds, of voices without messages, of
> newsless winds, listen to the vowel sounds and crackling dentals, to the low
> harsh gutturals of empty anguish, now riding the curve of a preacher's
> rhythm I heard long ago in a Baptist church, stripped now of its imagery: No
> suns having hemorrhages, no moons weeping tears, no earthworms refusing
> the sacred flesh and dancing in the earth on Easter morn. Ha! singing
> achievement, Ha! booming success, intoning, Ha! acceptance, Ha! a river of
> word-sounds filled with drowned passions, floating, Ha! with wrecks of
> unachievable ambitions and stillborn revolts, sweeping their ears, Ha! . . .
> the sound of words that were no words, counterfeit notes singing
> achievements yet unachieved, riding upon the wings of my voice. . . .[48]

This passage parodies speech rituals the invisible man encountered at the
black college. As a parody on "the black rite of Horatio Alger," it also signifies
a subversion of a teleological understanding of time.[49] Through its mocking
tone as well as its rhythmic complexity, this excerpt suggests the validity of
time concepts other than the rational-linear time patterns advocated by the black
college teachers and their white patrons. Ellison's "rush of sound" is constantly
penetrated by surreal imagery. Moon and sun are multiplied and personified.
The narrator's associations of these terms for planets with "tears" and
"hemorrhages" appear paradoxical. Thus any mode of rational thinking becomes
distorted. Rhythmically, Ellison produces an oracular flow of words, sounds,
and images occasionally interrupted by the exclamation "Ha!" The mocking
tone accompanies the counterrhythmic effect of this brief exclamation.

---

[47]   Ellison 542 (italics mine).

[48]   Ellison 111.

[49]   Ellison 109.

Moreover, the short interruption of the flow recalls breaks in jazz through which rhythmic tension is achieved. The phrases in between these exclamations are of different syntactical structure and length. They range from single words via elliptic phrases to sequences of short sentence units. Ellison, thus, achieves a polyrhythmic effect. Avoiding complete sentences, he undermines a linear narrative pattern. Accordingly, time is divided into a series of momentary impressions.

Ellison's shifts in style illustrate an overall movement from stasis to kinesis. At the same time detaching the narrative from mimetic representation, his writing evokes the steady movement of jazz toward new boundaries. As we have seen, Ellison moves steadily away from a pattern of notation or score to a more spontaneous, improvising voice. "Listen to me, the bungling bugler of words playing thematic variations," the narrator announces.[50] He transforms the historical material, changing his narrative voice into a performative mode. The mood expressed by the voice recalls the blue note in blues and jazz where it is a means of strong emphatic expression, reflecting and creating a condition of high arousal.[51] Technically the blue note is achieved by pulling or hammering the strings of a guitar, for instance. This technique detaches the music from fixed notation and intensifies the expression of strong emotional involvement in the act of performance.[52] Expressing his anger about the invisibility of African Americans, Ellison adopts the blues mood to focus on emotional responses to history; personal history functions as a gateway to history on a larger scale.

As the changes of narrative voice illustrate, language functions as medium to evoke various time levels. In some instances, the narrator's mode functions as a black commentary on white views of history. Whenever this is the case, the technique of mocking and parodying calls forth a clear cultural distancing. By counterpointing culturally diverging concepts of time Ellison succeeds in building up tension; generally accepted notions about historical progression are put into question. Hence, the apparently stable temporal system of mainstream culture begins to dismantle on the level of narrativity. Time shifts indeed occur in the novel frequently. Prologue and epilogue are set chiefly in the present. In both segments the invisible man's narration roams through time, sometimes prophesying the future—"All sickness is not unto death, neither is invisibility"[53]—, at other times recalling the past: "One night I accidentally bumped into a man, and perhaps because of the darkness he saw me and called me an insulting name."[54] The self-conscious voice is not confined to prologue and epilogue, though. It repeatedly appears in the main body of the novel,

---

50   Ralph Ellison 111.

51   Alfons Dauer, Jazz: *Die Magische Musik* (Bremen: Carl Schuenemann Verlag, 1961) 306.

52   Helmut Grahl, *Die Folkblues Gitarre* (Frankfurt/Main: Tenuto-Musik-Edition, 1976) 48.

53   Ralph Ellison, *Invisible Man* 14.

54   Ellison 4.

commenting upon the ongoing events. Describing the atmosphere on campus, for instance, the narrative of the main plot resorts to a lyrical tone creating a pastoral picture of college life: "Oh, long green stretch of campus, Oh, quiet songs at dusk, Oh moon that kissed the steeple and flooded perfumed nights. . . ."[55] Suddenly this mode is interrupted by the self-conscious voice of the present questioning and mocking the former's romanticizing tone. "Why and how? How and why?. . . . And oh, oh, oh, those multimillionaires!"[56] In this musical allusion to jazz and ragtime, the image of the past turns into a wasteland through the mocking and self-conscious tone of the present. "I'm convinced it was the product of subtle magic, the alchemy of moonlight; the school of flowerstudded wasteland."[57]

The mocking tone of the narrative expression illustrates that humor and ambiguity, so prevalent in the blues, shape the content of the novel as it progresses. Trueblood's narration and Reverend Barbee's speech in honor of the college's founder—both part of African American oral culture—further intensify the "blackness" of Ellison's prose. Barbee emphatically tells the students about the founder's funeral:

> Black, black, black! Black people in blacker mourning, the funeral crape hung upon their naked hearts; singing unashamedly their black folk's songs of sorrow, moving painfully, overflowing the curving walks, weeping and wailing beneath the drooping trees and their low murmuring voices like the moans of winds in a wilderness. And finally they gathered on the hill slope and as far as the tear-wet eyes could see, they stood with their heads bowed singing.[58]

Barbee refers to the heritage of black folklore when he describes the mourning congregation's singing. The songs express a sense of pain and hardship. Moreover the "low murmuring voices" suggest the multiplicity of voices at work in *Invisible Man*, reminiscent of jazz's polyphonic progression. In the prologue Ellison has already signalled the jazzy movement of the novel when the protagonist descends into a mental Dante-like underworld listening to Armstrong's blues "What Did I Do to Be so Black and Blue". Ellison writes: "The unheard sounds came through, and each melodic line existed of itself, stood clearly out from all the rest, said its piece, and waited patiently for the other voices to speak."[59] In Ellison's rendering, jazz's structural matrix represents the ideal basis for a dialogical approach to history. A variety of cultural expressions are necessary parts of a truly American historical discourse which can only be seen as a complex net of interpenetrating notions of time.

---

[55] Ellison 36.

[56] Ellison 36-37.

[57] Ellison 37.

[58] Ellison 129.

[59] Ellison 8.

The changing tempos throughout the protagonist's mental descent into the depths of Armstrong's blues make us aware that it is music as well as language which can provide us with aesthetic models for negotiating culturally different views of the historical process.

The invisible man's journey into an awareness of time differences, both cultural and aesthetic, does not precede according to a linear pattern, as we should expect by now. Narrative voice, in *Invisible Man*, not only expresses time conceptions it also inserts temporal changes within its own progression. Like the "boomerang image" it is based upon a back and forth movement which also effects the syntactical and semantic level of the novel.[60] The repetitive appearance of the words "bled" and "blood" in the protagonist's speech at Tod Clifton's funeral results in shifted meanings, dependent on the context the words are placed in:

> He fell and he kneeled. He kneeled and he bled. He bled and he died. He fell in a heap like any man and his blood spilled out like any blood; red as any blood, wet as any blood and reflecting the sky and the buildings and birds and trees, or your face if you looked into its dulling mirror—and dried in the sun as blood dries. That's all. They spilled his blood and he bled.[61]

In the first sentences and the last sentence of the above quotation the words "blood" and "bled" are exclusively connected with Tod Clifton as an individual. In the middle passage—"red as any blood, wet as any blood"—, however, the word "blood", placed in another context, is related to humankind as a whole, thus implying a common bond between all men and women. Accordingly, it counterpoints the previous word-individual association by a word-collective association. Rhythmically, the syntax-word pattern of the first two sentences illustrates a complex structure. A basic rhythmic progression emerges from the parallel arrangement of the sentences. Yet, Ellison adds an improvising and counterpointing solo voice when he shifts the syntactical order of words. The repeated terms "kneeled" and "bled", for instance, occupy front and end positions alternately. The quotation as a whole parallels the overall structure of the novel that progresses not in a linear manner but, similar to a jazz improvisation, shifts back and forth between basic theme and variations. From a word-individual association in the beginning, to a word collective association in the middle passage, Ellison returns to the former in the end. In sum, Ellison's style translates jazz techniques on the levels of narrative voice, structure, and

---

60 Similar to a blues or jazz musician who manipulates sound—pulling or hammering the strings of a guitar—Ellison plays on phonetics and semantics throughout the novel. Two examples shall suffice here to illustrate my point: "Call me . . . a thinker-tinker" (7) and "I yam what I am" (260). In both cases the phonetic quality of the words "thinker" and "yam" is almost preserved, only slightly moderated. The quasi-repetitions "tinker" and "am" are semantically different, though. While blues and jazz musicians resort to the distortion of sound for affective impact, Ellison primarily applies this technique to make a pun.

61 Ellison 445.

time. Thus he emphasizes music's key role for cultural development and orientation within African American communities. Especially the interaction of individual and collective in jazz bears social implications for Ellison transcending mere artistic concern:

> For true jazz is an art of individual assertion within and against the group. Each true jazz moment (as distinct from the uninspired commercial performance) springs from a contest in which the artist challenges all the rest; each solo flight, or improvisation, represents (like the successive canvases of a painter) a definition of his identity: as individual, as member of the collectivity and as a link in the chain of tradition.[62]

Individual assertion requires a sense of self. This, according to Ellison, presupposes a close attachment to cultural roots. Singing the blues, Trueblood gains a sense of self:

> All I know is I ends up singin' the blues. I sings me some blues that might ain't never been sung before, and while I'm singin' them blues I makes up my mind that I ain't nobody but myself and ain't nothin I can do but let whatever is gonna happen, happen. I made up my mind that I was goin' back home and face Kate; yeah and face Matty Lou too.[63]

The singing of the blues evokes a sense of identity. Moreover the blues has a cathartic effect because it enables Trueblood to face up to the demands of social reality. Deciding to go back home, Trueblood differs from the roaming bluesmen of the folk blues era in particular. "Goin' back home" metaphorically expresses his reunion with his family as well as with his cultural roots. Telling his story over and over again, Trueblood draws on the African American oral tradition in order to survive economically in mainstream commodity culture. To Baker, the blues sung and told by Trueblood bears artistic and commercial dimensions. As he points out, "the complexities of American culture, however, function in a way that enables the sharecropper to reconcile his merchandizing role as oral storyteller and his position as the antinomian trickster."[64] The triumph of the trickster reveals Baker's view of the blues as a subversive force.

---

[62] Ellison, *Shadow and Act* 234.

[63] Ralph Ellison, *Invisible Man* 66-67.

[64] Houston A. Baker, Jr., "To Move Without Moving: Creativity and Commerce in Ralph Ellison's Trueblood Episode," *Black Literature and Theory*, ed. Henry L. Gates, Jr. (New York: Methuen, 1984) 221-48; 241. Throughout his writings Baker has stressed the historical development and social functioning of the blues. Baker elucidates: "Originating in the field hollers and work-songs of the black agrarian south and becoming codified as stable forms by the second decade of the twentieth century, the blues offer a language that connotes a world of transience, instability, hard luck, brutalizing work, lost love, minimal security, and enduring human wit and resourcefulness in the face of such discouragements" (236). To Baker, the blues represents an artistic expression of suffering as well as one of catharsis. See also Houston A. Baker, Jr., *Long Black Song: Essays in Black American Literature* (Charlottesville: The UP of Virginia, 1990) 33-35.

Trueblood's story gains him a reputation within the white community; and, when Mr. Norton gives him a hundred dollar bill, Trueblood emerges from folk artist to paid artist. This transformation from folklore to the status of commercial arts finds its historical parallel in blues' and jazz's major breakthrough in the 1920s. More persuasively than ever before, African American culture became audible and visible in the American arts. Louis Armstrong became the embodiment of this major cultural breakthrough with a series of jazz tunes taking the market by storm. For various reasons, he represents the jazz musician *par excellence* for Ellison's use of jazz in *Invisible Man*. In the early days of New Orleans jazz, performers divided themselves in two basic categories. Those who could read music were labelled "musicianers" and those who improvised, "jazzed" or "ragged" called themselves jazzmen. Since Ellison is very much concerned with artistic form, a purely "ragging" or "jazzing" musician as artistic model would have betrayed his intention as artist. Armstrong, however, combined both traditions. At first, Armstrong clearly belonged to the group of jazzmen. His pure improvisations with King Oliver in the latter's Creole Jazz Band illustrate Armstrong's primary approach to jazz.[65] Yet, especially under the influence of his second wife Lil Hardin, he also turned to reading, writing, and arranging music. This evokes parallels to Trueblood's story. Like Armstrong, Trueblood turns to a larger structural frame—his family and the country quartet—to perform his story.

Armstrong's position in the world of jazz is twofold. First of all, he was a musical pioneer of the first rate. Without his experiments the function of solos in subsequent jazz styles would be inconceivable.[66] Both as instrumentalist and singer Armstrong broke new ground for generations of jazz musicians to follow. The talking effects of his trumpet playing and the instrumental quality of his singing voice characterized Armstrong's musical interpretation of his oral heritage. Emotion and technique alike formed the basis for his art. In a similar way, Ellison links emotional expression with technique, when he puts his narrative voice through a chain of emphatic and syntactic changes. Indeed, both artists fuse emotional message with technical accuracy.

Apart from Armstrong's revolutionary function in the world of jazz, he more than any other of his contemporaries succeeded in popularizing jazz. Through Armstrong's music jazz became audible in the United States and its international

---

[65]   See also Max Jones and John Chilton, *Die Louis Armstrong Story*, trans. Karl Ludwig Nicol (Freiburg: Herder, 1972) 61.

[66]   Already in 1924 Louis Armstrong's mastering of time on the level of solo playing pushed Fletcher Henderson's and Don Redman's experiments with harmonic complexity, rhythmic intensity and solo flights toward greater innovation. As Erenberg sums up," while Armstrong built sweeping improvisations on traditional rhythmic, harmonic, and melodic patterns, quoting other tunes, exaggerating a song's distinctive features, or using a phrase for the whole, Redman and Henderson made the brass and reeds—organized into legitimate orchestral sections—emulate the improvising soloist." Lewis A. Erenberg, *Swingin' the Dream: Big Band Jazz and the Rebirth of American Culture* (Chicago: U of Chicago P, 1998) 8.

popular fame in the era of swing would be unthinkable without Armstrong's innovative handling of solo and rhythm playing.[67] It is interesting to observe that Ellison picks one of Armstrong's popular tunes—"What Did I Do To Be So Black And Blue"—as essential musical matrix for the development of the prologue. Thus Ellison underscores that he aims at a fusion of folk or popular art with the high art of literature. As Ellison makes clear, this seems the most appropriate way for an African American artist to keep his individuality during an active participation in mainstream culture.

All this requires constant acts of balance in between diverging cultural identities. Hence, there is a dialogical dimension the African American artist has to resort to. In jazz, the interdependence of improvisation and a mastery of form provides a valid model since the art of improvisation needs to be embedded within a framework that provides structural grounding. A solo in jazz would run the risk of losing its musical effect if it were no longer related to the playing of the other band members. Convincingly, Ellison transfers this sense of improvisation from jazz to the world of literature. "Jazz taught Ellison a respect for limits, even as it revealed the possibility of overcoming limits through technique. It was the blues, however, that taught him to discern in this paradox an emblem of the human condition," Robert Bone points out.[68]

Indeed, only through artistic constraint—the process of constant repetition and revision—does Trueblood's storytelling achieve a mastery of form which enables him to sell his story. "He cleared his throat, his eyes gleaming and his voice taking on a deep, incantatory quality, as though he had told the story many, many times."[69] As Trueblood's case illustrates, Ellison does away with the primitivist myth of the intuitive black musician. Instead, he stresses that form and revision are essential to African American music and art in general. Improvisation, controlled through the mastery of form, is metaphorically circumscribed in the passage of the incest act where Trueblood keeps moving "without movin'."[70] Singing the blues, Trueblood gains control over his personal condition and gives artistic shape to his guilt-ridden conscience. As Ellison suggests, black movement outside the world of art is under the control of the white power structure. So, the arts remain one of the very few niches left to develop and protect African American cultural roots. Within the aesthetic

---

[67]   See Miles Davis and Quincy Troupe, Miles Davis: *Die Autobiographie*, trans. Brigitte Jakobeit (Hamburg: Hoffmann und Campe, 1990) 99. Frequently Armstrong has been critized by critics and fellow musicians such as Miles Davis and Dizzy Gillespie for popularizing jazz by playing the entertainer and grinning into the face of white racism. For Gillespie's critique see also Jon Panish, *The Color of Jazz: Race and Representation in Postwar American Culture* (Jackson: UP of Mississippi, 1997) 12-13.

[68]   Robert Bone, "Ralph Ellison and the Uses of the Imagination," *Ralph Ellison: A Collection of Critical Essays*, ed. John Hersey (Englewood Cliffs: Prentice Hall, 1974) 95-114 ; 99.

[69]   Ralph Ellison, *Invisible Man* 53.

[70]   Ellison 59.

sphere, African Americans can preserve their cultural heritage which is needed for a potential social change from within the system.

As Ellison makes emphasizes, Armstrong's music calls for action. The novelist clearly suggests political action. Yet, the protagonist still chooses to remain underground, writing his narrative. His story of anger, hatred, and revelations in black on white resembles the music of Louis Armstrong who "bends that military instrument into a beam of lyrical sound."[71] Similar to Armstrong's revolutionary experiments with musical time, the invisible man's act of lighting the underground with 1,369 lights represents an act of rebellion. Taping white electric power, he lightens his hole and the light enables him to give form to his self as well as warmth to his dungeon. At the same time he withdraws energy from the white system thus modifying the latter's substance. In this context Ellison provides no answer to the question if this act of subversion may lead to a final disruption of white mainstream culture. The riddle if African American time conceptions could alternate their white counterparts beyond an aesthetic level remains unsolved. Obviously, though, Ellison rejects any form of change which involves racial violence, despite the fact that the prologue also bears the potential of violent action. When the invisible man is insulted by a white man, calling him "a nigger," it is only the awareness that the white counterpart is blinded by racism that prevents the invisible man from slitting the white man's throat. Here Ellison plays with the notion of militant race struggle but dismisses it in favor of subversion from the underground. As Ellison's description of Armstrong's trumpet playing indicates, art transforms aggression into an act of creative subversion. Hence, Ellison embraces an integrationist attitude, preferring a steady social and cultural change to radical or militant rebellion.

To me, it is Ellison's embrace of multiplicity within American society that prevents him from formulating a radical African American aesthetic. In the textual rendering of a diversity of time zones, Ellison expresses his recognition of "the beautiful absurdity" of American identity.[72] To him, the culturally and aesthetically eclectic and synthesizing nature of jazz represents the supreme expression of the American spirit. Jazz, then, gives voice to a constantly changing history and personal identity. Ellison discerns in blues and jazz, and finally in writing, a medium to express his existentialist view of history as chaotic and absurd. In his view, identity itself is essentially temporary. Ellison's protagonist, for instance, adopts new roles according to the historical circumstances surrounding him. The idealistic college student, the political activist, and finally the improvising artist mark significant stages of the protagonist's metamorphoses. According to Ellison's historical imagination, the individual is bound to keep moving. While the author of *Invisible Man*

---

71   Ellison 8.

72   Ellison 546.

considers the ideology of order and discipline reductive, on the one hand, he regards living in chaos as apparently unethical on the other.

Whether the invisible protagonist will return to public life remains open to speculation. Cooke denies that there could be a return to a social function. He sees the protagonist estranged from his own cultural heritage and incapable of intimacy in human relationships.[73] If we share Cooke's belief, we would have to assume that the invisible man's plunge out of history is as final as Tod Clifton's fall after the latter's disillusionment with socialist and black utopia. Tanner, on the other hand, believes that the protagonist will return to the social world above and will have something to contribute to it.[74] With a nod to Hortense Spillers, I suggest that the invisible man will give up his refusal of historical commitment. According to Spillers, "he must emerge: Spatially underground, he will come up into the light of the day again with his dark-skinned self, a little more noble and fierce than when he entered."[75] It is obvious that he has no concrete social role in mind when he suggests a return to the history above ground. However, in the opening sentences of the prologue, the naming motif, so prevalent in the male blues tradition, stresses the self-confidence the protagonist has gained after numerous metamorphoses: "I am a man of substance, of flesh and bone, fiber and liquids—and I might even be said to possess a mind."[76] He is now well equipped with the blues rhetoric, with improvisational skills, and an ethical outlook based upon social responsibility and diversity.

Since Ellison seems concerned with depicting his protagonist's assertion more against the group than within the group, Ellison focuses on individual development. Hence, he locates the resonsibility for the invisibility of black culture in the United States in the individual actions of African Americans and whites alike. The invisible man expresses this attitude in the epilogue: "The fact is that you carry part of your sickness within you, at least I do as an invisible man."[77] Clearly Ellison is less interested in developing a larger social vision for African Americans in the United States. Yet, the invisible man's plea for diversity implies cultural and social dimensions, as form and content of *Invisible Man* indicate. Ellison's thematic "riffs", stylistic improvisations with time and form as well as his pluralist outlook not only create a masterpiece of

73 Michael G. Cooke, *Afro-American Literature in the 20th Century: The Achievement of Intimacy* (New Haven: Yale UP, 1984) 106-07.

74 Tony Tanner, "The Music of Invisibility," *Ralph Ellison*, ed. Harold Bloom (New York: Chelsea House Publishers, 1986) 37-50; 49-50.

75 Hortense Spillers, "Ellison's Usable Past: Toward a Theory of Myth ," *Speaking for You: The Vision of Ralph Ellison*, ed. Kimberly W. Benston (Washington, D.C.: Howard UP, 1987) 144-58; 149.

76 Ellison 3.

77 Ellison 562.

using musical time in fiction but also shape the matrix for postmodern and contemporary black writers to experiment with blues and jazz as concerns the creation more outspoken social and communal visions.

IV. Crossing Temporal Boundaries: Toni Morrison— Individual and Communal Concepts of History

More than their literary predecessors—Hughes and Ellison—, who emphasize the individual's vision of history, contemporary African American novelists draw on music to develop historical visions based upon communal and social aspects. Whereas Hughes and Ellison still explore the significance of black music for African American culture in general and the individual in particular, contemporary writers such as the Nobel Prize winner Toni Morrison relate musical rhythm and group improvisation to concepts of time within a network of communal ties.[1] Hence, Morrison's novel remains close to what Sandra A. Zagarell labels "the narrative of community."[2] Describing the aesthetic features of this literary genre mainly developed by women writers in the 19th century—Sarah Orne Jewett, George Eliot and Harriet Beecher Stowe among others—, Zagarell emphasizes that space and time are bound to local life. Narratives of community ignore chronological time patterns; instead, they prefer process over progress. And, spatially, they focus on a specific geographical place. The formal aspects of this narrative tradition in the 19th century "reflected its commitment to rendering the local life of a community to readers who lived in a world the authors thought fragmented, rationalized, and individualistic."[3] Clearly, Morrison shares this perception of social environment as well as many of the genre's formal requirements.[4]

---

[1]   In general one may claim that the contemporary generation of African American writers has absorbed the cultural significance and musical techniques of blues and jazz so that they are capable of experimenting with them more freely. Hence, Morrison's use of musical elements appears clearly embedded within a larger cultural concept and, naturally, more abstract in comparison with the literary adaptations of African American music in texts by Hughes and Ellison. She prefers to select cultural and aesthetic models from the musical modes which can be appropriated for the literary discourse. Her literary use of music then is more detached from blues and jazz as musical or commercial art forms than that of Hughes and Ellison.

[2]   For discussions of communal values and the interaction of individual and community see also Patrick Bjork, *The Novels of Toni Morrison: The Search for Self and Place Within the Community* (New York: Lang, 1992), Denis Heinz, *The Dilemma of "Double-Consciousness": Toni Morrison's Novels* (Athens: U of Georgia P, 1993) and Jan Furman, *Toni Morrison's Fiction* (Columbia: U of South Carolina P, 1996).

[3]   Sandra A. Zagarell, "Narrative of Community: The Identification of a Genre," *Revising the Word and the World: Essays in Feminist Literary Criticism*, eds. Vèvè A. Clark, Ruth-Ellen B. Joeres, and Madelon Sprengnether (Chicago: U of Chicago P, 1993) 249-78; 254.

[4]   In an interview with Stepto Morrison explains that "I felt a very strong sense of place, not in terms of the country or the state, but in terms of details, the feeling, the mood of the community . . . I think some of it is just a woman's strong sense of being in a room, a place, or in a house."

Due to the fact that community functions on a larger cultural scale—issues of race and gender enter the picture—, Morrison changes this genre from a specifically African American perspective. On the level of time and space, she adds complexity and multiplicity playing on forms of temporal negotiation present in the African American musical discourse. Morrison draws on those aspects of the musical heritage that are basic and central to African American musical rhythm and interaction in general. Accordingly, she does not resort to the more innovative modes of jazz to experiment with history and narrative structurally. While her multiple views on history display her postmodern sensibility for cultural differences, her narrative strategies look backward to more traditional forms of reconstructing the past in *Song of Solomon* (1977).[5]

Blues and jazz, in particular, shape Morrison's conceptions of cultural memory in *Song of Solomon*. Reflecting on what it means to own your history or the memory of it, she explores how memory is created, reinvented and transmitted in African American discourse and what political consequences result from historical constructions within these processes.[6] Throughout the novel, music launches diverse acts of remembering or rememorizing. The blues, especially, becomes an important touchstone in Morrison's attempt to evoke former and present images of a vital black community life. As Morrison's use of music underscores, the blues represents an African American extension of Voodoo and other African cultural elements. Thus to Morrison, it expresses a consciousness of black culture and heritage linking black communities in America with those in Africa.

Remembering then represents an act of crossing national and cultural boundaries. Hence, it requires an awareness and acceptance of fluid temporal concepts which shift from one cultural background to another. In order to come

---

Robert B. Stepto, "Intimate Things in Place: A Conversation with Toni Morrison," *Chant of Saints*, eds. Robert Stepto and Michael Harper (Urbana: U of Illinois P, 1979) 213-29; 213.

[5]   In her novel *Jazz* (1993), Morrison's diction and syntactic rhythms display stronger musical influences on the level of form. Yet, more than any other of her texts, *Song of Solomon* exposes the musical influence on the representation of time and history in fiction. For a discussion of Morrison's narrative voice in *Jazz* see Jan Furman, *Toni Morrison's Fiction* 96-102.

[6]   The process of reconstructing history within a minority discourse often resorts to unorthodox means of historical documentation. Frequently writers resort to oral history—storytelling—or products of popular culture. Cf. Hannah Möckel-Rieke, "Introduction: Media and Cultural Memory" *Amerikastudien / American Studies* 43.1 (1998): 5-17; 6. Two rather different discourses on cultural memory have emerged in recent years, as Sabine Bröck points out. While Western European intellectuals pursue a rather disengaged focus on memory discussing the latter as a "mnemonic technique" or as a "human faculty" , postcolonial critics and writers are less concerned with technique; rather they seek for "a recuperation of lost history." According to Bröck, "Toni Morrison's work stresses how interested, how invested cultural memory actually is, precisely because it is an act of mediation. Her project is part of a wider effort to politically own memory and not to discuss it in merely formal terms." Sabine Bröck, "Postmodern Mediations and Beloved's Testimony: Memory Is Not Innocent," *Amerikastudien / American Studies* 43.1 (1998): 33-49; 33-34.

to terms with the complex temporality involved in the process of remembering, Morrison develops a sublime vision of history fusing linear and cyclical time patterns. Thus she transfers the method of superimposing various rhythms in jazz onto a literary level. Within the narrative progression different sources of history and various memories interact.

Analogous to her intention to draw upon elements of interaction within African American music, Morrison avoids extended references to any actual blues or jazz musician in particular. Hence she signals no aesthetic preference for a specific blues or jazz style.[7] Instead, her use of music is based upon the latter's social and cultural significance which explains why jazz-related experiments with spelling and syntax hardly ever enter the narrative progression in *Song of Solomon*. Morrison inserts temporal and communal aspects in a subtle and unobtrusive way. Still, Pilate's recurring blues performances—in private and public settings—make music a constant presence underlying the thematic and structural set-up of the novel. Pilate's shifting of places for her singing performances, moreover, documents that music functions as a bridge between personal and political time. African American music turns into an aesthetic backbone for Morrison's experimentation with history.

To Morrison the novel and history are closely related. In her conception of the literary genre the novel turns into a narrative of shared memories. It becomes a mirror, albeit subjective and fictitious, of communal history. Describing the function of the novel, Morrison points out that "it can do exactly what blues or jazz or gossip or stories or myth or folklore did." To her the novel represents "a common well-spring of ideas" and involves the active participation of the reader. Talking about the reader's relation with the characters in the novels, she says: "The people he may not know but there is some shared history."[8]

In the novel's close connection with the concerns of the people, Morrison detects in the genre a contemporary extension of traditional folk art. Especially painting and music are important sources of influence for all her novels. In an interview with Claudia Tate she reveals her intention to apply the techniques of the above art forms to the novel: "I only have twenty-six letters of the alphabet, but I don't have colors or music. I must use my craft to make the reader see the colors and hear the sounds."[9]

Morrison is not a trained musician like Ellison, nor is she as intensively involved with blues and jazz as Reed and Shange are, but there is a strong familial background in music that informs her craftmanship as a writer on the

---

7   While references to rural musical forms dominate in Song of Solomon, urban blues and jazz
        infiltrate Morrison narrative voice in her novel Jazz .

8   Quoted in *The World of Toni Morrison: Explorations in Literary Criticism*, eds. Bessie W.
        Jones and Audrey L. Vinson (Dubuque: Kendall Hunt, 1985) 145-46.

9   Quoted in Claudia Tate, ed. *Black Women Writers at Work* (New York: Continuum, 1983) 120.

levels of both form and content.[10] The blues song in *Song of Solomon* derives from her Alabama family heritage. "My mother and my aunts play and sing all the time."[11] What makes blues and jazz such an important impact on her writing is the tremendous communal force she finds in the music. To her they are reminiscent of the Greek chorus and the services of the Black church. The audience is always actively involved, an act of communication takes place.

In *Song of Solomon*, Morrison invites the reader to join her characters on a journey through the history of black communal life.[12] She portrays a family that is fragmented and riven by the corrupt values of a sick society. Referring primarily to the years from the Great Depression until the early 1960s, Morrison depicts how sexist and racist ideology destroys familial as well as communal ties within the black community. Poorer blacks, like Guitar and the militant group the Days, turn to violent action against white racism, while the African American bourgeoisie sells out to the decadent ways of white America. The family of Macon Dead and Ruth Foster Dead with their three children Lena, Corinthians, and Milkman are representative of the black middle-class. The family symbolizes a lack of values and orientation in large parts of the black community. Adopting the attitudes and rules of white America, the family, as its name implies, lives in a sterile ambience, estranged from African American cultural traditions. Father as well as son neglect and oppress the female members of the family. Macon Dead rules his family as well as his tenants in an autocratic manner. Macon's sister Pilate, though, pursues a radically different way of life. She rejects her brother's selfish interests in obtaining money and property. Instead, she preserves and embodies black folk wisdom and values. Together with her daughter Reba and her granddaughter Hagar she lives in a household centered around family and community concerns. Guided by Pilate, Milkman gradually breaks out of the materialistic setting of the Dead household. In the second part of the novel Milkman leaves his familiar environment to head South. This journey leads him deep into the core of black history and culture, as he traces the roots of his own family back to the times of slavery.

Within the framework of this temporal movement, Pilate's old blues song 'O Sugarman' bears importance to both theme and structure in *Song of Solomon*. Very early in the novel Morrison establishes Pilate as the keeper of the blues tradition. It is her singing when Robert Smith jumps off the roof of the Mercy

---

[10]   This may be part of the reason why Morrison takes a more detached approach to musical form than the other writers discussed in this study.

[11]   Quoted in Wilfred D. Samuels and Cleonora Hudson-Weems, *Toni Morrison* (Boston: Twayne Publishers, 1990) 4.

[12]   As Carole Boyce Davies stresses, the notion of travelling is a vital aspect of African American women's fiction. This is also true for the works of Toni Morrison since all of her novels function through tropes of change and movement. See Carole Boyce Davies, *Black Women, Writing and Identity: Migrations of the Subject* (London: Routledge, 1994) 148-49.

hospital that gives his "flight" a magic and mythic touch. As part of the African American blues tradition the song also spans a historical dimension since it links Smith's "flight" with the storytelling about flying Africans among blacks during times of slavery. The desire for freedom expressed in this blues song draws a continuous historical line from the first landing of African slaves to the plot of *Song of Solomon*. As Susan L. Blake explains in her discussion of black folklore in the works of Ralph Ellison, 'flying' is of great significance to folklore and myth in various cultures:

> Flying is a predominant motif in black American folklore as well as in Western myth; its meanings vary from one tradition to another. In Greek mythology, flying represents the superhuman power of the gods; in Freudian psychology, it symbolizes male sexual potency; in black American folklore, it means freedom. In a folk context the aspiration to fly recalls Harriet Tubman's dream of flying over a great wall, the numerous references in spirituals to flying to freedom in Jesus, the Sea Islands legend of the Africans who rose up from the field one day and flew back to Africa, and the humorous folktale of the Colored Man who went to heaven and flew around with such abandon that he had to be grounded but who boasted that he was "a flying black bastard" while he had his wings.[13]

Resorting to the treasure of African American folk art, Morrison underscores the meaning of tradition for cultural assertion. Since "flying" also stands for a model of mastering and changing time, Morrison links "flight" with a journey through time, back to the past in particular. Still, Pilate's blues song transcends the aesthetic function of preserving cultural memory. It occurs at various places in the novel and in each new context it assumes further meaning. Thus Pilate's blues song not only represents a central theme but also a major structural device in Milkman's search for roots and identity. As the novel progresses, its plot signifies upon central tropes in the blues. The blues song in *Song of Solomon* mimics the function of the chorus in jazz, then. As Bohlaender and Holler explain, the chorus in jazz signifies the refrain upon which the musicians improvise together or from which solo improvisations derive.[14] In the novel the blues sung by Pilate contains the tropes upon which Morrison plays riffs throughout the novel. An excerpt from the lyrics of Pilate's blues song reveals the most important of them:

> O Sugarman don't leave me here / Cotton balls to choke me / O Sugarman don't leave me here / Buckra's arms to yoke me / Sugarman done fly away /

---

13   Susan L. Blake, "Ritual and Rationalization: Black Folklore in the Works of Ralph Ellison," *Ralph Ellison*, ed. Harold Bloom (New York: Chelsea House Publishers, 1986) 77-99; 83.

14   Carlo Bohlaender and Karl Heinz Holler, *Reclams Jazzführer* (Stuttgart: Reclam Verlag, 1970) 749.

Sugarman done gone / Sugarman cut across the sky / Sugarman gone home.[15]

The central tropes of the chorus of the blues song are "flying" and "home". The lines of the first stanza circumscribe another trope—"love"—that Morrison links thematically with the other two tropes. The basic mood of the first stanza indicates the singer's communal longing in the face of an oppressive environment. In the course of *Song of Solomon* these tropes display that Morrison's sense of history is closely attached to the life of the community. Taken together, they function as the basic texture that Morrison improvises upon within the novel. Put briefly, the blues song represents a lyrical prophecy and summary of Milkman's journey into selfhood, communal responsibility, and cultural rootedness.

Morrison extends the act of signification so that the tropes bear meaning for other characters and contexts, too. She thus plays with the principle of repetition and difference, crucial to blues and jazz as well as to other vernacular forms in African American culture.[16] In the writing of Morrison, 'signifyin(g)' establishes the dialectics of home and homelessness, departure and arrival, and motion and stasis. Similar to riffs in jazz, Morrison creates a pattern of repetition and variation juxtaposing different conceptions of 'flying' in both materialistic and spiritual terms. More precisely 'flying' assumes spatial, temporal, and spiritual meaning in *Song of Solomon*. It has social implications since attitudes toward flying mark each character's relationship to time and the larger community. Robert Smith's flight symbolizes his departure from communal ties. Milkman's final leap, on the other hand, signals his return to communal responsibility. The sublime version of 'flying' finally is embodied by Pilate: "Without ever leaving the ground, she could fly."[17] Her sense of flying is rooted in a belief in communal values including the communication with dead ancestors as well as new-born relatives: "You just can't fly on off and leave a body," Pilate says.[18] Pilate is not afraid of death; neither is she is bogged down by material concerns. After years of wandering she has reached a spiritual

---

15   Toni Morrison, *Song of Solomon* (New York: Signet, 1977) 49.

16   In the context of critical theory, Gates links the structure of signifyin(g) explicitly to music, when he discusses patterns of repetition and difference in African American culture. He points to a Jelly Roll Morton recording of Scott Joplin's "Maple Leaf Rag": "Morton's composition does not 'surpass' or 'destroy' Joplin's; it complexly extends and tropes figures present in the original. Morton's Signification is a gesture of admiration and respect. It is this aspect of Signifyin(g) that is inscribed in the black musical tradition in jazz compositions such as Oscar Peterson's 'Signify' and Count Basie's 'Signifyin'. . . . It is this principle of repetition and difference, this practice of intertextuality, which has been so crucial to the black vernacular forms of Signifyin(g), jazz—and even its antecedents, the blues, the spirituals, and ragtime." Henry L. Gates, Jr., *The Signifying Monkey* (New York: Oxford UP, 1988) 63-64.

17   Toni Morrison, *Song of Solomon* 340.

18   Morrison 336.

equilibrium, now supporting and nourishing the community of Darling Street. Her "flight" is spiritual. Milkman first can only imagine himself flying by airplane, a fact which underscores the materialistic attitude he has taken on following the footsteps of his father. "The airplane ride exhilarated him, encouraged illusion and a feeling of invulnerability."[19] When he leaps at the end he has embraced the familial and historical past and has found spiritual grounding that makes him "ride the air." Now he can merge with the community of his flying ancestors from Africa. Smith, on the other hand, falls from the cupola. His wings—the color imagery of red, blue, and white evoking the national flag of the United States—cannot hold him; he cannot ride the air. His contact with the folk has always been dominated by money and number. Smith lacks what Pilate possesses, the ability to break through strictly linear conceptions of time. Clock-time determines his life until the very last when he commits suicide after announcing the precise date of his "flight": "At 3:00 P.M. on Wednesday the 18th of February, 1931, I will take off from Mercy and fly on my wings."[20]

In a similar way Morrison plays variations upon themes such as love, freedom, and history. As the suggestive richness of the blues song indicates, all these themes and variations are intertwined and interdependent. Beyond its structural function, the blues becomes a memory-evoking force in *Song of Solomon*:

> Surrendering to the sound, Macon moved closer. He wanted no conversation, no witness, only to listen and perhaps see the three of them, the source of that music that made him think of fields and wild turkey and calico. . . . As Macon felt softening under the weight of memory and music, the song died down. The air was quiet and yet Macon Dead could not leave.[21]

These images called forth in Macon's memory are part of his past in the South. The music takes him out of everyday life and pulls him toward the house of the sister whom he has avoided for such a long time. Music, here, interrupts the flow of time. Magnetically attracted by the singing of the three women, Macon enters a timeless stage on which memory and imagination begin to fuse. He not only remembers moments of his childhood with Pilate, he also starts picturing Pilate's face to himself while she is singing: "Singing now, her face would be a mask; all emotion and passion would have left her features and entered her voice."[22] Music, in this context, sets off a spiritual journey that allows Macon to remember as well as to imagine. The blues then represents a grounding in the present which frees the listener from a teleological outlook.

---

[19]   Morrison 222.

[20]   Morrison 3.

[21]   Morrison 29-30.

[22]   Morrison 30.

From the blues temporal platform, he is able to engage in his mind's ability to absorb various time experiences and to react or act accordingly.

Within this context, individual and collective improvisations in blues and jazz function as an artistic model for individual survival in a social setting. Hence, jazz is more than an aesthetic model for Morrison as concerns the rendering of content and form in *Song of Solomon*. The art of the jazz musician to improvise individually and collectively assumes existential significance in the reactions of individual characters to the vicissitudes of time and the needs of the community. In blues and jazz, improvisation implies constant communication on at least two levels. Individual and collective improvisation require constant mediation between the participating musicians. Especially in the early days of blues and jazz performances, improvisation also included the interaction between musicians and audience. Musicians responded to the shouts and comments from the audience; since they depended on tips they often had to play "hot" or "sweet" upon the audience's request. Improvisation then also meant economic survival.[23]

Socially, improvisation in *Song of Solomon* suggests a change of the regular hierarchy of male-female relationships and class differences.[24] Morrison thus places the individual solos of her characters against a background of economic oppression and sexual repression. Skillfully, Morrison puts her characters repeatedly in situations where they are urged to improvise. Some—Corinthians and Porter—succeed; others—Robert Smith and Hagar—fail. Lena and Corinthians, for instance, experience moments of change during which improvisation determines the decision-making. Lena revolts against male dominion in the Dead house in her verbal assault upon Milkman:"You've been laughing at us all your life. Corinthians. Mama. Me. Using us, ordering us, and judging us. . . . Our girlhood was spent like a found nickel on you."[25] Corinthians, on her part, breaks through the barriers of social caste and parental expectations to make love to poor Porter in the shabby apartment that he rents from Corinthians' father. She feels "bathed, scoured, vacuumed, and for the first time simple."[26]

Henry Porter experiences in his relationship with Corinthians a social alternative to the cold masculine world of the Days. Symbolically, sexuality as a union of two individuals functions as an expression of historical transition on a larger scale. Corinthians breaks through the repressive structure of bourgeois

---

[23] See also my discussion of time levels in New Orleans jazz and the act of reception in chapter I.

[24] For a more intense discussion of class-consciousness in Toni Morrison's work see Doreatha D. Mbalia, *Toni Morrison's Developing Class Consciousness* (Selinsgrove: Susquehanna UP, 1991).

[25] Toni Morrison, Song of Solomon 216. For a discussion of Milkman's sexist attitudes see also Missy Dehn Kubitschek, *Toni Morrison: A Critical Companion* (Westport: Greenwood Press, 1998) 82-83.

[26] Morrison 201.

values; Porter leaves behind the reductive view of history based upon the death-and-revenge pattern underlying the Days' ideology, since he joins Corinthians who had moved to a small house in Southside. Hence, sexual union also implies a subversion of class and caste barriers, for Porter is one of Macon Dead's tenants and belongs to the lower-class blacks the Dead family looks down upon.

As the vicissitudes in Corinthians' and Porter's ways of life show, Morrison always illustrates historical change by means of individual cases. Similar to Corinthians' rebellion against the bourgeois narrowness of the Dead family, Milkman's sexual union with Sweet should be understood as an act of liberation. He breaks through his own shell of egotistic profit-orientation to take his part in a truly social relationship. For the first time Milkman does not exploit the woman he spends time with. Before his date with Sweet he had abused Hagar's passion and the help of his sisters. Toward Pilate and his mother Ruth he had shown only indifference. His making love to Sweet then indicates Milkman's willingness to merge into a larger community. Translating the emphatic and cathartic moment of improvisation in blues and jazz in social as well as sexual terms, Morrison embraces a historical vision which propagates a return to family and community.

While the individual improvisation marks a subjective response to time, community signals a diversity of stories giving voice to wide range of historical experiences. Translating the multiplicity of historical conceptions present in a communal framework in terms of structure, Morrison contrasts and superimposes linear and circular patterns. Within the emerging dialectical process Morrison's play with opposites becomes essential to *Song of Solomon*. And jazz, as an intercultural art form, provides the aesthetic model for rendering dialectics on a narrative level.

In jazz, it is especially the emphasis on rhythm that allows for a dialectical art, as opposed to Western music that is tempo-based. As Berendt points out, a "both this and that" attitude and rhythm belong to dialectics as well as to jazz.[27] The highest function of rhythm, according to Berendt, lies in its capacity to connect opposites.[28] To Berendt, swing—the rhythmical principle behind jazz—can only be comprehended as a temporal phenomenon. In *Die Story des Jazz* (1975) he points out that he sees in swing a rhythmic pattern oscillating between the magical time of African culture and the measured time of European culture. Tempo, characteristic of European music, belongs to the world of progress, a world in which things drift apart, where opposites become more distinct. Rhythm that is swinging back and forth, however, as Berendt concludes, aims at balancing opposites and at negotiating between them.[29] What swing does in jazz, the juxtaposition and fusion of different time patterns effect

---

[27]   Joachim E. Berendt, *Die Story des Jazz: Vom New Orleans zum Rock Jazz* (Stuttgart: Deutsche Verlagsanstalt, 1975) 191.

[28]   Berendt 189.

[29]   Berendt 191.

in *Song of Solomon*. A balancing of opposites—Guitar's mechanical view and Hagar's natural view—occurs in Pilate's embrace of past, present, and future, evoking an African sense of time, as will be discussed at a later point. Like polyrhythm in jazz, the fusion of time patterns signifies a connection between American and African cultures. LeRoi Jones, for instance, sees in the rhythm of jazz a strong link between African and African American musical traditions. In *Blues People* (1963) he points out that

> the most apparent survivals of African music in Afro-American music are its
> rhythms, not only the seeming emphasis in the African music on rhythmic,
> rather than melodic or harmonic qualities, but also the use of polyphonic or
> contrapuntal, rhythmic effects. [30]

In *Song of Solomon* the literary adaptation of these rhythmic effects takes the shape of diachronic, circular, and—in the figure of Pilate—synchronic conceptions of time. Linearity is suggested by the historical time span ranging from the years of the Civil War to Milkman's confrontation with radical black aesthetics in the 1960s. The first part of the novel covers the years from Milkman's birth in the early thirties to the sixties. Through Macon's and Pilate's accounts of the past the reader gains insight into the family heritage. We learn about Milkman's grandfather who owned a little farm, "Lincoln's farm," after the Civil War. The years of Jim Crow experience and segregation which lasted until the middle of the twentieth century are implied repeatedly in the novel. Ruth, for instance, is the first black woman to give birth inside the hospital. Finally, the killings by the Seven Days connote the militant black movements in the 1960s. As Guitar tells Milkman, the origin of the group dates back to the year 1920: "It got started in 1920, when the private from Georgia was killed after his balls were cut off and after that veteran was blinded when he came home from France in World War I."[31] Within this progressive temporal frame Morrison thus interpolates crossreferences. Accordingly, Smith's flight from the cupola and Guitar's final attack on Milkman link black radical movements from the 1920s with those of the 1960s. Since these periods also mark cyclically reappearing heydays of black influence on white culture, especially music, Morrison's view of historical connections inserts repetition within progression.[32]

In Morrison's rendering then repetitive elements are translated into circular forms of narrativity. Recurring patterns like that of violence run like a thread through *Song of Solomon*. Milkman's grandfather, for instance, is killed when he defends his farm against white intruders. Milkman, too, faces violence on his trip South which leads him directly into a violent confrontation with the men of

---

[30]   LeRoi Jones, *Blues People* (New York: William Morrow and Company, 1963) 25.

[31]   Toni Morrison, *Song of Solomon* 156.

[32]   Blues, rhythm'n blues, and soul were the most influential African American forms of music
       during that period.

Shalimar. On a larger cultural scale, violence reappears in the cruel politics of the Seven Days, a radical organization that revenges each killing of a black person by a white. The pattern comes full circle in the end, for Milkman encounters a final physical assault when Guitar intends to kill him.

At first the way the two parts of *Song of Solomon* are arranged creates the impression of a more linear structural frame behind the novel's plot. Yet, as Morrison's concern with the interrelation of content and form manifests, her understanding of history could not be expressed by means of a straightforward narrative progression. Part I, if you will, contains the philosophical and historical matrix that prepares Milkman's journey to the South. Part II, then, actually portrays this journey dramatically. While progressing, part II plays "riffs" on part I. As the stories of Pilate, Ruth, and Macon illustrate, part I is full of memories of the family's past. Not surprisingly, several time layers overlap in this part of the novel. A sense of simultaneity is already generated at the opening of the novel when Smith's flight from the cupola of the Mercy hospital announces Milkman's birth. The juxtaposition of death and birth in the very beginning of the novel implies a circular principle behind Morrison's choice of structure. And circles continue to influence the form of the novel. At the center of these circular arrangements stand Pilate and her house. Almost magnetically the members of the Dead family—Macon, Ruth, and Milkman—are successively drawn to the house that keeps on looking like "a safe harbor."[33] A movement back and forth, hence, between the dead house on Not Doctor Street and the equilibrium of Pilate's home full of song and life characterizes part I.

Milkman's historical quest in part II follows a circular pattern as well. In a very subtle manner Morrison turns this trip South into a series of circular movements. Milkman's wandering between the worlds of his father and his aunt finds parallels in three consecutive circular movements bringing him closer to his roots and cultural heritage. It is also a journey which brings Milkman back to the cradle of African American music. From the Danville community and Circe's house he wanders to the cave and from there he hikes back to Danville. In the Shalimar section Morrison interpolates another two circles. Milkman joins the hunting crew in Shalimar and returns to Sweet's home in Shalimar once the hunt is over. And, finally, he returns with Pilate to Solomon's Leap to bury the bones of Pilate's father in the wilderness where Milkman's first violent encounter with Guitar took place. In vertical terms, too, Morrison resorts to a circular pattern. When Milkman travels South the series of means of transport circumscribe a downward movement from sky to earth. He starts out via airplane, then changes to bus and car. To get to the cave he has to travel by foot. In the cave, finally, he is even forced to move ahead on his knees in his search for Pilate's gold. In material terms this movement marks a continuous process of renunciation. Morrison closes the circle again by juxtaposing this process with a spiritual uplifting. Milkman's final leap toward Guitar demonstrates that the

---

[33]   Morrison 135.

former has learned to fly "without leaving the ground." Thematically, the pattern comes full circle when death and flight on Solomon's Leap recall Smith's flight into death during the opening section of the novel. Likewise, song marks the beginning and the end of the novel. Pilate's singing voice is superseded by Milkman's when the novel fades out.

Cultural memory then is transmitted from one person to another. Milkman, so Morrison suggests, continues to preserve and hand down to the next generation those aspects of African American history that Pilate and the Shalimar community have provided him with. The blues song becomes the medium for carrying on a continuous process of telling and retelling history. And as textual form the blues lyrics are open for improvisation. Hence, they provide the ideal aesthetic basis for including new material, adding new stories, and reinventing lost material in the moment of composition and performance.

Morrison makes use of this aesthetic flexibility when she explores different versions of natural and mythical understandings of time which are predominantly associated with feminine views of history. The mythical view of temporality becomes the most piercing, though, as Morrison's act of naming her characters shows:

> No character in *Song of Solomon* possesses an ordinary designation; instead, Morrison links characters with archetypal figures that span centuries and hemispheres: Omar, Circe, Hagar, Guitar, Singing Bird. Fusing East and West, Native American and Afro-American, Christian and Classical Tradition, all of *Song of Solomon*'s names resound with association.[34]

Jane Campell's explanation illustrates that Morrison's understanding of the sublime view of history keeps on shining through despite all the vicissitudes in the novel. The sublime place, to Morrison, is marked by its sociability and hospitality. The course of the novel reveals that this place could be everywhere. Milkman encounters at least two spatial settings that provide him with a sense of the sublime—Pilate's home in Darling Street and the community of Shalimar.

The spirit of the sublime is embodied by Pilate, the "lady who had one earring, no navel, and looked like a tall black tree".[35] Her understanding of time is mythic, not historical or chronological. Her birth out of death—her mother dies while in labor—, her fearlessness in the face of death, and her communication with the dead expose that she embraces an African conception of time where past, present, and future exist simultaneously.[36] Not only does she transcend temporal categories, she is also a wanderer in space. She is indeed a blueswoman, metaphysically related to the wandering bluesmen of the folk

---

34   Jane Campell, *Mythic Black Fiction: The Transformation of History* (Knoxville: The U of Tennesee P, 1986) 146.

35   Toni Morrison, *Song of Solomon* 38.

36   See also George P. Rawick, *From Sundown to Sunup: The Making of the Black Community* (Westport, Conn.: Greenwood Publishing, 1972) 31-40.

blues period, roaming from town to town, from state to state.[37] In a larger historical sense she stands for generations of migrating individuals and families throughout African American history. If it had not been for her grandchild Hagar's longing for a stable social home, we may assume, Pilate would have kept on wandering. "Besides, she wanted to keep moving."[38] More than once she is compared to a bird. On her way through space she collects rocks from every place she has been to. This demonstrates that she is close to nature and earthbound after all. The fact that she is born without a navel emphasizes the mythic ambience surrounding her. It also marks her off-centredness in relation to the societal standards of Not Doctor Street, which are based on money and status rather than culture and community. The lack of a navel then does not imply that she is antisocial. What makes her different from the roaming bluesmen is her social act of settling down to provide shelter for her family. And the spirit of wandering lives on in the music Pilate, Reba, and Hagar are making in their house in Darling Street. The spiritual quality of music is personified by Pilate herself. Already at her first appearance in the novel she is linked with music. Her singing accompanies Mr. Smith's free fall from the cupola of the Mercy hospital. Her humming during this suicidal scene is followed by her prophecy of Milkman's birth the next morning, as she approaches Ruth in the crowd of spectators. Morrison, then, emphasizes very early in the novel that Pilate's understanding of time is more complete than that of any other character. It encompasses birth and death, memory and vision.

Just like her music, Pilate belongs to the world of blues. She is a practitioner of Voodoo rites, a believer in Voodoo prophecy, a singer of blues songs expressing suffering and transcendence. In this context African American music represents a sign of both existential and aesthetic survival, a source of cultural pride and expansion, and perhaps most important, an alternative value-system. As an extension of satirical songs and songs of praise in African cultures, the blues signals cultural difference in America.[39] Due to the fact that elements of Voodoo and magic in blues songs invoke an emphasis on the unconscious and instinctual elements of the human psyche, it is not surprising that Pilate does not fit in the rational business world of her brother Macon.[40] It is Macon himself

---

[37]   Cf. Arrigo Polillo, *Jazz: Geschichte und Persönlichkeiten*, trans. Egino Biagioni (München: Piper/Schott, 1991) 41-43.

[38]   Toni Morrison, *Song of Solomon* 145.

[39]   See for the historical and musical origin of the blues Alfons M. Dauer, *Jazz: Die Magische Musik* (Bremen: Carl Schünemann Verlag, 1961) 307-08.

[40]   The blues lyrics comprise elements of dream, desire, and magic. In the blues the power of magic survives in allusions to diverse charms, spells, and rituals. References to various magic powders, potions, and talismans are common in blues lyrics. Muddy Waters' "My John the Conqueror Root," Willie Dixon's "I'm Your Hootchie Coochie Man," and Lightnin' Hopkins "Mojo Hand" are just a few examples that mark the blues as a musical extension of Voodoo in

who suggests that she is related to the values and way of life of a more ancient
culture, that of Africa:

> If you ever have a doubt we from Africa, look at Pilate. She look just like
> Papa and he looked like all them pictures you ever see of Africans. A
> Pennsylvania African. Acted like one too. Close his face up like a door.[41]

Her way of life as the keeper of a wine house, her mysterious brass box, and
her belief in the healing function of music show her in clear opposition to the
belief and value-system of white and black Christianity. It is Pilate who
concocts a love potion for Macon Dead so that Ruth can conceive a baby son.
Pilate also leaves a Voodoo doll on Macon's chair when the latter desperately
pursues the abortion of the child. She thus is mainly linked to black magic and
folklore in *Song of Solomon*. She prefers natural light to electric light as well as
natural clothes to extravagant clothing.[42] Her close alignment with African
American folklore is further expressed in her playing the black trickster when
she gets Milkman and Guitar out of jail.[43] She fools the white policeman, lying
to him and pretending to be a humble and subservient black woman. In general,
she is rooted in a world that is stigmatized as superstitious, primitive, and
devilish, not only by white people but also by Macon who, drawing upon
Christian imagery, compares Pilate with a snake. In Voodoo, ironically, snakes
embody magic power. To Macon, however, Pilate is in part a devilish person
not to be trusted. Morrison seems to view her as an embodied extension of the
very early African American community, in which music and Voodoo coexisted
and played a central role. Julio Finn describes the communal life as follows:

> Music was their birthright, a communal possession to be shared by one and
> all. From the cradle blacks lived in a world of music. Someone was always
> singing—weeping and singing, working and singing, laughing and singing,
> dying and singing. Musically speaking, it was a rich and inspiring
> experience. In the same way, they lived in the mysterious sphere of
> Hoodoo—a world of invisible happenings, of magic charms and spells,

---

the United States. Giving voice to an eclectic outlook, the blues lyrics counteract any form of
dogmatic belief system.

[41]   Toni Morrison, *Song of Solomon* 55.

[42]   See Morrison 50, 206.

[43]   Byerman discusses the element of resistance in folklore elucidating that "folklore serves in
literature as the antithesis of closed oppressive systems. Closed systems may be political,
economic, cultural, religious, racial, sexual, aesthetic or philosophical: they may be black or
white, male or female, psychological or physical. They seek to suppress individuality,
community, imagination, voice, freedom, or even life itself by imposing a homogeneous order
on a heterogeneous reality. . . . Folk characters display fluid identities, folk tales and songs are
given in different versions, and folk values are adapted to changing circumstances; in all the
writers improvisation continually occurs. Keith E. Byerman, *Fingering the Jagged Grain*
(Athens: The U of Georgia P, 1985) 3-4. Pilate displays these flexible identities intellectually
and physically as well as through her relation to time and space.

presided over by conjure men and *mambos*, who were in touch with the
highest powers. Both were part of their inheritance, inalienable legacies
bequeathed to them by their people.[44]

Pilate functions as a conjure woman in the novel. It is she who predicts
Milkman's exact birth date. It is Pilate's voice that heals Reba's and Hagar's
sorrows. And it is Pilate's voice that like a charm puts a spell on both Macon
and Milkman. Her power also appears stronger than that of the Christian
church, as the scene of Hagar's funeral service demonstrates. Pilate only joins
the service when it is halfway through and silent mourning dominates the
atmosphere. Her voice and singing carry a lot more spiritual power than that of
the minister or the Baptist choir preceding her.[45] Pilate breaks the silence of the
congregation. Her words "toss like stones into a silent canyon."[46] It is not a song
of mourning that she sings standing at Hagar's coffin; it is a song of
reassurance. And its words are of secular, not religious concern. Obviously,
Morrison is aware of the fact that blues and theology are not as distant from one
another, as popularized views of the music constantly stress. Secular and sacred
elements overlap in the blues tradition and both express a spiritual longing.[47]
They differ on a temporal level, though. While the church points to a life after

---

[44]   Julio Finn, *The Bluesman: The Musical Heritage of Black Men and Women in the Americas*
(London: Quartet Books, 1986) 146.

[45]   Here Morrison resorts to the technique of signifyin(g) in African American culture and draws
on modes of contest in African American music. In general the term signifyin(g) appears in
relation to the Dozens. "The Dozens," as Lawrence W. Levine explains, "was an oral contest, a
joking relationship, a ritual of permitted disrespect in which the winner was recognized on the
basis of verbal facility, originality, ingenuity, and humor." Lawrence W. Levine, *Black Culture
and Consciousness* (New York: Oxford UP, 1977) 347-48. The game of verbal insult proceeds
according to a call-and-response pattern. As concerns music, Mezzrow and Wolfe refer to
cutting contests between young musical talents when they describe signifyin(g) as a form of
performance which applies to verbal as well as musical texts. These cutting contests represent
musical versions of the ritualistic verbal duels. Cf. Mezz Mezzrow and Bernard Wolfe, *Really
the Blues* (New York: Random House, 1946) 230-31.

[46]   Toni Morrison, *Song of Solomon* 323.

[47]   See also Jon Michael Spencer, *Blues and Evil* (Knoxville: The U of Tennessee P, 1993).
Spencer points out that the close relationship between the blues, prayer, and religious belief has
been either denied or ignored by musicologists and anthropologists. Spencer then revises
classical attitudes about the relation between blues and religion. He mentions preaching, prayer,
and eulogy as kinds of blues expressions (49). And he provides concrete examples: "Blues
singers not only prayed in moments of "instant religion," which was perhaps the real test of
fundamental religious belief (one's feeling of extra-dependency), but also spoke theologically in
the aftermath of tragedy. Uncountable blues singers bemoaned their loss of a lover and the pain
of going to the funeral or burial, and they did so in lyrics that tended to show agreement with
the ritual traditions of the church. When the woman Robert Wilkins 'did love and like' passed
away, Wilkins sang in his "I'll Go with Her Blues" that he dressed himself in black so he could
show the world he indeed wanted her even though he could not get her back" (47-48).

death, the blues, as Pilate's song reveals, holds out for "paradise now."[48] In the course of *Song of Solomon* this blues attitude becomes central for a feminine concern with the present and its potential for rewriting or changing history.

Both the causes and final epiphany of Milkman's journey into his true humanity are guided and accompanied by women. Although Morrison avoids overdichotomizing gender in *Song of Solomon*, Zora Neale Hurston's opening of *Their Eyes Were Watching God* (1937), which sets apart male and female visions, bears similarities to Morrison's treatment of male and female characters:

> Ships at a distance have every man's wish on board. For some they come in with the tide. For others they sail forever on the horizon, never landing until the Watcher turns his eyes away in resignation, his dreams mocked to death by Time. That is the life of men. Now, women forget all those things they don't want to remember, and remember everything they don't want to forget. The dream is the truth. Then they act and do things accordingly.[49]

As Hurston puts it, men are seldom aware of the present. Instead they cling to vague visions of the future. Women, on the contrary, confront all time categories directly. Their handling of cultural memory is selective. Hence, experiences of the past are interpreted and judged for their future significance. Most important, the newly gained image of the past becomes transformed into actions in the actual present. Thus they shape the future course of their private lives as well as that of history on a larger scale.

Similar to Zora Neale Hurston's gender distinction, Morrison seems to divide the black community into male and female worlds. Morrison plays here on the gender conflict in the blues tradition. She also signifies on the differences between the wandering bluesmen, who preferred the solo performance, and the classical female blues singers, who favored the group setting. Accordingly, Morrison selects primarily male characters in order to expose their difficulties with family and communal ties. While women tend to be portrayed in smaller communal settings—family and neighborhood—with a strong sense of social commitment, male characters are generally presented as solitary individuals. Their meeting ground is the barroom, the business world, the hunting ground. They leave home to chase their dreams of historical or material fulfillment. History is not set in domestic spheres; instead, men turn to the public platform since history, to them, is still produced by the media and measured out in numbers. The Days subscribe to the rationalized, male version

---

48   Paul Garon, *Blues & the Poetic Spirit* (New York: A Da Capo Paperback Press, 1979) 136. Although Garon and Spencer agree on the temporal aspects of the blues, Garon sees no link between the blues and the church. To the latter, the blues dismisses "divine systems of reward and punishment" thus representing an "uncompromisingly atheistic" art form (6). In Garon's assumptions we see a dominant European perspective on the blues, while Spencer looks at the music from within African American culture.

49   Zora Neale Hurston, *Their Eyes Were Watching God* (Urbana: U of Illinois P, 1978) 9.

of history. Their view of history is largely shaped by the news on the radio, and the historical role they choose for themselves reduces human existence to statistics; for each black person killed by a white person a member of the Days murders a white counterpart in return to reestablish "historical balance." Clearly their view of history is based on hatred and revenge: their sense of time is mechanical. Consequently each group member has been deformed into a Monday or Tuesday killer; their human potential has been twisted into an administrative form of killing. Finally, they have become incapable of building or participating in a life-sustaining communal setting; the dream of community "mocked to death by time."

In a similar way Macon Dead's conception of history makes him a victim of mechanical time. There is no space in his life for the enchanting singing in Pilate's home. The power of memory and catharsis conveyed by the blues hardly influences Macon's sense of time. His life as landlord and businessman is dictated by the ticking of the clock. There is not a glimpse of humanity when Macon insists on the punctual collection of the rent. He believes in progress and the power of property: "Own things. And let the things you own own other things. Then you'll own yourself and other people too."[50] To look back only drains your strength to realize your material vision. This is the advice Macon Dead gives his son.

One of the few male characters in *Song of Solomon* who seems able to approach Pilate's understanding of time is Guitar. He is full of passion and rich in intellectual insights. Guitar's psychological scrutiny of Hagar's distorted love and Milkman's materialistic obsession shows the immense human potential he carries in himself. However, unlike Pilate, Guitar has no sense of music; unlike Milkman, Guitar never starts to sing. He is named after the instrument he wanted to play so desperately as a child. But he never gets the guitar he wanted to win so badly in a contest in his hometown. He remains what his name implies: an instrument that is played upon. Ideas of history are imposed upon him and he is incapable of responding with an individual sense of time and experience. Accordingly, his tremendous potential for passion and insight turns into racist activism; he is even willing to kill. As regards the tension between individual and community, Guitar fails to reconcile individual and collective concerns. In his outlook the human being is reduced to race, love turns into hatred. "The disease they have is in their blood, in the structure of their chromosomes," Guitar says of white people.[51] He continues his assault with the following words: "White people are unnatural. As a race they are unnatural."[52] Similarly, he fails to differentiate among the diverse spectrum of black culture. To Guitar, all black people should unite in their struggle as racial warriors

---

50   Toni Morrison, *Song of Solomon* 55.

51   Morrison 158.

52   Morrison 157.

against white dominion. He does not recognize the richness of black cultural heritage; rather, his world view mirrors a reductive black and white picture ensuing from a crucial childhood experience. The accident of his father and the indifference of his white employer—he sends Guitar candies for consolation— haunts him all his life and causes his final fall. His potential for compassion gives way to a thirst for gold and a longing for revenge. Guitar, at last, never learns to liberate himself from the images of the past. There is no vision for a future life in Guitar's relation to time either. "Guitar and the Days chose never to have children. Shalimar left his, but it was the children who sang about it and kept the story of his leaving alive."[53] Similar to Macon, Guitar and the Days never absorb the psychological power of the blues which draws on memory and transcends the past.

While Guitar's passion turns into an outer-oriented aggression aiming at destruction, Hagar's unanswered passion for Milkman, finally becomes a destructive force directed against herself. She represents the loving woman who never finds control over her passion. In Hagar,

> there was the wilderness of the Southside. Not the poverty or dirt or noise, not just extreme unregulated passion where even love found its way with an ice pick, but the absence of control. Here one lived knowing that at any time, anybody might do anything. Not wilderness where there was system, or the logic of lions, trees, toads, and birds, but wild wilderness where there was none.[54]

Whereas Guitar succumbs to the depersonalized mechanical version of history blinding the members of the Days, Hagar, on her part, is trapped by natural time. As Stephanie Demetrakopoulos points out, "for Hagar, time is only cyclical, tied to feminine rhythms; she cannot comprehend the irrevocable passage of linear time."[55] Like "a restless ghost, finding peace nowhere and in nothing," she attempts to kill Milkman toward the end of each menstrual cycle.[56] She cannot accept that her lover has left her. Moreover she cannot endure that love and passion are transitory. Morrison's description of Hagar's hair as "standing out from her head like a thundercloud" captures Hagar's wild and chaotic nature; she is detached from strong familial ties and social responsibility.[57] Her life lacks a clear attachment to the community surrounding her. She "needed what most colored girls needed: a chorus of mamas,

---

[53]   Morrison 336.

[54]   Morrison 138.

[55]   Karla F.C. Holloway and Stephanie A. Demetrakopoulos, *New Dimensions in Spirituality: A Biracial and Bicultural Reading of the Novels of Toni Morrison* (New York: Greenwood Press, 1987) 98.

[56]   Toni Morrison, *Song of Solomon* 127.

[57]   Morrison 128.

grandmamas, aunts, cousins, sisters, neighbors, Sunday school teachers, best girl friends, and what all to give her the strength life demanded of her."[58]

The absence of a chorus from Hagar's life shows that she does not possess social grounding.[59] Her personality lacks stability, and her blackness represents a sign of inferiority to her; she hopes to win Milkman's love by buying all the things white people like. If one compares her spontaneous shopping tour with a musical improvisation one can conclude that her solo is completely out of touch with the playing of the community. She desperately moves in a world far away from the heritage of her culture and home. She buys all the things advertised by white commodity culture in order to regain her earlier attraction for Milkman. "He loves silky hair. . . . And lemon-colored skin." [60] The way she dresses and puts on her make-up suggests that she wants to adapt her appearance to white standards of beauty:

> Hagar stripped herself naked there, and without taking time to dry her face or feet, she dressed herself up in the white-with-a-band-of-color skirt and matching bolero, the Maidenform brassiere, the Fruit of the Loom panties, the no color hose, the Playtex garter belt and the Joyce con brios. Then she sat down to attend her face. She drew charcoal gray for the young round eye through her brows, after which she rubbed mango tango on her cheeks. Then she patted sunny glow all over her face. Mango tango disappeared under it and she had to put it on again. She pushed out her lips and spread jungle red over them. She put baby clear sky light to outwit the day light on her eyelids and touched bandit to her throat, earlobes, and wrists. Finally she poured a little youth blend into her palm and smoothed it over her face.[61]

Reba's and Pilate's unorthodox way of living cannot provide the social conditions to give shape to Hagar's wilderness. Hagar has clearly not inherited her grandmother's strength for solitary wandering. The final shopping scene describes a last attempt on Hagar's part to regain youth, to recapture the moments of a love long gone. In the end she dies of a broken heart, never having learned to cope with the fact that people, times, and places are bound to change.

---

58 Morrison 311.

59 In Greek culture, chorus originally meant a place for dance; in later periods the term referred to dance combined with song, as well as to the dancers. The traditional form of the Greek chorus consists of a leader and a masked chorus, and the presentation of the leader is continuously interrupted by the calls of the chorus; the calls represent a sort of refrain. See Werner Digel and Gerhard Kwiatkowski, eds. *Meyers Grosses Taschenlexikon*, vol. 4 (Mannheim: Bibliographisches Institut, 1983) 299. In African American culture this dialectical pattern is primarily present in the call-and-response pattern in the church services and various forms of sacred and secular music. Despite cultural differences, chorus in general implies communication and interaction.

60 Toni Morrison, *Song of Solomon* 319.

61 Morrison 318.

A similar troubled relationship to the flux of time characterizes Milkman's mother, Ruth Foster Dead. Time and space in Ruth's world are largely static. Although she resorts to Pilate's conjure power to reawaken Macon's sexual interest in her, Ruth's bourgeois conception of life keeps her far removed from the fluid and improvisatory nature of black folklore and music. While Pilate and Milkman embody the blues musician who keeps wandering and improvising, Ruth seeks continuity only. The water mark on the mahogany table in the dining room is a metaphor for her fixation on things static and stable. It becomes to her what the sun signifies to the prisoner and the sea to the keeper of the lighthouse, "some stable visual object that assured her that the world was still there; that this was life and not a dream."[62] On the level of social reputation this finds its expression in her overt concern with keeping and displaying her inherited status. With reference to her father's house and his reputation as a professional man, she justifies her feeling of social supremacy in the community of Not Doctor Street. The family Sunday drives in the Dodge sedan, her invitations for tea, and her concern with the water mark are nothing but desperate attempts to keep the memories of a privileged past alive. Her character requires continuity, not change. Just like Hagar she cannot deal with transitoriness. And, unlike Pilate, she cannot synthesize past, present, and future; nor is she capable of accepting death as part of the natural cycle. She has not the imaginative power of Pilate, who keeps on communicating with her dead father spiritually. Rather, she seeks physical contact with her deceased father, as her embrace of his body on the latter's death bed and her visits to lie on his grave illustrate. Thus she also tries to regain the lost love of her father in the physical contact with her son Milkman. Again Ruth displays a distorted relation to time passages since she keeps on breastfeeding her son despite the fact that he is much too old to be still fed with mother's milk. The present is dead for Ruth, a hope for the future is only projected when she attempts to protect her son Milkman from Hagar's violent passion. Nothing but the past remains, and Ruth withdraws into an idealized niche of private history.

Contrary to his mother's static relation to time—she lives in an imaginatively constructed past—, Milkman learns how to travel through time. Yet, in the beginning, he is unable to look backward; things past are things to be shunned. The family car ride on a Sunday afternoon reveals his bothered relation to the past:

> But riding backward made him uneasy. It was like flying blind, and not knowing where he was going—just where he had been—troubled him. He did not want to see trees that he had passed, or houses and children slipping into the space the automobile had left behind.[63]

---

62   Morrison 11.

63   Morrison 31-32.

In the boy there is not yet a desire for memory nor a potential for vision. In order to comprehend Pilate's relation to history, Milkman has to leave his immediate historical context of Not Doctor Street, a world of business interests and cold personal relationships. His journey takes him South, from an urban environment into a rural setting. Thus Morrison intensifies the dialectical process Milkman has to undergo on his way to define his place in history. The tension of opposite values in the juxtaposition of Darling Street and Not Doctor Street is heightened by the clash of the rural South with Milkman's urban manners. It becomes obvious at this point that Morrison's play with opposites is essential to the understanding of her fiction.

Milkman slowly moves into a conflict between economic and cultural values. The tension indicated lies in the clash between individual fulfillment—property and wealth—and the immersion into cultural and communal ties. In his initial indifference toward the problems and concerns of others, especially women, and his embrace of his father's materialistic ideology, Milkman, similar to Hagar, is completely out of touch with the larger community life. Indeed, his life circles around his own self until he heads off South.

This journey is closely related to the question of how Milkman is going to define his place in history. Is he going to accept the belief in history as an endless progress in materialistic terms, as his father does? Or is going to share Guitar Bains' revenge-pattern that measures history in terms of hatred and statistics? And we know by now that, to Morrison, neither one can be the sublime vision. As in her other novels, Morrison sets out to subvert both of these male historical concepts in *Song of Solomon*. Keith E. Byerman expounds that Morrison shows the exploitative nature of reductive sign systems. "She dramatizes the destructive power implicit in the control of various symbolic systems."[64] Milkman's hunger for gold displays what a strong hold his father's value system has on him. In order to disrupt this system he needs to change his goals. As Byerman continues, "the revision of goals makes possible a loosening of the control of logocentrism so as to achieve a black selfhood that negates that control."[65] Flexibility and change then supersede a purely teleological outlook. Milkman turns away from the thirst for gold to immerse himself into his cultural heritage and he breaks through a linear pattern of time to embrace music and folk culture.

At first glance it may seem strange that Morrison chooses a male protagonist in *Song of Solomon* to achieve selfhood, but she makes clear throughout the novel that Milkman's personal and spiritual growth would be impossible without female critique and guidance. This form of female protection starts already before Milkman's birth. His primary guide through life—Pilate—becomes the spiritual source of his life for it is she who reawakens Ruth's and

---

64   Keith E. Byerman, "Beyond Realism: The Fictions of Toni Morrison," *Toni Morrison*, ed. Harold Bloom (New York: Chelsea House Publishers, 1989) 52-62; 55.

65   Byerman, "Beyond Realism" 56.

Macon's sexual desires and it is she who keeps them from aborting him. In addition, Milkman's search for Pilate's gold makes him enter a realm of myth as he encounters the old black woman Circe. Circe's age is unknown. The community, as Reverend Cooper tells Milkman, has thought her dead for a long time. But she has survived the decay of the Butler family and seems to outlive all the material wealth, once the pride of the rich white family, that collapses as time goes by. Circe lives outside material history, and time, reduced to numbers, does not matter to her. She gives Milkman the impression, "as though seventy-two, thirty-two, any age at all, meant nothing whatsoever to her."[66] In spite of her apparently high age—"She was old. So old she was colorless"—her voice is young and her body seems forever "committed to constant change."[67] Continuously seeking for renewal, Circe embodies the spirit of jazz. She displays fluid identities. As healer, deliverer, and breeder of dogs she assumes a spiritual role. She is closely linked with nature, as Pilate is, and explains to Milkman the way into the wilderness, to the cave where Milkman hopes to find Pilate's treasure.

The subsequent journey through the wilderness is not only spatial but spiritual as well. It is in the face of nature that, for the first time in his life, Milkman has to rely upon himself. And the regulation of mechanical time, so powerful in the world of his father, becomes meaningless in the wilderness. Symbolically, his watch still "ticked, but the face was splintered and the minute hand was bent," after the crossing of the creek.[68] This crossing suggests a sort of rebirth. At one time, Milkman is completely under water, and when he has reached the other side of the creek he succumbs to the power of nature. "He lay back on the grass and let the high sunshine warm him. He opened his mouth so the clear air could bathe his tongue."[69]

Still the greed for gold drives him forward toward the cave. It is anger and exhaustion Milkman experiences when he finds out that the cave is empty. "There was nothing. Nothing at all."[70] This experience is crucial to a journey consisting of a series of situations in which Milkman's materialistic outlook and desire are confronted with absence or opposites. Circe, before, had rejected Milkman's offer to give her money, explaining to him that she could be free without it. Her run-down home, just one room left to be destroyed by the dogs, marks a clear opposite to Milkman's wealthy home in Not Doctor Street.

After having left the cave he encounters another situation that teaches him that the meaning of money is relative. Fred Garnett, a black man, gives him a lift to the next bus station. When Milkman wants to pay for the Coke and the lift

---

[66]   Toni Morrison, *Song of Solomon* 243.

[67]   Morrison 242.

[68]   Morrison 252.

[69]   Morrison 252.

[70]   Morrison 255.

he violates Garnett's code of hospitality: "I ain't got much, but I can afford a Coke and a lift now and then."[71]

Milkman's journey is not only spatial but spiritual in that it requires a series of metamorphoses in his character. He exchanges the role of the rent collector for the role of the folklorist. Talking with the members of the Danville and Shalimar communities, Milkman gets obsessed with the details and secrets of his family history. Morrison carries him through the realms of nature, myth, and sexuality to the world of art. Milkman finally takes on the role of the artist when he sings to Sweet. "He sang all the way: 'Solomon'n Ryna Belali Shalut.'"[72] His singing assumes a social and ritual function when he consoles the dying Pilate. "Sugargirl don't leave me here / Cotton balls to choke me / Sugargirl don't leave me here / Buckra's arms to yoke me."[73] To be sure, Milkman is not a musician—he "had no singing voice that anybody would want to hear"—but like a jazz musician he learns to adapt his solos to the playing of the group.[74] Milkman's individual improvisations on his way South—the search for the cave, the fight in the store in Shalimar, and the nightly hunt—gradually shift to improvised actions that lead to communal ties. He joins the men of Shalimar in the verbal celebration of the successful hunting. His relationship with Sweet expresses his growth. He is now able not only to take but also to give:

> He soaped and rubbed her until her skin squeaked and glistened like onyx. She put salve on his face. He washed her hair. She sprinkled talcum on his feet. He straddled her behind and massaged her back. She put witch hazel on his swollen neck. He made up the bed. She gave him gumbo to eat. He washed the dishes. She washed his clothes and hung them out dry. He scoured her tub. She ironed his shirt and pants. He gave her fifty dollars. She kissed his mouth. He touched her face. She said please come back. He said I'll see you tonight.[75]

As I have mentioned, the give-and-take interlude between Milkman and Sweet illustrates that Milkman begins to comprehend the importance of communal ties. A final epiphany occurs in the scene when he listens to the children sing and play. Pilate's old blues song appears in a different version in the form of a ring-game. Already in the early decades of 20th century Elsie Parson had collected several ring games from the folk heritage of the Sea Islands in South Carolina. Most of these ring games follow a call-and-response pattern in which a leader and the ring interact. "Jump Over Yonder" and "Have

---

71 Morrison 257.

72 Morrison 306.

73 Morrison 340.

74 Morrison 340.

75 Morrison 289.

you seen my turkey" are just two examples.[76] The ring rotates slowly anti-clockwise. Between leader and ring a shouted colloquy takes place. Frequently the children use songs while performing these ring-games. "The Farmyard" and "Nancy Beulah" are two of the songs used.[77] Most of them are interspersed with nonsense words similar to the "come booba yalle, come booba tambee" of "O Solomon don't leave me here."[78] Basically these nonsense phrases have a rhythmic effect accompanying the movement of the ring. Pilate's song signifies upon this traditional children' song. And Milkman not only remembers Pilate's version but starts to identify his own family background with names mentioned throughout the rounds of the children. "[T]he children, inexhaustible in their willingness to repeat a rhythmic, rhyming action game, performed the round over and over again. And Milkman memorized all of what they sang."[79] A new temporal awareness is indicated by the repetitiveness of the rhythm as well as by the movement which is anti-clockwise. Teleology turns into a seemingly timeless space.[80]

Milkman's sojourn in a strange environment detached from the dictate of money and clock-time opens his mind for a new consciousness of speech and language. He drops his family name "Dead" given to his grandfather after the liberation from slavery, when he introduces himself to Miss Byrd. "My name is, uh, Macon, and I'm visiting here for a few days."[81] Gradually Milkman learns to recognize the importance of the act of naming for African Americans in the reconstruction period and the years thereafter. Houston A. Baker explains that

> the simple English word *name* has an awesome significance for black American culture that it can never possess for another culture; the quest for being and identity that begins in a nameless void exerts a pressure on the word *name* that can only be understood when one understands black American culture.[82]

Since Morrison considers language always embedded within culture, the act of liberation from an oppressive culture requires semantic and political change. Symbolically, the family name "Dead" stands for the sterility and stasis ensuing

---

76   Elsie C. Parsons, *Folk-lore of the Sea Islands, South Carolina* (New York: The American Folk-Lore Society 1923) 200-01. For a discussion of ring plays see also Bessie Jones and Bess Lomax Hawes. *Step It Down: Games, Plays, Songs, and Stories from the Afro-American Heritage* (Athens: The U of Georgia P, 1972) 87-120.

77   Parsons, *Folk-lore of the Sea Islands* 184, 180.

78   Toni Morrison, *Song of Solomon* 306.

79   Morrison 306.

80   For a discussion of rational and teleological time concepts and their dissolving see also Homi K. Bhabha., *The Location of Culture* (London: Routledge, 1994) 142.

81   Toni Morrison, *Song of Solomon* 290.

82   Houston A. Baker, Jr., *Long Black Song: Essays in Black American Literature and Culture* (Charlottesville: The UP of Virginia, 1972) 120.

on the tranquil acceptance of white middle-class values. An active participation within history, however, involves the tackling of existing forms of discourse, for it is through language that history comes into being.

Milkman plunges into American history through his newly developed awareness of words and names:

> He read the road signs with interest now, wondering what lay beneath the names. The Algonquins had named the territory he lived in Great Water, *michi gami*. How many dead lives and fading memories were buried in and beneath the names of the places in this country. . . . Names that had meaning. No wonder Pilate put hers in her ear . . . . He closed his eyes and thought of the black men in Shalimar, Roanoke, Petersburg, Newport News, Danville, in the Blood Bank, on Darling Street, in the pool halls, the barbershops. Their names. Names they got from yearnings, gestures, flaws, events, mistakes, weaknesses. Names that bore witness. Macon Dead, Sing Byrd, Crowell Byrd, Pilate, Reba, Hagar . . . Muddy Waters, Pinetop, Fats, Lead-belly. . . .[83]

Places, people he knows, and African American musicians merge when Milkman contemplates the history of the country on his way back home. Linking locality with music, Morrison plays on a strong sense of place deeply rooted in the blues tradition. His personal history fuses with the history and the culture of the African American community. According to Susan Willis, Milkman

> reconstructs a dialectic of historical transition, where individual genealogy evokes the history of black migration and the chain of economic expropriation from hinterland to village, and village to metropolis. The end point of Milkman's journey is the starting point of his race's history in this country: slavery.[84]

In *Song of Solomon* the facts or data of history books are superseded by a memory that has its roots in oral culture and is thematically related to blues. In an essay Joyce Wegs relates the experience of pain and loneliness of all the major characters to a feeling of blues.[85] Similar to jazz—the musicians play around notes—Morrison circumscribes historical facts, playing on individual emphatic responses to historical conditions. Just like the jazz musicians who detach themselves from spatial fixation such as score and notation, Morrison, the writer, frees herself from historical data, to remember that which could not be precisely recorded but which continues to exist in storytelling, in music, in cultural patterns, and in the literary imagination. Macon's sexual memories of

---

83   Toni Morrison, *Song of Solomon* 333-34.

84   Susan A. Willis, "Eruptions of funk: historicizing Toni Morrison," *Black Literature and Theory*, ed. Henry L. Gates, Jr. (New York: Methuen, 1984) 263-83; 270.

85   See Joyce Wegs, "Toni Morrison's Song of Solomon: A Blues Song," *EILWIU* 9 (1982) 211-23.

his wife Ruth illustrate the interplay of memory and vision in the process of reconstructing the past:

> There had been a time when he had a head full of hair and when Ruth wore lovely complicated underwear that he deliberately took a long time to undo. . . . And in almost twenty years during which he had not laid eyes on her naked feet, he missed only the underwear. Once he believed that the sight of her mouth on the dead man's (her father's) fingers would be the thing he would remember always. He was wrong. Little by little he remembered fewer and fewer of the details, until he finally had to imagine them, even fabricate them, guess what they must have been.[86]

To remember, then, engages acts of recollection as well as acts of imagination. And these acts are necessarily highly subjective. The various stories in the novel that make up history are expressions of individual destinies. As Elizabeth Schultz stresses, "the neighborhoods in Morrison's novels have the vitality and integrity of a multi-dimensional personality."[87] To Morrison the sum of individual memories verbally expressed constitutes a record of history different from linear, logocentric systematization.

Comparing Ellison's and Morrison's narrative structure, Melvin Dixon points out that "Morrison undercuts the hegemony of Ellison's preferred narrative strategy . . . by enlarging the structure to encompass multiple lives and points of view as her characters aim for motion, not stasis."[88] To resort to an analogy to jazz, one can say that Ellison seems to emphasize the solo or the individual consciousness whereas Morrison puts emphasis on the solo embedded within group improvisation or the individual's role in a communal context. This act of sharing and participating is essential to black culture as a whole, as Morrison points out in a conversation with Gloria Naylor. Black folk "have never taken directions well, they've always participated . . . whether it was political or blues singing, or jazz . . . ."[89] History, then, is never complete, but made up of various different stories in the novel. These stories sound as the black folk would tell them, "meanderingly, constantly retold, constantly imagined within a framework."[90] For Morrison "the postwar model of the text as a system of discourse composed of floating signifiers" opens up no abyss.

---

86   Toni Morrison, *Song of Solomon* 16.

87   Elisabeth Schultz, "The Novels of Toni Morrison: Studies of the Individual and the Neighborhood," *Essays on the Contemporary American Novel*, eds. Hedwig Bock and Albert Weinheim (München: Max Hueber Verlag, 1986) 281-304; 281.

88   Melvin Dixon, *Ride Out the Wilderness: Geography and Identity in Afro-American Literature* (Urbana: U of Illinois P, 1987) 137.

89   Gloria Naylor and Toni Morrison, "A Conversation," *The Southern Review 21* (1985) 567-93; 574.

90   Nellie McKay, "Toni Morrison: Interview," *Contemporary Literature* 24 (Winter 1983) 413-29; 427.

The semiotically freed word levels the way for new thinking.[91] Language is semiotically liberated to suggest more diversity and complexity than the fixed relationship between signifier and signified in logocentric thinking would allow.[92] Pilate reveals Morrison's own ideological foundation when she explains the relativity of blackness to Milkman. "There're five or six kinds of black. Some silky, some woolly. Some just empty. Some like fingers. And it don't stay still. It moves and changes from one kind of black to another."[93] This is not only Morrison advocating a rich, diverse black culture but also Morrison propagating her belief in history as being constantly in motion and exposed to change. Coherence, both on the psychological level of the individual and on the aesthetic level of the artist, can only be achieved by accepting flux and embracing contraries. This implies that it is always important to approach the opposite, the other.

As Morrison's focus on individual destinies emphasizes, African American culture cannot be reduced to a small scale of cultural manifestations. On the contrary, African American culture is rich and diverse. Pilate, Hagar, Ruth, Guitar, and Milkman are but a few characters giving shape to its manifold facets. So Morrison keeps on moving back and forth between the individual and the communal level to iterate that culture, like history, remains in motion constantly. Fluidity resists any ordering pattern. Hence, ambivalence, so prevalent in the blues lyrics, also characterizes many temporal aspects of *Song of Solomon*. Morrison repeatedly reminds the reader that there is more than one way of looking at things. Perspectives from an individual and from a communal point of view most often differ from each other or even clash with one another. Milkman's freedom in the first part of the novel ensues from the oppression of his sisters at home and his indifference toward Hagar's possessive love for him. Milkman's freedom in the second part of the novel sharply contrasts with his former state of freedom. The second part portrays a state of freedom that is to be more highly valued, according to Morrison's concern with the net of individual and communal interests. Milkman's gradual process of liberation is based upon his merging with the Shalimar community, his love-making with Sweet, and his refound love for his aunt Pilate and his mother Ruth: "From the beginning his mother and Pilate had fought for his life, and he had never so much as made either of them a cup of tea."[94]

---

91   See Vincent B. Leitch, *Deconstructive Criticism* (New York: Columbia UP, 1983) 15.

92   See Jacques Derrida, *Of Grammatology*, trans. Gayatri Spivak (Baltimore: The John Hopkins UP, 1976) 3-5. For a discussion of the subversive function of language in the work of Toni Morrison see also Dwight A. McBride, "Speaking the Unspeakable: On Toni Morrison, African American Intellectuals and the Uses of Essentialist Rhetoric," *Toni Morrison: Critical and Theoretical Approaches*, ed. Nancy J. Peterson (Baltimore: The Johns Hopkins UP, 1997) 131-52; 149-50.

93   Toni Morrison, *Song of Solomon* 40.

94   Morrison 335.

Milkman's new social consciousness counteracts the disruptive effect that history has had on the African American community from the early days of slavery on. The system of slavery aimed at and partially succeeded in breaking up the African American family unit. Physical separation has been followed by psychological isolation. That Pilate is born without a navel and collects rocks from all the places she attends on the search for her roots stands as a grotesque symbol for the uprootedness of many African Americans on the American continent. The communal ties –so essential to African and African American neighborhoods– have further been dismantled during the migration years from a rural to an urban setting and through the rapid expansion of a mass commodity culture. Not surprisingly, Morrison chooses the 1960s for the setting of the novel. As she makes us understand, the historical development in this period goes hand in hand with the loss of a collective consciousness –the lore and rituals of ancient communities. Milkman regains at least part of the heritage when he travels South; he remembers all of the children's rhymes and ploughs through his family history. The ambivalence accompanying his sojourn in the South –his thirst for Pilate's gold mixes with his yearning to know more about his ancestors– remains until the very end of the novel. Milkman's leap is indeed an act of liberation, but his future destiny Morrison leaves unprophesied.

Using jazz as an artistic paradigm with social as well as aesthetic implications, Morrison naturally picks an open ending for the novel. She offers no fixed solutions. Letting various circles—both temporal and spatial—intersect, Morrison faces the reader with multiple perspectives on history. The various representations of history—from Hagar's uncontrolled wildness without form to the total control of mechanical time as in the organization of the Seven Days—illuminate different degrees of a loss of freedom in *Song of Solomon*. Freedom for the individual and the collective only seems possible in terms of adjustment, in terms of compromise. Obviously, Morrison's notion of freedom calls forth parallels to the function of solo in jazz since individual flights lose their musical impact as soon as they are no longer grounded in the band playing. Morrison's belief in change, then, cannot be viewed as a radical individual act. Change needs to be embedded in a communal context.

Accordingly, history continues to be a field of force where the interplay of individual and collective energies reigns. And the improvisational abilities necessary to play blues and jazz are as important socially since improvisation is constantly needed in defining one's historical role. Perhaps the most distinguished expression of the interrelation of nature, language, art, and social action occurs in the hunting scene:

> In distinctive voices they were saying distinctive, complicated things. That long *yah* sound was followed by a specific kind of howl from the dogs. The low *howm howm* that sounded like a string bass imitating a bassoon meant something the dogs understood and executed. . . . All those shrieks, those rapid tumbling barks, the long sustained yells, the tuba sounds, the drumbeat sounds, the low liquid *howm howm*, the reedy whistles, the thin *eeee's* of a

cornet, the *unh unh unh* bass chords. It was all language. . . . Before things were written down.[95]

The sounds of nature are associated with sounds of a jazz performance. Here Morrison refers to the talking effects in jazz and links them with a basic form of communication. To relate the multiple levels of interaction in African American music to social rituals, Morrison chooses the archetypal hunting scene where Milkman is placed in a setting where communication takes place between the different hunters as well as between man and nature. Clearly, African American music has not only paved the way to heritage and past, it has also provided him an access to communal living. Compared to Langston Hughes' dance section *in Not Without Laughter*, Morrison's use of music appears completely detached from any direct relation to the world of music. This underscores that music becomes more and more abstracted and contextualized in contemporary African American fiction. Indeed, in Morrison's novel, blues and jazz shape artistic and social aesthetic alike. And it is through music—Pilate's singing, the children's song, and all the blues musicians such as Muddy Waters and Leadbelly—that Milkman is pulled out of the purely materialistic world view and drawn into a holistic sense of history.

Using blues and jazz for reconstructing a communal vision of history, Morrison sets an important example for contextualizing blues and jazz within a narrative about cultural politics. Since she focuses on those elements in blues and jazz which stand for continuity primarily, her call for change is iterated through a rather traditional narrative voice, though. Among the more experimental postmodern writers discussed next, such as Ishmael Reed and Ntozake Shange, African American music evokes radical critiques of narrative structure, diction, and cultural politics alike. Therefore aspects of racial and gender politics interact with experimental forms of jazz as these writers produce new ways of conceiving culture and history from multicultural and feminine perspectives.

---

[95]   Morrison 281.

V. Musical Time and Multicultural Aesthetics: Ishmael Reed and a Denial of Closure

Ishmael Reed's play with indeterminacy in *Mumbo Jumbo* (1972) penetrates the content and structure of the novel. His artistic intention behind the novel seems to be to dismantle anything static, time concepts included. In terms of literary tradition, Reed then continues what Mikhail Bakhtin describes as a process of subverting ancient hierarchizations of temporalities within the genre of the novel.[1] To Bakhtin, the novel bears at its core "a new way of conceptualizing time."[2] Different from the epic which stresses an absolute past, the novel is in direct contact with everyday reality. On a temporal level as well as otherwise it represents a genre that continues to examine itself and subject its forms to change and review. Bakhtin's claim that the novel expresses "plasticity itself" gains new validity when we take into account that Reed draws on extra-literary sources for rewriting history in *Mumbo Jumbo*.[3] Bakhtin links the reconceptualization of time in the novel with the genre's origin in folklore. Reed, on his part, turns to artistic modes outside the literary discourse which have also emerged from a folk heritage, blues and jazz in particular. Drawing on these musical modes, he re-shapes time conceptions and their implications for concepts of race and culture.[4]

Since bebop compositions, improvised around arbitrarily exchangeable musical components, play such an important role in Reed's "signifyin(g)" on

---

1   Bakhtinian ideas in this essay are taken from the following texts: M.M. Bakhtin, *Rabelais and his World*, trans. Helene Iswolsky (Cambridge, Mass.: MIT Press, 1965), *Problems of Dostoevsky's Poetics*, trans. R.W. Rotsel (Ann Arbor: Michigan: Ardis, 1973), and *The Dialogic Imagination: Four Essays by M.M. Bakhtin*, trans. Caryl Emerson and Michael Holquist (Austin: U of Texas P, 1994). In relation to carnivalesque elements I refer to: Michail M. Bachtin, *Literatur und Karneval: Zur Romantheorie und Lachkultur*, trans. Alexander Kaempfe (Frankfurt/Main: Fischer Taschenbuch Verlag, 1990).

2   M.M. Bakhtin, *The Dialogic Imagination: Four Essays by M.M. Bakhtin* 38.

3   Cf. M.M. Bakhtin, *The Dialogic Imagination* 39.

4   As Günter H. Lenz emphasizes, "Afro-Americans today, Neo-HooDooism, cannot simply adopt the African sense of time and spiritual universe, but have to reconstruct it in the context of their Western history, have to acknowledge how archetypes and traditional patterns changed over time, and in which forms they have been realized in modern history." "Ishmael Reed," *Essays on the Contemporary American Novel*, eds. Hedwig Bock and Albert Wertheim (München: Max Hueber Verlag, 1986) 305-34; 317. As concerns the intercultural dimension of shaping and re-shaping cultural identities see also Samuel Mattias Ludwig von Schiers, *Concrete Language: Intercultural Communication and Identity in Maxine Hong Kingston's The Woman Warrior and Ishmael Reed's Mumbo Jumbo* (Dissertation: Universität Bern, 1994) and Robert Young, *Intercultural Communication: Pragmatics, Genealogy, Deconstruction* (Clevedon: Multilingual Matters LTD, 1996) 32-56.

widely shared assumptions about race and culture, this chapter pursues a performative shape in analysing Reed's text. My analysis thus displays Reed's playing "riffs" on genre, structure, and history. Since a constant tendency to disrupt and renew characterizes Reed's third novel, my approach explores the element of revolt in blues and jazz—rhythmic and otherwise—, which has an impact on Reed's vision of a multicultural society as well as on literary theme and form. His historical and aesthetic vision responds to previous ideas about racial difference and the interrelation of tradition and innovation by both black and white thinkers. Reed's "riffs" reveal his responses to W. E. B. DuBois, T.S. Eliot, Hegel, and more recent black aesthetic critics such as Addison Gayle, Jr., while he develops his individual vision of history and form.

W.E.B. DuBois's famous definition of the African American double-consciousness in *Souls of Black Folk* has intrigued African American writers and critics alike in their endeavors to develop historical and theoretical models for a better understanding of African American culture:

> (T)he Negro is a sort of seventh son, born with a veil, and gifted with second-sight in this American world,--a world which yields him no true self-consciousness, but only lets him see himself through the revelation of the other world. It is a peculiar sensation, this double-consciousness, this sense of always looking at one's self through the eyes of others, of measuring one's soul by the tape of a world that looks on in amused contempt and pity. One ever feels his twoness—, an American, a Negro; two souls, two thoughts, two unreconciled strivings; two warring ideals in a dark body, whose dogged strength alone keeps it from being torn asunder.[5]

Ishmael Reed responds to DuBois's dualistic tension at the heart of African American cultural productivity with a dialogical voice. Various concepts of time and culture enter into a dialogue, as Reed unfolds different narrative strategies in *Mumbo Jumbo*. Hence, he turns binary oppositions into communicating opposites, as he plays on and undermines dualistic thinking. Once conceptions like DuBois's 'double-consciousness' become rigid or static, once they are accepted as constant historical facts, they become reductive and restrictive to Reed. To him, DuBois's conception bears not only great potential for artistic creativity—two cultures meet—but also presents a potential trap. Insisting on the dualistic principle, DuBois runs the risk of preserving barriers of racial difference and racial bias, thus locking the doors for cultural renewal in American society. In blues and jazz especially, Reed detects dialogical art forms subverting dualistic systems. As Reed uses these musical patterns, they turn into cultural modes of expression defying the signs and metaphors of controlling systems. "In *Mumbo Jumbo* Reed spells out his vision of the alternative to society as control," Kathryn Hyme points out.[6]

---

5   W. E. B. DuBois, *Souls of Black Folk 1903: Essays and Sketches* (New York: NAL, 1969) 45.

6   Kathryn Hyme, "Ishmael Reed and the Problematics of Control," *PMLA* 108.3 (May 1993): 506-18; 509.

Ishmael Reed's affiliation with blues and jazz is not only apparent in allusions, references, and structural devices in his novels, poems, and essays.[7] Together with the avant-garde musician Kip Hanrahan, Reed produced two albums titled "Conjure". The first album, released in 1983, presented poems by Reed arranged to blues and jazz music. Blues musician Taj Mahal and jazz virtuosos such as Lester Bowie and David Murray contributed to the production of the album.[8] As critic and commentator on the African American music scene, moreover, Reed has been active throughout his writing career. Most of his essays are devoted to jazz and jazz musicians. "The Old Music", "Music: Black, White and Blue", and "Remembering Josephine Baker" are but a few examples, all gathered in Reed's essayistic autobiography *Shrovetide in Old New Orleans* (1978). Central to Reed's understanding of the significance of jazz as aesthetic model for the artist is, without doubt, his admiration for the bebop musician Charlie Parker, an admiration that shines through in Reed's novels and poems alike. As Reed repeatedly emphasizes, jazz embodies a master model for artistic innovation within a tradition in the figure of Charlie "Bird" Parker.

That Reed points to bebop in particular requires a brief excursion into the history of jazz. Bebop marked an important renewal of formal and improvisational elements in jazz toward the end of the heyday of the swing era. Like almost all new directions in jazz the bebop avant-garde in the 1940s was led by black musicians, above all Charlie "Bird" Parker and Dizzy Gillespie. Their emphasis on polyrhythmic elements such as in Gillespie's African-Cuban jazz and their numerous performances with African musicians and dancers signified a reorientation to the African elements of jazz.[9] The bebop style had a distinct formal build-up to which the tunes adhered: the theme played in unison at the beginning, then a string of long, fast, difficult improvisations, and as a conclusion again the theme played collectively. The rhythm section (including

---

[7]   See Peter Nazareth, "An Interview with Ishmael Reed," *Iowa Review* 13.2 (1982):117-31. In this interview Reed talks about the influence of jazz on his writing: "I am influenced by jazz. I used to play the trombone in jazz bands and nightclubs. When I was going to university I would do that. That's the way the solos go. That's the way you improvise and that's what I do, twist and turn. One phrase calling another phrase to mind. I think it's orderly, though, and I think it makes sense; it's connected. There's more variety and surprise, it's more entertaining and more interesting to the serious reader" (129). "Discontinuity. In jazz one can make associations that on the surface do not seem to have anything to do with anything, but when you think of the entire process, it makes sense. It is unified. I think that's what I do in my work. The reader has to pay attention, has to keep up with it, but it's no different from someone starting off with a melody or tune and then improvising on it or merely alluding to it. That's what I try to do" (120). The interaction between jazz and writing, poetry in particular, was most intense in the late fifties and the sixties. For a historical and critical study of poets and writers belonging to the Umbra group, Howard poets or Village poets see Aldon Lynn Nielsen, *Black Chant: Languages of African-American Postmodernism* (Cambridge: Cambridge UP, 1997) 38-77.

[8]   See Hans Peter Schwerfel, "Mister Multikult," *Zeitmagazin* 17 (April 1992): 61-64; 62.

[9]   Iron Werther, *Bebop* (Frankfurt/Main: Fischer Verlag, 1988) 52.

percussion, bass, piano) played diverse rhythms which overlapped, hence creating a density much more complex than the standard four beat rhythm of swing tunes. Thus bebop represented a new black alternative to the popularized swing.[10]

More than in earlier styles of jazz, bebop represented jazz at an extremely individualistic end of the improvisation-communal dialectic.[11] Parker's solos, for example, appear to leave the common rhythmical basis of the band for a moment only to be on beat again shortly afterward.[12] Hence, his "solo flights" represent radical experiments with Armstrong's mastering of time on an individual level. In their emphasis on innovation and improvisation in composition and performance bebop musicians become suitable spokesmen for Reed's own "Neo-HooDoo" aesthetic. "Charlie 'Yardbird (Thoth)' Parker is an example of the Neo-HooDoo artist as an innovator and improvisor," Reed confirms in his "Neo-HooDoo Manifesto".[13] More explicitly Reed delineates his artistic concern in "The Neo-HooDoo Aesthetic":

> Gombo Févi
>
> A whole chicken—if chicken cannot be / had, veal will serve instead; a little ham; / crabs, or shrimps, or both, according to the/taste of the consumer; okra according to the / quantity of the soup needed; onions, garlic, / parsley, red pepper, etc. Thicken with plenty of / rice. (Don't forget to cut the gombo or okra.) /
>
> Gombo Filé /
>
> Same as above except the okra is pulverised and oysters are used / Why do I call it "The Neo-HooDoo Aesthetic"? /

---

10   Turning their back on the swing tradition also represented a cultural statement. Bebop was regarded as a truly black musical and cultural expression. Arnold Shaw points out, that the black boppers basic concern was "to create something that "Charlie", meaning white musicians could not steal—as Charlie had done with Swing (The new jazz was unabashedly antiwhite, and that included audiences as well as musicians)." Arnold Shaw, *Black Popular Music in America* (New York: Macmillan, 1986) 161-62.

11   Indeed, as concerns the improvisation-community dialectic, bebop takes one of the most individualistic stances in jazz. Stearns, for instance, points out that bebop musicians had to struggle hard to keep their solo flights in touch with the rest of the band: "At Minton's, a musician launched upon a new chorus and then stopped short, leaving his successor to pick up the pieces." On stage many a bebop musician put on a mask of "hunched preoccupation, of somnabulistic concentration." Some of them even performed with back to the audience; some of them walked off the stand after having finished a solo. It is also important to mention that a lot of bebop musicians rejected the image of the African American entertainer as embodied by Armstrong in the swing tradition. Marshall W. Stearns, *The Story of Jazz* (New York: William Morrow & Company, 1970), 222, 221.

12   Peter Niklas Wilson and Ulfert Goeman, *Charlie Parker* (Schaftlach: Oreos Verlag, 1988) 37.

13   Ishmael Reed, *Conjure* (Amherst: U of Massachusetts P, 1972), 21.

The proportions of ingredients used depend / upon the cook![14]

Tradition remains a necessary matrix for every artist, as Reed's analogy between recipe and art forms suggests. However, the role of the "cook" is essential to Reed's vision of the artist's possibility to shape the tradition according to his own will. Clearly, Reed pursues a highly idiosyncretic approach to history in which the author's choice is decisive for the emerging conceptions of time and process. His aesthetic is emphatically anti-dogmatic, and he boldly claims his own place in American literature. His "Manifesto", on the one hand, signifies a response to Eliot's "Tradition and the Individual Talent"; although Reed stresses the importance of tradition he is more concerned with the individuality of the artist: "The proportions of ingredients used depend upon the cook." On the other hand, it is a sharp refusal of the doctrines of the Black Aesthetic Movement in the 1960s. Reed rejects the reduction of art to a mere instrument of political statement and action. He does not deny the political implications of art. Yet, he refuses to succumb to prescribed ideologies.

His view of history, then, is quite different from that of African American fictions ideologically based upon the conventions of the socio-realist tradition. And jazz informs Reed's historical imagination decisively. "What if I write circuses, a novel can be anything it wants to be," Loop Garoo announces in *Yellow-Back-Radio-Broke-Down*, Reed's second novel, thus expressing the latter's own concern.[15] Indeed Reed's desire for freedom of form finds many parallels in the history of jazz styles. His use of form, especially in *Mumbo Jumbo*, expresses the perhaps utopian concept of a multicultural society. In *Mumbo Jumbo* above all Reed advocates a multicultural aesthetic, an aesthetic that pursues openness, not closure. Berndt Ostendorf's account of jazz illustrates why Reed's adaptation of jazz techniques in *Mumbo Jumbo* is so suitable for Reed's literary and social ambitions:

> In the history of jazz, the tangle of black-white relations is particularly complex, but also paradigmatic for an understanding of what makes American culture what it is. Jazz also represents a testimony to a black coming of age in American culture: It announces the break into audibility and visibility, and it marks a black appropriation not only of instruments, techniques, and strategies of music making but also of the public sphere and the market.[16]

In the endeavor to make white America more multi-ethnic, to "blacken up" American culture is of the essence for Reed. In his concern with a multicultural aesthetic, black culture thus occupies a specific position. Voodoo, the ancient

---

14   Reed 26.

15   Ishmael Reed, *Yellow-Back-Radio-Broke-Down* (New York: Doubleday, 1969), 36.

16   Bernd Ostendorf, "Ralph Waldo Ellison: Anthropology, Modernism, and Jazz," *New Essays on Invisible Man*, ed. Robert O' Meally (New York: Cambridge UP, 1988): 95-121 ; 110.

African religion, embodies the undogmatic spirit Reed feels to be a necessary basis for a multicultural whole. To him Voodoo is spiritual as well as physical: spiritual in the sense that it functions as a matrix for a harmonious coexistence between nations and cultures; physical in the sense that it is always connected with music and motion. "When I'm looking at HooDoo, I'm looking at dance . . . and singing, songs, drums. . . ."[17]

Blues and jazz, represented by Jes Grew in Reed's *Mumbo Jumbo*, are the carriers of Voodoo culture in the 20th century. To Reed they are extensions of an ancient African culture and therefore of historical significance. The continuity of history and tradition implied here becomes central to Reed's view of history. History, in *Mumbo Jumbo*, is seen as an infinite series of stories that needs to be complemented and corrected continuously. The story can never be complete, the picture never finished. The history-making of *Mumbo Jumbo* is only part of an ongoing process. As Reed makes explicit, the writing of *Mumbo Jumbo* ceases on "Jan. 31st, 1971 3: OO P.M." in "Berkeley, California."[18] Giving the novel a definite place in time and space, he emphasizes that *Mumbo Jumbo* can only provide one way of looking at history. This way is naturally subjective and framed by the cultural and historical here-and-now surrounding the particular writer.

The plots and subplots of the novel revolve around the culture war between the white Atonist path and the Mu'tafikah, a militant wing of the Jes Grew movement. The main story of the novel dramatizes the conflict between these opposed groups. The conflict is both cultural and religious since the Atonist Wallflower Order stands for the Judaeo-Christian tradition, whereas the Jes Grew movement represents the African American tradition. Jes Grew, a music and dance epidemic, is spreading all over America. White America is horrified: "if this Jes Grew becomes pandemic it will mean the end of Civilization As We Know It."[19] In order to stop the epidemic the Wallflower Order tries to get hold of Jes Grew's sacred text. The ancient HooDoo detective LaBas attempts to save the text to guarantee Jes Grew's survival. Both fail, though, since Abdul Hamid, black cultural nationalist, burns the Text. Even though Jes Grew subsides in the end, Papa LaBas optimistically announces its comeback: "Is this the end of Jes Grew? Jes Grew has no end and no beginning. . . . We will miss it for a while but it will come back, and when it returns we will see that it never left. . . . We will make our own future Text. A future generation of young artists will accomplish this."[20] Reed's claim that Jes Grew is without beginning and end suggests a continuous presence of African American culture in the United

---

17   Robert Gover, "An Interview with Ishmael Reed," *Black American Literature Forum* 21.1 (1978):12-19; 12.

18   Ishmael Reed, *Mumbo Jumbo* (New York: Avon Books, 1972) 249.

19   Reed 7.

20   Reed 233.

States. While it functions outside a linear temporal progression it represents a subcultural force. But it also shares a utopian outlook with mainstream culture, a belief in the future presence of African American culture within a larger American cultural framework. The repetitive structure that Reed locates behind history indicates that historical and cultural phenomena come and go; they resurface in a different shape at an unknown point in the future. As paradigm for his assumptions he uses the periods of highest artistic production within the African American community. The strong visibility of African American art in the Harlem Renaissance gives way to a less noticeable presence in the following decades. Yet, it returns with even more artistic and political impact in the Black Arts movement of the 1960s. Reed's prophecy that Jes Grew reappears at a later point in time may already be true if we think about the contemporary spreading of African American rap music across the continents.

Shifting time sequences in *Mumbo Jumbo*, Reed achieves a disruption of temporal hierarchy as perceived by Western cultures at large. In Reed's re-writing of history, white civilization and culture is characterized by hypocrisy and art piracy. White art never reveals the true sources of its achievements. Although, according to Reed, white art emerges out of black or Eastern origins, it pretends to be original and independent. To give evidence to his thesis he refers to Greek and Roman mythology deriving from the myths of ancient Egypt. As PaPa LaBas's recollection of the Set and Osiris myth underscores, Reed places the African culture of Egypt at the origin of Western civilization, thus parodying the idea of white supremacy. LaBas refers to Greek culture as an extension of Egyptian culture: "Dionysus taught the Greeks the Osirian Art which lasted until the Atonists in the late 4th century B.C. convinced the Emperor Constantine to co-sign for the Cross." La-Bas continues: "The Greeks established temples to these Egyptian-derived mysteries where people would go out of their heads so that the gods could take them over."[21] In Reed's parody of history Egyptian mysteries, still celebrated by Greeks and Romans, turn into paranoia and hysteria in the terminology of Christianity and modern psychology. "Exorcism becomes Psychoanalysis, Hex becomes Death Wish, Possession becomes Hysteria."[22]

White culture, however, cannot only be accused of hiding its actual sources but also of depriving Eastern and African nations of their cultural identity. Thousands of art objects from the Asian or African continent can be found in European and American museums. Again, white societies enrich their cultural spectrum by "borrowing" artifacts from countries once conquered and occupied by them. Reed describes their museums as "pirate dens."[23] Conversely, in *Mumbo Jumbo* Reed propagates a cultural diversity, rejecting both a

---

[21]   Reed 192.

[22]   Reed 244.

[23]   Reed 94.

predominant white Atonist aesthetic and the radical black aesthetic expressed by Abdul Hamid, who wants to unite blacks by force:". . .we need a strong man, someone to 'whip these coons into line.' Let the freedom of culture come later!"[24] Hamid is criticized by LaBas and his assistant Black Herman, both attesting that nobody is allowed to judge people's tastes, both putting emphasis on the necessity of diversity for the creation of a free society and a free world.

> Yes, LaBas joins in, where does that leave the ancient Vodun aesthetic: pantheistic, becoming, 1 which bountifully permits 1000s of spirits, as many as the imagination can hold. Infinite Spirits and Gods. So many that it would take a book larger than the Koran and the Bible, the Tibetan Book of the Dead and all the holy books in the world to list, and still room would have to be made for more. And I resent you accusing us of taking advantage of the people, Black Herman joins in. Why have you established yourself as an arbiter for the people's tastes?[25]

On an intertextual level, Reed's cultural criticism is also directed against black aesthetic critics such as Addison Gayle and Clarence Major. He rejects their dogmatic and collective approach to black art. To Reed, *The Black Aesthetic*, edited by Gayle, represents a homogenizing concept of a black aesthetic. Numerous critical and creative voices included in this anthology propagate a view of black art as functional, collective, and always politically engaged. In his foreword, Gayle expresses an all-out black ideology: "The problem of the de-Americanization of black people lies at the heart of the Black aesthetic."[26] According to Gayle, all black artists should unite as political warriors against white America. A similar collective view of black artistic engagement underlies Clarence Major's selection of poems in *The New Black Poetry*, an anthology of young black poets. In his introduction Major emphasizes the synthesis of art and politics as well as the necessity of a collective spirit behind social change.[27] Accordingly, he condemns individualism and the capitalist spirit. Obviously Reed refers to critics like Gayle and Major when he develops types such as Abdul Hamid, Muslim and black nationalist, and W. W. Jefferson, black critic with affiliations with the marxist school. They both advocate homogenizing approaches to politics and art.

In order to reestablish cultural multiplicity the Mu'tafikah, a militant wing of the Jes Grew movement, launches an art crusade, delivering Asian and African art objects back to the vernacular places where they once were designed and manufactured. Primarily, however, Reed's ideal of multiculturalism is

---

24   Reed 230.

25   Reed 39.

26   Addison Gayle, Jr., ed. *The Black Aesthetic* (New York: Anchor Books, 1972), xxiii.

27   See Clarence Major, ed., "Introduction," *The New Black Poetry* (New York: International publications, 1969).

accompanied by the aesthetic phenomenon of Jes Grew manifesting itself, chiefly in music and dancing. It is an expression of high sensuality and physical motion, and thus compensates for the extreme rationality and focus on consciousness in Atonist art and society. Jes Grew mainly refers to jazz music. "Jes Grew, the Something or Other that led Charlie Parker to scale the Everests of the Chord. Riff fly skid dip soar and gave his Alto Godspeed. Jes Grew that touched John Coltrane's Tenor."[28] In the broader sense, it stands for the musical creations and innovations made by African Americans under most unfavorable conditions—in the days of slavery, for instance—during their American experience. On the one hand, Jes Grew manifests survival and creativity; on the other hand, Jes Grew bears a culturally revolutionary potential. It is not by chance that Reed refers to the two most stunning jazz innovators, Parker and Coltrane. It is in jazz and blues that Reed locates a cultural and psychological counterforce to the white power structure. Jes Grew embodies what Franklin Rosemont finds in the blues:

> The 'Devil's music'—that is, the music of the damned, the music of the excluded—embraces the revolutionary principle of evil which Hegel long ago recognised as the form in which the motive force of historical development presents itself. Through its 'deliberately obscure language of concealment' (Oliver 1968: 11) one finds in the blues old but neglected truths gushing forth in geysers of inspiration prophesying the eventual triumph of the damned over those who now hold the reins of power.[29]

Reed figuratively attacks the rational concepts of the white power structure through music and physical motion. Western civilization, in Reed's parody, seems without body. "No where in the New Testament does Jesus Christ dance."[30] Reed indeed plays on general assumptions about the differences between black and white cultures. Jesus Christ, Marx, and Freud are caricatured in Reed's burlesque assault upon Western civilization. The continuous progress of science and philosophy is reversed into regression into madness and destruction. The Dionysian world of black magic in *Mumbo Jumbo* becomes the carrier of true humanity. Throughout the text of the novel Reed interpolates data, graphics and comments referring to war, destruction of nature, and militancy on the part of Western culture. He roams through space and time, synthesizing the age of the Crusades, slavery, World Wars I and II, and the contemporary Vietnam War. Indeed, the history of Western Civilization forms a chain of religious and racial discrimination. The decade of the 1920s, in which Reed chooses to situate the main plot of the mystery story, signals a dead end for Western culture. The ruins of World War I and the crash of the stock market

---

[28]   Reed 241.

[29]   Franklin Rosemont, "Preface," to Paul Garon, *Blues and the Poetic Spirit* (New York: Da Capo Press, 1979) 7-15; 14.

[30]   Ishmael Reed, *Mumbo Jumbo* 183.

at the end of the decade symbolize the spiritual death of a culture which has defined its existential essence as economic and scientific progress. A Faustian spirit, Reed maintains, propels the white power structure. Its history bears the burden of a centuries-old tradition of exploitation, both cultural and socioeconomic.

In *Mumbo Jumbo*, this status quo is not only jeopardized by the subversive forces of African American music and dance. The black speech idiom, too, threatens to undermine the ruling system. Hinckle Von Vampton, the ancient Knight Templar and LaBas' antagonist, attempts to stop the spreading of Jes Grew, launching the magazine "Benign Monster" and creating a "Talking Android." By learning and adopting the specific black language code of Harlem, the "Talking Android" is thought of as reaffiliating the disloyal whites and blacks addicted to Jes Grew to the mainstream of Western civilization. This undertaking is finally prevented by PaPa LasBas and Black Herman, who unmask the intruder.

Overall, Reed approaches history as a jazz musician would the work of his musical ancestors. History becomes indeed a field for improvisation. In the manner of a jazz musician Reed plays his variations on different historical epochs. On his journey through space and time he thematically focuses on three historical aspects. First, the content and form of the novel signify a reevaluation of the Harlem Renaissance. The setting for the first part of the novel is Harlem of the 192Os. As Lenz explains,

> *Mumbo Jumbo* is a literary re-vision of the Harlem Renaissance, using the interplay and tension of fiction and of history to reveal its hidden dynamic and meaning, its limitations as well as its deep impact on African-American literature and culture of the present time.[31]

Reed does away with the view of the Harlem Renaissance as an artistic failure. Instead, the artistic movement of the 1920s represents an important touchstone for Reed's endeavor to create a positive image of blackness. While it has been common among literary critics to consider the Harlem Renaissance a failure—black aesthetic critics point to the lack of political engagement among black writers of the time—Reed's celebration of African American cultural expression in *Mumbo Jumbo* foreshadows Baker's eloquent dispute of the above view in *Modernism and the Harlem Renaissance.* And like Baker, Reed claims that African American writing should not be judged according to Anglo-American critical assumptions. "[T]hey must adopt our ways, producing Elizabethan poets," Biff Musclewhite propounds.[32] Whereas white modernist art expresses a feeling of loss and alienation, the Harlem Renaissance signals a beginning to African Americans. To Baker it marks the beginning of a conscious participation in modern history, at least in its discursive form. Reed

---

31   Günter H. Lenz, "Ishmael Reed" 320.

32   Ishmael Reed, *Mumbo Jumbo* 130.

primarily values the Harlem Renaissance as an expression of a culture grown self-confident. To him it is not so much a movement as it is the manifestation of many individual artistic voices that found their way to the publishing market. The poet Major Young speaks for Reed in *Mumbo Jumbo*: "Is it necessary for us to write the same way? I am not Wallace Thurman, Thurman is not Fauset and Fauset is not Claude McKay, McKay isn't Horne. We all have our unique styles."[33] To Reed, the Harlem Renaissance marks a pivotal period of black creativity and artistic freedom.

Second, his portrayal of the 1920s in *Mumbo Jumbo* signals a commentary on the Black Arts Movement in the 1960s and the ideological battles of that time. As a continuous historical thread, finally, the war between black and white cultures runs through the various textual and visual parts of the novel. In order to give the plots and subplots of *Mumbo Jumbo* a still larger historical range, Reeds draws upon the myth of Set and Osiris which takes us back into ancient Eqypt. Again, the myth not only helps explain many of the mysteries of the detective plot of the novel but also comments upon the above two decades. "Time is a pendulum. Not a river," as Reed quotes Arna Bontemps.[34] He rejects a linear conception of time; time, like a pendulum, is constantly in swing, back and forth. History, then, in Reed's presentation in *Mumbo Jumbo*, bears similarities to jazz in that it progresses in a pattern of repetition and variation. Reed uses the model of temporal complexity present in jazz's polyrhythmic progression not only to superimpose different historical periods upon one another. In addition, he makes them enter a dialogical framework in which they function as a critical commentary on each other.

The novel at hand is certainly Reed's formally most experimental. It represents an extension of the genre of the novel to a collage of written and visual parts. Thus Reed aesthetically confirms what Bakhtin expresses theoretically: that the novel by its very nature is not canonic.[35] The influence of cubism and film-making penetrates especially the visual set-up of *Mumbo Jumbo*. The opening of the novel is reminiscent of the prologue of a film.[36] Moreover the novel ends with a reference to film: "Freeze frame."[37] Adapting the techniques of collage—its equivalent in jazz would be polyrhythm—to literature, Reed synthesizes narrative, dialogue, illustrations, graphs, photoduplications, newspaper clips, footnotes, epigraphs, anagrams, and a bibliography into a history-making work of art. What is true for his cowboy-artist Loop Garoo is true for Reed, too:

---

[33]   Reed 117.

[34]   Reed 249.

[35]   Cf. Mikhael Bakhtin, *The Dialogic Imagination* 39.

[36]   Henry L. Gates, Jr., *The Signifying Monkey* (New York: Oxford UP, 1988) 227.

[37]   Ishmael Reed, *Mumbo Jumbo* 249.

> Loop seems to be scatting arbitrarily, using forms of this and adding his own. He's blowing like that celebrated musician Charles Yardbird Parker—improvising as he goes along. He's throwing clusters of demon chords at you and you don't know the changes.[38]

Reed's multiplicity of textual and visual forms in *Mumbo Jumbo* is not only reminiscent of collage and film-techniques; as the explicit reference to musical chord changes indicates, concepts of musical time shape the sudden shifts from medium to medium within the novel's textual progression as well as the way in which various time levels interact. Quick changes in musical time function as matrix for Reed's surprising back and forth movements on a temporal level. Like the bebop tunes of Reed's "Neo-HooDoo artist" *par excellence*, Charlie Parker, Reed's structural set-up in his third novel translates Parker's aesthetic of improvisation. In the history of jazz, Parker's improvisations have been referred to as "formulaic approach" or mosaic technique.[39] Many of the musical phrases are independent components and can be exchanged almost arbitrarily in the progression of jazz pieces based upon either chromatic or diatonic chord structures. Whenever Parker played various versions of one title they differed decisively. The exchangeability of various textual forms seems true especially for the first part of *Mumbo Jumbo*. The interpolation of photographs and statistics illustrating the potential for militancy and destruction in white civilization appears arbitrary, chosen at random. Beyond the "formulaic approach", fast tempo and frequent citations characterize Parker's improvisations. He plays more than six quarter notes per second during many improvisations. Playing four quarter notes per second, he is even capable of shifting to double time.[40] The fast-paced shiftings in tempo function as an aesthetic model for Reed's quick temporal movements between past, present, and future.

Apart from many bebop phrases that he created himself, Parker had a tremendous repertoire of popular tunes including melodies from Broadway and television. Frequently, citations from popular music and classical music appear briefly in Parker's lines. As Wilson and Goeman say, the use of citations in Parker's improvisations includes a message for the audience. As far as the numerous women in the audience were concerned, the messages were more or less explicitly sexual.[41] Reed's use of citation parallels Parker's musical use in that it transcends purely artistic concerns. The use of citations in *Mumbo Jumbo*—quotations, and statistics, for instance—shapes Reed's social and cultural criticism. Citations comment upon the culture war between black and white, frequently associating "black" with vitality and "white" with destruction.

---

[38]   Ishmael Reed, *Yellow-Back-Radio-Broke-Down* 154.

[39]   Peter N. Wilson and Ulfert Goeman, *Charlie Parker* 38.

[40]   Wilson and Goeman 37.

[41]   Wilson and Goeman 35-36.

What emerges is a polyphonic novel based upon a carnivalesque structure in which dialogues between various media and ideologies lead to laughter which is comic and tragic at the same time. Reed's novel textually expresses a form of Bakhtinian dialogism that identifies writing as both a subjective and communicative, or in other words, an intertextual mode.[42]

Intertextuality also bears signs of intercultural processes. The multiplicity of forms from different cultural sources in *Mumbo Jumbo* parallels the syncretic nature of jazz. In the course of the music's history, a fusion of Euro-American, African, Latin-American, and Oriental influences has informed the diverse styles of jazz. Technically Reed achieves the fusion of African American and Euro-American art forms through reducing narrative components to fragments. He then combines the latter into new forms of meaning. This process can be illustrated by Reed's use of structure and language.

The structure of his fiction roots itself in fragmentary plots, which at first proceed parallel to one another without obvious connections. Yet, in the course of the novels the action and content of each plot unit disclose their meaning for the text as a whole. Meaningful correlations between the various plots gradually come to the surface, as diachronic and synchronic time elements overlap. Moreover, through thematic or structural motifs which are the key to understanding the interaction between the plots, Reed's novels, in spite of the absence of closure, assume a sense of coherence. In *Mumbo Jumbo*, the use of a mythic level circumscribing and explaining the dichotomies and divisions in the novel helps to resolve mysteries and link subplots.

In general, Reed's language convinces by its immediacy and spontaneity. Sentences are kept short. Ellipses, sometimes reduced to a single word, mixed with shorter forms of grammatically incomplete sentences, shape a fast-paced rhythm through which the text verbally progresses:

> A true sport, the man of New Orleans, spiffy in his patent-leather brown and white shoes, his plaid suit, the Rudolph Valentino parted-down-the-middle hair style, sits in his office. Sprawled upon his knees is Zulu, local doo-wack-a-doo and doo-do-dee-odo fizgig.[43]

> Hi-yellow. pimply-faced and epicene, rose to speak.[44]

> He is a large negro man with sharkskin suit, alligator shoes, skinny brim hat, pencil-thin mustache, Johnny Walker eyes.[45]

---

[42] See also Julia Kristeva, "Word, Dialogue and Novel," *The Kristeva Reader*, ed. Toril Moi (Oxford: Blackwell, 1992) 34-61; 39.

[43] Ishmael Reed, *Mumbo Jumbo* 5.

[44] Ishmael Reed, *The Last Days of Louisiana Red* (New York: Avon Books, 1976) 78.

[45] Reed 124.

In the above passages Reed's verbal rhythm is syncopated, reminiscent of jazz. The syncopation is visually achieved by connecting words with hyphens. Phonetic fragments such as "voo", "do", "dee", etc. are transformed through hyphenization into a new extended sound unit. Thus they are reminiscent of the scat-singing technique in jazz. They recall among others Dizzy Gillespie's version of Joe Carrol's "Oo-Shoo-Be-Doo-Be."[46] In terms of musical performance, scat-singing represents an improvised singing of syllables without semantic significance. Syllables such as "do" and "be" mark onomatopoetic imitations of instrumental phrases. Scat-singing, as Bohlaender and Holler point out, is also present in religious music such as shouts and spirituals as well as in Voodoo. Here the improvised singing becomes an expression of heightened religious ecstasy.[47] As concerns the jazz tradition Ella Fitzgerald remains perhaps the most prolific interpreter of scat-singing, as her versions of the "Cow Cow Boogie" and "Waiting for the Junkman" show.[48] In Reed's writing, the use of these sound syllables that bear resemblance to nursery rhyme nonsense underscores Reed's willingness to play in dealing with language and structure. But he changes the temporal quality of syntactical structures, too. Moving back and forth between a narrative voice that covers large time spans and a staccado-like syntax emphasizing the particular moment, Reed's narrative rhythms translate various time conceptions syntactically. The polyphonic set-up of the novel thus gains a polyrhythmic equivalent on a narrative level.

The open form Reed chooses underscores his denial of any sense of closure. A view of history as something static necessarily collapses. As *Mumbo Jumbo* manifests, static versions of history must be deceptive in the end. Instead, the novel mirrors the kinetic energy Reed assumes behind historical processes. The genre Reed chooses, the mystery story, as well as the content and structure of the novel, implies Reed's embrace of openness. He frees form to a collage of 'add this and that' so that the text of *Mumbo Jumbo* could indeed be complemented endlessly. *Mumbo Jumbo*, then, is a novel on the search for form. Like the unresolved mysteries of the novel, the open form creates a mood of uncertainty. The novel as a whole questions the rational order of Western thought. Hence, it shares the dialogism of Menippean and carnivalesque discourses, "translating a logic of relations and analogy rather than substance and inference." As Kristeva goes on, "from within the very interior of formal logic, even while skirting it, Menippean dialogism contradicts it and points toward other forms of thought."[49] As opposition against Aristotelian logic,

---

[46] Dizzy Gillespie, *Paris Concert* (GNP Crescendo Records 9006, 1972).

[47] Carlo Bohlaender and Karl Heinz Holler, *Reclam Jazzführer* (Stuttgart: Reclam Verlag, 1970) 785.

[48] Ella Fitzgerald, *New York: Recordings 1943-50* (Delta Music GmbH 57 554-8, 1991).

[49] Julia Kristeva, *The Kristeva Reader* 55. Kristeva discusses Bakhtin's writings in the context of carnivalesque and Menippean structures. She traces these discourses back to Menippus of Gadara, a philosopher of the third century BC. As she explains, Menippean discourse is both

Reed's *Mumbo Jumbo* as a representative of polyphonic novels appears to disapprove of ways of thinking based upon formal logic exclusively. Indeed, it is a fierce attack on any form of monolithic thinking. Primarily Reed's verbal assault aims at Christianity and its faith in a single God. But Reed goes further in his endeavor to undermine the established Western thought system. At first the frequent appearances of the numbers '1' and '2' suggest a dualistic principle behind the novel. Like his poem "Dualism" *Mumbo Jumbo* signifies a parody of dualistic reduction:

> i am outside of
>
> history. i wish
>
> i had some peanuts, it
>
> looks hungry there in
>
> > its cage
>
> i am inside of
>
> history. its
>
> hungrier than i
>
> thot[50]

The two-headed Papa LaBas, detective and NeoHooDooist, cannot solve all the mysteries of the plots and subplots of the novel. To Reed, dualistic thinking falls short of explaining the complexity of history. Symbolically, the 'two heads' of PapaLaBas do not suffice to explain all the riddles within the text. He is not an infallible Sherlock Holmes or Dupin.[51] And many students walk out on him, as he lectures on a New York campus in the 1960s, for they consider him anachronistic and out of his mind. Through LaBas, Reed dismantles the dualistic thought system based upon binary oppositions. The former's two-headedness, however, stands for a form of dialogue, too, which Reed's envisions in order to come to terms with the historical process. Dialogism, as

---

"carnivalesque" and "serious." And it is "politically and socially disturbing" (52). In terms of literary history, Kristeva maintains that Menippean structures are at the origin of the subversive and polyvocal novel. Important for the discussion of Reed is that Menippean texts are characterized by ambivalence. Hence, they do not transmit fixed, stable messages (54). For Bakhtin's discussion of Menippean elements see Michail M. Bachtin, *Literatur und Karneval: Zur Romantheorie und Lackkultur* 47-60.

50   Ishmael Reed, *Conjure* 50.

51   Reed's total rejection of absolutist thinking explains the undercurrent element of self-parody in his novels. "One thing common to my fiction, essay, and poetry, they don't claim to know all the answers," Reed admits. Ishmael Reed, *Shrovetide in Old New Orleans* (New York: Doubleday, 1978) 7.

Reed develops it, indicates multiple participants in a communicative framework.

In Reed's historical imagination various perspectives of history are played off against one another. Thoughts on history and culture from such different characters as Biff Musclewhite, Abdul Hamid, Berbelang, and LaBas keep the reader's mind wandering until they are filtered and framed with Reed's own multicultural outlook in the omniscient narration in the second part of the novel. And within the framework of his dialogical approach to history he explores the problematics of narrativity itself. In *Flight to Canada*, Reed's fourth novel, he asks, "Where does fact begin and fiction leave off?"[52] Likewise, in *Mumbo Jumbo*, Reed juxtaposes actual newsflashes with fictitious ones to suggest how vague, actually, the borderline between history and myth, reality and imagination is. Resorting to hyperbole, he draws upon extreme and esoteric manifestations of history, mixing them with grotesque and surreal literary devices. In doing so, he makes clear that the most unbelievable is often fact. Conversely, he advocates his belief in the imagination as being capable of creating reality: "Art can reflect and create reality."[53] In *Mumbo Jumbo*, then, Reed synthesizes the recording and ordering function of the non-fiction writer with the creative and innovative role of the fiction writer.[54] Thus he makes obvious that different understandings of how to experience and express temporality merge in the writing process of the novel at hand.

As we have seen, dialogism supersedes dualistic thinking in Reed's writing. In order to underscore that history goes beyond binary oppositions such as rich and poor, black and white, Reed not only doubles the numbers—"22"—but introduces the number "3" and its multiples. "The 3, Hubert, Hinckle and W. W.", "PaPa LaBas, Black Herman, T Malice and 6 tall Phyton men", and "about 9 men" represent three examples of Reed's playing with numbers.[55] More and more numbers are added. Continuously, Reed dissolves anything static. Knowledge and history alike are bound up in a kinetic process. The force behind continuous change is Jes Grew, the voiceless but swinging protagonist of the novel which embodies jazz and its manifestations during the 1920s:

> Actually Jes Grew was an anti-plague. Some plagues caused the body to waste away; Jes Grew enlivened the host. Other plagues were accompanied by bad air (malaria). Jes Grew victims said that the air was as clear as they had ever seen it and that there was the aroma of roses and perfumes which had never before enticed their nostrils . . . Jes Grew is electric as life and

52   Ishmael Reed, *Flight to Canada* (New York: Bard, 1976) 18.

53   Joe David Bellamy, ed., *The New Fiction: Interviews with Innovative American Writers* (Urbana: U of Illinois P, 1974) 135.

54   Elisabeth Plessen, *Fakten und Erfindungen* (Frankfurt/Main: Ullstein Materialien, 1981) 26.

55   Ishmael Reed, *Mumbo Jumbo* 162, 182, 172.

characterized by ebullience and ecstasy. Terrible plagues were due to the wrath of God; but Jes Grew is the delight of the gods.[56]

As Reed puts it, Jes Grew is thoroughly anti-authoritarian.[57] Ideologically, Jes Grew becomes Reed's companion in the parody of the standard Western forms of knowledge, primarily science and history. The "plague" is nothing that can be brought into focus or categorized; "once we call it 1 thing it forms into someting else."[58] This bears obvious parallels to the development of jazz itself. In a rapid manner—in less than a century—jazz has produced a variety of styles, including ragtime, Dixie, swing, bebop, modern and free jazz. Like jazz, Jes Grew moves geographically from the South to the North. Alain Locke "compared jazz to an 'epidemic' that spread rapidly and transformed tempo, technique, and themes in popular music. Like James Weldon Johnson, who called ragtime a music that 'jes grew', Locke depicted jazz as an infectious sound that had grown quickly to reach a large audience by the thirties."[59] Reed stylizes 'jes grew', James Weldon Johnson's term for African American folk music, into a culturally revolutionary form. Critics like Garon and Ensslen have also pointed out the blues' potential for mockery and rebellion. In its fidelity to humor, desire, and fantasy, "the blues generates an irreducible and, so to speak, habit-forming demand for freedom and what Rimbaud called 'true life'."[60] Ensslen detects in the blues a specific tendency for hyperbolic, humorous, and ironic exaggeration.[61] In *Mumbo Jumbo* Reed draws upon exactly these characteristics attributed to the blues to turn "Jes Grew" into a subversive form. Humor in *Mumbo Jumbo* includes folk humor, slapstick, and black humor, as the deportation scene of W. W. Jefferson illustrates:

---

[56]   Reed 9.

[57]   Imagination, in *Mumbo Jumbo*, is closely associated with sensuality and sexuality. The dance epidemic of the 1920s frees the body and the spirit of the repressed. Without possibility for renewal, so Reed, Western civilization resembles a repressed "id" turning to acts of violence and madness. Reed mocks Freud and plays on Freudian terms when he lets Jes Grew destabilize the white mind. With its heavy reliance upon sexuality and desire, Jes Grew marks a frivolous challenge to the bourgeois ethics of the white Protestant mainstream. Blues lyrics dealing with sexuality and desire are primarily at home in the classic urban blues form. See Otto Werner, *The Origin and Development of Jazz* (Dubuque: Kendall/Hunt, 1984) 17.

[58]   Reed 7.

[59]   Kathy J. Ogren, *The Jazz Revolution: Twenties America & the Meaning of Jazz* (New York: Oxford UP, 1989) 124.

[60]   Paul Garon, *Blues and the Poetic Spirit* (New York: Da Capo Press, 1979) 64. On a temporal level, according to Garon, the blues represents a hedonistic and rebellious form, since it holds out for pleasure and fulfillment in the here-and-now. See for this also my discussion of Hager's funeral scene in the Morrison chapter of my study.

[61]   Klaus Ensslen, *Einführung in die schwarzamerikanische Literatur* (Stuttgart: Kohlhammer, 1982) 22.

The 3 deacons accompanying Rev. Jefferson kneel as Rev. Jefferson stretches his hands toward the heavens. Lawd we axes you to pray over this boy . . . mmmmmm mmmmmm An' deliver this child away from these naked womens . . . mmmm And sweet black mens. And save his soul from torment . . . mm. . . . Rev. Jefferson slugs Hinckle Von Vampton with a fist that has toted many a grain sack and tamed many a horse. Hinckle kind of floats to the rug, out cold. Hubert "Safecracker" Gould tries to flee through the door but is grabbed quickly by the 3 other deacons who've accompanied their pastor from Ré-mote Mississippi. . . . Rev. Jefferson walks toward his son with an open 12-foot sack and doesn't stop until he gets him all the way. One squirming shoe shows and he pushes that in too.[62]

Fantasy shines through in Reed's embrace of surreal elements, the two heads of PaPa LaBas, for instance. As Garon's selection of blues lyrics in *The Poetic Spirit* reveals, a sense of ambiguity and ambivalence underlies quite a number of blues lyrics and performances.[63] The blues carries on the tradition of the 'double entendre' going back to the work songs in times of slavery. The 'double entendre' signifies a code disguising desires such as the longing for freedom or sexual fulfillment. Traditionals like "Follow the Drinking Gourd"[64] and blues songs like "Cave Man" are examples of the continuing presence of the 'double entendre' in African American folk music.[65]

Reed already plays with the 'double entendre' in the title of his third novel. According to the *Oxford Advanced Learner's Dictionary*, 'mumbo jumbo' stands for "gibberish" or "meaningless or obscure ritual."[66] The etymological origin of the expression lies in Swahili. "The phrase derives from the common greeting *jambo* and its plural *mambo*, which loosely translated mean 'What's happening?'"[67] This question describes exactly the reader's primary reaction to the various texts of *Mumbo Jumbo*. And, as Reed's superb, complex structure of the novel shows, *Mumbo Jumbo* means anything but gibberish. The sense of ambivalence and ambiguity accompanying the first reading of the novel is intended on Reed's part. Thus the reader's mind is bound to keep thinking and reflecting. Not only does he or she wonder in what way the different subplots relate to one another; the reader is also kept busy finding out who are the good and who are the bad guys in the novel. Characters like Thor Wintergreen, a white member of the Mu'tifikah who becomes a betrayer going over to the Atonists, embody this sort of ambivalence penetrating the polyvocal parts of *Mumbo Jumbo*.

---

62   Ishmael Reed, *Mumbo Jumbo* 162-64.

63   See Paul Garon, *Blues and the Poetic Spirit* 76-86.

64   Otto Werner, *The Origin and Development of Jazz* (Dubuque: Kendall/Hunt, 1984) 16.

65   Paul Garon, *Blues and the Poetic Spirit* 79.

66   *Oxford Advanced Learner's Dictionary of Current English* (London: Oxford UP, 1974) 565.

67   Henry L. Gates, *The Signifying Monkey* 221.

The ambiguity constantly present in Reed's text infects the reader's sense of time, too. She cannot follow a linear or chronological pattern. Instead she has to reorient her understanding of time structures in the novel repeatedly. The question 'What's happening?' expresses the fact that the reader finds herself on a journey through time. And she has to adjust her own comprehension of temporal progression to the various time layers at work in Reed's text. Hence, an intertextual dialogue on questions of time emerges throughout the reception process.

Reed expands this interaction from a textual to a transcultural level. Jes Grew subverts, changes, and keeps on changing itself. Beyond its presence as impersonal protagonist within the texts of *Mumbo Jumbo*, Jes Grew functions as a matrix for a thinking beyond cultural boundaries in both a social and aesthetic dimension. Thus he subverts generally accepted assumptions about black and white cultures. As James Snead elucidates, "'Black culture' is a concept first created by Europeans and defined in opposition to 'European culture.'"[68] Snead goes on to discuss Hegel's distinction between European and African culture, pointing out the dualistic juxtaposition of improvisation, circularity, tribe, and nature on the African continent as opposed to logic, progress, state, and history on its European counterpart. Hegel's view of Africa is static, his view of Europe kinetic. In the above juxtaposition it becomes obvious that—from a white point of view—African and black cultures in general are outside history and situated in a natural context. Euro-American cultures, on the contrary, are considered engine and part of history at the same time. To Hegel, history moves toward the revelation of God: "This Good, this Reason, in its most concrete forms is God. God governs the world, the actual working of his government—the carrying out of his plan—is the History of the World."[69] He further argues that history possesses an underlying rational structure. It is purposeful and good. In its overall movement it represents progress and linearity. However, black cultures are not part of it.

In response, Reed historicizes black culture, particularly through continuous references to Haiti. "But little Haiti resists. It becomes a world-wide symbol for religious and aesthetic freedom."[70] Toussaint's successful slave rebellion against the French in 1796, his prevention of Spanish and British invasions as well as Haiti's resistance against the American invasion in 1915 seem to influence Reed's choice of Haiti as a symbol of black survival. Despite numerous attempts at christianization, Voodoo, for instance, remains a dominant spiritual force in Haiti until the present.

---

[68]   James A. Snead, "Repetition as a Figure of Black Culture," *Black Literature and Literary Theory*, ed. Henry L. Gates, Jr. (New York: Methuen, 1984) 59-79; 62.

[69]   G.W.F. Hegel, "Introduction to the Philosophy of History," *The European Philosophers: From Descartes to Nietzsche*, ed. Monroe C. Beardsley (New York: The Modern Library, 1960) 537-608; 569.

[70]   Ishmael Reed, *Mumbo Jumbo* 72.

Since Reed places black cultures back into an historical context, the supposedly "always already there" moves back into a historical dimension exposed to constant change. Reed thus liberates 'Black Culture' from the Euro-American (Hegelian) world view and links its new image with a sense of time representative of Africa and Voodoo. In contrast to the linear and teleological concept of history, Reed develops a syncretic and synchronic view of history built upon musical time; for jazz thematically transforms syncretism into an art form, always adding, changing, and improvising. The synchronicity in the structure of the novel—reminiscent of polyrhythmic simultaneity—can be seen in the disruption of a linear narrative progression. Reed achieves this temporal effect by introducing numerous events taking place simultaneously. At first, these actions seem to have no interrelation whatsoever. The further the novel progresses the more penetrable the structural links become, however. Finally, through LaBas' revelation in his account of the Set and Osiris myth, Reed's structural design, albeit flexible and open, becomes fully visible. LaBas' linear, straightforward narration lifts the veil to most of the mysteries presented in the synchronic parts preceding it. Reed, then, uses the diachronic conclusion to comment upon the various narrative threads of the novel. He also applies it to delineate a historical survey of Hoodoo from the beginning of the world, from Osiris' mother "the sky Nut" and "his father Geb", the earth, to the presence of Hoodoo in the United States in the 1960s in the figure of PaPa LaBas.[71] Yet the diachronic nature of this narration should not conceal the fact that, in Reed's view, history moves back and forth. In fusing events from various centuries and cultures, he propagates the idea that history bears a repetitive pattern. In the synchronic ordering of diachronically different events, he builds up an intensity that mirrors the exploitative and destructive forces behind Euro-American history.

Reed's choice of Jes Grew as protagonist for his novel shows that jazz signifies the sublime artistic model for Voodoo metaphysics and his own "NeoHooDoo" aesthetic. Reginald Martin describes the syncretic flexibility of Voodoo historically, as follows:

> During the great cultivation period of Voodoo in the Caribbean, 1650-1800, West Africa itself was undergoing great religious change due to the influence of Islam and Hinduism. Consequently, Voodoo (Hoodoo is the United States' version) returned to an African religious landscape already greatly altered and different from the original Yoruban landscape it had left behind. Presently, one finds aspects of all of the aforementioned religions, along with icons and practices from each, present in Voodoo. Thus, Voodoo, a religion formed under the pressure of degrading social conditions to give human beings dignity and a connection with helpful supernatural forces, thrives because of its syncretic flexibility; its ability to take anything, even ostensibly negative influences, and transfigure them into that which helps

---

71   Reed 184.

the horse. It is bound by certain dogma or rites, but such rules are easily changed when they become oppressive, myopic, or no longer useful to current situations.[72]

Mumbo Jumbo's syncretic text borrows from various cultures. The Western genre of the detective novel is interspersed with African American folklore and African myth. Besides Standard English, Elizabethan English, and Black English stand side by side in Reed's novel. Time and language then cross cultural boundaries in Reed's aesthetic rendering of history. This act of transgression is important for Reed, for only a transcultural outlook can prevent mass culture from falling into a deadening paralysis.[73] Thus Reed translates on a narrative level Bakhtin's belief that "the new cultural and creative consciousness lives in an actively polyglot world" and that "[t]he period of national languages, coexisting but closed and deaf to each other, comes to an end."[74] Any other attitude would lead to cultural stasis, as the role of the "Talking Android" in the person of Woodrow Wilson Jefferson manifests. He, in *Mumbo Jumbo*, leaves rural Mississippi where people believe in "haints and things; and spirits and 2-headed men, mermaids and witches," to hit the big city of New York.[75] Jefferson represents a black comic version of the Faustian spirit. He is just one of many examples illustrating that Reed's irony aims at black and white. As an ambitious young man he wants to make a career by any means. In Reed's rendering, his flight to New York parodies the classical quest for freedom by way of migrating north that one discerns in African American writing. What he finds up North, however, is not the desired state of freedom. Instead, he ends up being caught in a system where hierarchy and imitation are of the essence. From the very beginning Reed portrays him as naive. Though he does not always understand the content of writings by Marx and Engels, "he liked the style. Objective, scientific, the use of the collective We, Our."[76] Reed's irony is at its best when he makes Jefferson walk the streets of New York in the search for the long dead Karl Marx and Friedrich Engels. When Jefferson has finally found a position with the "Benign Monster" magazine, he works hard to imitate the style of his grand idols. He is not capable of producing anything authentic. Although his editor Von Vampton urges him to "avoid those Marxist-Engelian and sociological clichés", Jefferson's will to imitate makes him the ideal candidate to be used for the task of the "Talking Android."[77] Throughout

---

[72] Reginald Martin, *Ishmael Reed and the New Black Aesthetic Critics* (New York: St. Martin's Press, 1988) 71.

[73] Time levels of different cultural background interact in Mumbo Jumbo. In doing so Reed avoids hierarchical structures as concerns concepts of history and culture.

[74] Mikhael Bakhtin, *The Dialogic Imagination* 12.

[75] Ishmael Reed, *Mumbo Jumbo* 32.

[76] Reed 32.

[77] Reed 89.

his writings Jefferson simply repeats already existing concepts of rhetoric and history, not being concerned with their relevance for the present. Accordingly, he does not succeed in creating an individual sense of time. Jefferson, in terms of music, never manages to play his "solo flights". And he never comprehends the dynamics between tradition and innovation, so essential to jazz and other art forms. Jefferson, instead, becomes a manipulated cultural warrior for a Jes Grew-free world—a propagator of cultural stagnation. In psychoanalytical terms he represents the adolescent growing up in a patriarchal world in which the father figure is the measure of all things. Ironically, it is his father Reverend Jefferson who sticks him in a "12-foot cotton sack" and brings him back home after having found out that his son "had left the teachings of d church."[78]

Von Vampton's and Jefferson's failure to stop Jes Grew has a double meaning. First, it signifies the delusion that white culture is powerful enough to silence black culture; "They thought that by fumigating the Place Congo in the 1890s when people were doing the Bamboula the Chacta the Babouille the Counjaille the Juba the Congo and the Voodoo that this would put an end to it."[79] Second, it displays white culture's inability for cultural renewal by itself.[80] Reed obviously refers to the strong impact of African art on modernist art, especially on painting and sculpture. Moreover he has in mind the tremendous influence of blues and jazz on pop and rock music in the 1960s. Hence, he places modernist and postmodernist art into a multicultural perspective and negates prejudices still considering African American culture inferior to and imitative of Western aesthetic models.

Von Vampton's critique of Jefferson's essay style, for instance, echoes eighteenth century beliefs that colored people are capable of imitating but not of innovating: "The books you read and all those articles. You quote Kant, James and Hegel very well but don't you think that you ought to liven it up a bit with some of that raggle-taggle?"[81] It was Kant who uttered his belief in the mental inferiority of blacks in his discussion of the beautiful and the sublime.[82] And Kant's thoughts were part of a heavy theoretical debate about black culture and

---

[78]   Reed 163-64.

[79]   Reed 9.

[80]   As Reed demonstrates in the novel, the minstrel tradition represents one of the central elements for cultural exchange and renewal in the United States. To him, it is a supreme example of the acculturation of African and African American elements by Euro-Americans. The minstrel shows also paved the way for African American music into the white mainstream. In the early nineteenth century the coon songs, for instance, marked the most popular musical form parodying black plantation songs, and during the performances the actors resorted to African American dances such as shuffles and cakewalk. See Alfons Dauer, *Jazz: Die Magische Musik* (Bremen: Carl Schuenemann Verlag, 1961) 337-38.

[81]   Reed 90.

[82]   See Immanuel Kant, *Observations on the Feelings of the Beautiful and the Sublime*, trans. John T. Goldthwait (Berkeley: U of California P, 1960), 111-13.

writing which called forth numerous white reviews of writings by black authors during the Age of Enlightenment. Technological renewal in particular was responsible for the fact that writing turned into an instrument of cultural classification. With the invention of the printing press, written discourse, on part of Western culture, became the master model for the proof of cultural superiority. Ultimately, this development had a strong impact on literary endeavors by African American writers, as Gates explains further:

> Literacy, the very literacy of the printed book, stood as the ultimate parameter by which to measure the humanity of authors struggling to define an African self in Western letters. It was to establish a collective black voice through the example of an individual text, and thereby to register a black presence in letters, that most clearly motivated black writers, from the Augustan Age to the Harlem Renaissance.[83]

Since the Text is not found in *Mumbo Jumbo*, Reed seems to suggest at least two things: first, that black culture continues to embrace both oral and written discourse; second, that there can be no master narrative of the black condition since black culture is as rich and diverse as its various artists. To Reed, a found Text would only disregard the complex nature of the black heritage. Such a single text by itself could not translate all the various temporal dimensions present in African American discourse and it would also bear the signature of a power structure, which suppresses what is different from the mainstream, "the other".

Since *Mumbo Jumbo* admittedly mirrors nothing but a temporary historical perspective, the Western assumption that the written arts are a higher form of recording history seems illusionary. According to Reed, culture and historical circumstances continue changing. Oral culture naturally reacts more promptly to changes than a notated or written system is able to. Thus both cultural expressions carry an equivalent significance in the transmission of history. In claiming this, Reed discards the primitivist myth frequently associated with African American oral culture, music in particular.[84] The complexity of Jes Grew, accordingly, suggests the high formal training needed in the performance

---

[83]   Henry L. Gates, *The Signifying Monkey* 131.

[84]   As Thomas Huke comments, many African American novelists develop and use the myth of the natural black musician in their writings. See Thomas Huke, *Jazz und Blues im afroamerikanischen Roman* (Erlangen: Hochschulverlag, 1990) conclusion. In most instances the black musicians' natural talent is regarded as a positive cultural force. Many white critics see in the lack of formal training a liberating factor in passionate and spontaneous creation. Early European jazz critics—Goffin, Delaunay and Panassie, to name but a few—primarily focused on energy and vitality in jazz thus helping forge the primitivist myth surrounding the aura of jazz to the present. The subsequent lines from Panassie illustrate why: "Primitive man has greater talent than civilized man. An excess of culture atrophies inspiration, and men crammed with culture tend to much to lay tricks, to replace inspiration by lush technique under which one finds music stripped of real vitality." From Hughes Panassie, *The Real Jazz* (New York: Smith and Durrel, 1942) 6.

of jazz. In his book on jazz, *The Imperfect Art* (1988), Ted Gioia refers to temporal differences but emphasizes that there is no difference in the sphere of mental activity as concerns the distinction of composition vs. improvisation:

> Jazz, like all art from an aural/oral tradition, reveals its rigors in ways different from notated/written arts. The absence of a permanent document, whether musical score or printed word, does not indicate that the mental processes involved in the creative act are any less evident in improvised art than in composed art. Improvisation merely changes the time frame of what takes place: it is spontaneous composition.[85]

Like a jazz musician, Reed clearly plays on the distinction between the oral and the written, dismantling both concepts and making boundaries between them permeable. Partly due to a sponanteous writing process, partly due to the author's intention, oral and written modes of expression undergo continuous metamorphoses in *Mumbo Jumbo*. As Norman Harris points out, black folklore is reevaluated in Reed's fiction by being liberated from a kind of static use. In Reed's fiction, folklore becomes something dynamic, fluid, adaptable.[86] Craig Werner, in a similar way, emphasizes the kinetic energy behind Reed's use of parody: "Reed's immediate aim is simply to keep the parodic focus moving in order to deny his readers the sense of certainty which produces stasis."[87] To Gates, finally, the kinetic power of parody in *Mumbo Jumbo* aims at the subversion of standard assumptions about African American culture and the African American novel in particular. Reed critiques not only "the metaphysical presuppositions inherent in Western ideas" but also "the African-American idealism of a transcendent black subject, integral and whole."[88] Indeed, *Mumbo Jumbo* is as eclectic as jazz.

As Gates's comments make clear, Reed sets out to write his very own account of the so-called black experience. And *Mumbo Jumbo* marks a further farewell to naturalist conventions in the African American canon. Yet, despite Reed's concern with parody and indeterminacy, the novel at hand does not indulge in play for the sake of play itself. Rather, Reed's experiments with genre and form converge with political and cultural criticism on the level of content. As the intertextual dimension of *Mumbo Jumbo* demonstrates, Reed has no problem in using metafictional techniques to make social and cultural

---

[85]   Ted Gioia, *The Imperfect Art: Reflections on Jazz and Modern Culture* (New York: Oxford UP, 1988) 33.

[86]   Norman Harris, "Politics as an Innovative Aspect of Literary Folklore: A Study of Ishmael Reed," *Obsidian* 5 (1979): 41-50; 41.

[87]   Craig Werner, "Poe and Ishmael Reed: The Insurrection of Subjugated Knowledge," *Poe and Our Times: Influences and Affinities*, ed. Benjamin Franklin Fisher IV (Baltimore: The Edgar Allan Poe Society, 1986): 144-56; 147.

[88]   Henry L. Gates, *The Signifying Monkey* 218.

criticism.[89] Especially since the publication of *Mumbo Jumbo* Reed has made obvious that his social criticism is directed at the cultural discrimination against minorities in the homogenizing mass culture of American society. He advocates individuality and diversity. In his plea for a coexistence of cultures— aesthetically expressed through his negotiations between culturally different concepts of time—, he demands the opening of mainstream culture and art canons to groups of innovative artists and representatives of minorities.

Reed's NeoHoodoo aesthetic marks his own response to and assault upon what he considers forms of historical reductionism. Therefore Reed relentlessly dismantles any point of view that dogmatically prescribes the way African American artists (minority artists in general) have to create. Moreover, like all innovators in jazz, Reed searches for new modes of expressing and rendering time. This rhythmic quest in music has also been accompanied by the longing for new spirituality, particularly in jazz forms after swing. In *Mumbo Jumbo* PaPa LaBas's Mumbo Jumbo Kathedral represents the sublime artistic and social space for the individual where time levels may interact and create new experience—aesthetic, social, and spiritual:

> PaPa LaBas' Mumbo Jumbo Kathedral is located at 119 West 136th St. The dog at his heels, Papa LaBas climbs the steps of the Town house. He moves from room to room: The Dark Tower Room the Weary Blues Room the Groove Bang and Jive Around Room the Aswelay Room. In the Groove Bang and Live Around Room people are rubberlegging for dear life; bending over backwards to admit their loa. In the Dark Tower Room, artists using cornmeal and water are drawing veves. Markings which were invitations to new loas for New Art. The room is decorated in black red and gold. A piano recording plays Jelly Roll Morton's "Pearls," haunting, melancholy. In the Aswelay Room the drums sleep after they've been baptized. A guard attendant stands by so that they won't get up and walk all over the place. PaPa LaBas opens his hollow obeah stick and gives the drums a drink of bootleged whiskey. Stunned by Berbelang's attack upon him as "anachronism," he has introduced some Yoga techniques.[90]

Past and present are vital parts of LaBas' Mumbo Jumbo Kathedral which clearly differs from its counterpart in the Roman-Catholic church. It seems that Reed takes the word "catholic" more seriously than the Roman-Catholic church does, for the Greek term *catholikos* means "for all, in general."[91] In its Greek meaning the term then implies openness. As regards Reed's historical vision, LaBas' Kathedral stands as a microcosm for a multicultural community inviting many different haints, beliefs, rituals, and ideas. From the drums of Africa to Jelly Roll Morton's "Pearls", the Kathedral accommodates all styles of black

---

[89]   See also Keith Byerman, *Fingering the Jagged Grain: Form and Tradition in Recent Black Fiction* (Athens: The U of Georgia P, 1985) 237.

[90]   Ishmael Reed, *Mumbo Jumbo* 55-56.

[91]   *Meyers Großes Taschenbuchlexikon*, vol. 4 (Mannheim: Bibliographisches Institut, 1983) 256.

music and dance. Blues and jazz not only evoke sexuality and sensuality, but call the spirits of creativity and sophistication, which unite in this open artistic setting.

Not surprisingly, Reed chooses Jelly Roll Morton as representative of African American music since the latter was one of the early jazz composers who managed to combine the earthy and expressive qualities of blues and jazz with formal sophistication. According to Williams, recordings and written documents show that "Morton was the first great master of form in jazz."[92] Morton, as an artist capable of mastering the dialogue between expressiveness and form, personal time and measured time, indeed deserves to be a prominent member of the Neo-HooDoo Cathedral, a secret place of communication and subversion, a rather unlimited space for multicultural renewal.

---

92   Martin Williams, *The Jazz Tradition* (New York: Oxford UP, 1993) 17.

VI. Blues, Jazz and Women's Time: Ntozake Shange and Feminine Visions of History

In "Women's Time," Julia Kristeva differentiates feminist positions in their relation to various forms of temporality.[1] Accordingly, she creates a dialectic which places feminist concerns both outside and inside the linear time of history and politics. Analyzing the women's movement in Europe in particular, Kristeva distinguishes three major stages of development. The first generation, demanding equal rights with men, advocated an egalitarian approach to change embedded within a linear conception of time. The second generation, however, emerging after 1968, pursued a more radical critique of patriarchy rejecting the male-centered view of history as progress completely. As a result, new conceptions of identity and temporality gained prominence. While identity was perceived as 'plural', and 'fluid', time was regarded as either 'mythical' or 'cyclical'. The identification with different notions of temporal movement definitely provided an alternative to the male discourse. Yet, the inspired social changes often fell prey to a counter-ideology which failed precisely because it placed itself outside a temporal dimension which it had set out to dismantle. According to Kristeva, the contemporary women's movement uses dialogical means to cross boundaries between teleological and cyclical time patterns to overcome these difficulties.[2]

Although Kristeva primarily discusses temporal modalities within European feminism, she also addresses transcultural questions related to time.[3] Hence, I think, her historicizing theory about temporality and the women's movement represents a valid point of departure for looking at feminine ways of rendering

---

[1]   See Julia Kristeva, "Women's Time," *The Kristeva Reader*, trans. Alice Jardine and Harry Blake, ed. Toril Moi (Oxford: Blackwell Publishers, 1992) 188-213; 190-93.

[2]   Discussing specifically feminine aspects of time, Kristeva points out that "as for time, female subjectivity would seem to provide a specific measure that especially retains repetition and eternity from among the multiple modalities of time known through history of civilizations. On the one hand, there are cycles, gestation, the eternal recurrence of a biological rhythm which conforms to that of nature and imposes a temporality whose stereotyping may shock, but whose regularity and unison with what is experienced as extra-subjective, cosmic time. . . . On the other hand . . . there is the massive presence of monumental temporality, without cleavage or escape, which has so little to do with linear time . . . one is reminded of the various myths of resurrection which, in all religious beliefs, perpetuate the vestige of an anterior or concomitant maternal cult." Kristeva, "Women's Time" 191. In this context Kristeva speaks of 'maternal time'.

[3]   She refers to conceptions of time that are related to mystical experiences being a vital part of numerous civilizations and to notions of time among marginal groups. Both temporal dimensions have a lot in common with Kristeva's idea of 'maternal time'. See Kristeva "Women's Time" 192, 195.

time within the African American discourse; for the tension between being outside or inside of history penetrates texts by African American women writers as well.

In *Sassafrass, Cypress & Indigo*, her first novel published in 1982, Ntozake Shange draws on blues and jazz to create a temporal dimension in which forms of private and public time interact consistently, even if the emphasis lies on the former. Throughout the text, different time levels meet in a primarily female communal context. Hence, Shange's playing on the female blues tradition marks a feminine and communal response to the bragging blues tradition of the solitary bluesman. Structurally this communal vision is expressed through a blues-derived call-and-response pattern which Shange establishes between mother and daughters, tradition and innovation, past and present. The blues, to Shange, becomes a vital cultural force tapping the historical heritage of black women and expressing a future vision of African American communal ties. Formally Shange expresses this hope for artistic as well as social renewal by adapting elements of bop, hard bop, and free jazz. "It is music, bebop, jazz that inform much of Shange's writing," as Sandi Russell points out.[4] Modern jazz's polyphonic form gives voice to her feminine message that expresses the female artist's hope for new forms and new possibilities.[5] Therefore fast-paced sound sequences and sudden shifts in rhythm shape her use of diction and syntax as well as the open nature of the novel's overall structure.[6]

Within the jazz tradition, the free jazz idiom emerged when the developments of hard bop were on their height. Bop itself had radicalized rhythmic experimentation: surprising double-time runs, broken lines of eigth notes, fast tempos. Hard bop, in the 1950s, differed from its stylistic predecessor through a change of the rhythm section's role, for drummers such as

---

4   Sandi Russell, *Render Me My Song: African-American Women Writers from Slavery to the Present* (New York: St. Martin's Press, 1990) 181.

5   Music critics such as John Litweiler see in the longing for formal innovation a basic principle of the jazz tradition. According to Litweiler, free forms in particular are of interest to the jazz musicians. "The quest for freedom with a small f appears at the very beginning of jazz and reappears at every growing point in the musis history." John Litweiler, *The Freedom Principle: Jazz After 1958* (New York: William Morrow and Company, Inc., 1984) 13. After bebop formal experiments grew even more radical, if we think of free jazz in particular.

6   The performative nature of blues and jazz with their emphasis on immediacy and intensity in particular informs the critical mode which I resort to in this chapter. My approach is concerned with unfolding a narrative about the novel, but it also aims at discussing the interrelation of Shange's prose and the musical discourse in an associative way. To me, this approach seems most appropriate to describe the presence of blues and jazz in a structurally polyvocal and complex novel such as the text at hand. Especially when I pursue a close scrutiny of Shange's adaptations of music on the level of syntax, structure, and time, the critical mode develops "anti-narrative flights". My approach to Shange's "riffs" on diction, syntax, structure and theme is performative then. Accordingly, associative shifts back and forth between blues, jazz, and their reflections in Shange's structural devices characterize the way the chapter progresses.

Max Roach and Art Blakey did not merely accompany the soloists; instead they engaged in an intense interplay with them. Thus the rhythm section and the soloists were equally important for the musical progression in hard bop which cleared the ground for free jazz forms in the late fifties and sixties.[7] Yet even radical innovators such as John Coltrane at large built their solos in a both linear and referential fashion so that they still represented a musically structured story to composers as well as performers.[8] Setting her stories in the context of the 1960s, Shange clearly selects contemporary forms of African American music to give voice to her feminine conception of history. At the same time she pays tribute to the blues revival of the time period, as she turns the blues mode into a central means for historical reconstruction.

In the novel Shange tells the story of the Effania family, which represents a matriarchal unit after the death of the father: an incident that goes back to a time before the opening of the plot. Telling stories about the growing up of Hilda Effania's three daughters—Cypress, Sassafrass, and Indigo—Shange explores the social, economic, and artistic possibilities for African American women in contemporary American society. Though the young black women's professional and social concerns differ clearly, all their lives are closely linked with the world of African American music in the 1960s and its dialectics of cultural heritage and renewal. Indigo improvises black tunes on the fiddle, Sassafrass absorbs the female blues tradition as a poet, and Cypress pursues an African American dance career.

Shange deals not only with the tension of tradition and innovation in music, though. She also juxtaposes traditional and modern ways of living. In the 1960s communities based upon black nationalist or socialist ideals were very popular among younger African Americans. Both Sassafrass and Cypress explore innovative forms of living. Shange then compares the values of the rural South with experimental ways of living when she contrasts Hilda's home with the social experiments of her daughters. And family and community values eventually shape the daughters' final decisions for social engagement. Indigo, the youngest of the family, becomes a midwife;[9] Sassafrass combines weaving with business interests, and Cypress, finally, fuses marriage with a dancing career. A synthesis of old and new social roles suggests that patterns of repetition and continuity intermingle with concepts of renewal. It also underscores Shange's belief that values of an earlier time period can be

---

[7]   See John Litweiler, *The Freedom Principle: Jazz After 1958* 14-19.

[8]   Cf. Jon Panish, *The Color of Jazz: Race Representation in Postwar American Culture* (Jackson: UP of Mississippi, 1997) 125-26.

[9]   See also Valerie Lee, *Granny Midwives & Black Women Writers* (New York: Routledge: 1996) 51-78. Lee extensively discusses the literary recovery of the granny midwife in contemporary writings by African American women writers such as Toni Morrison, Alice Walker, and Gloria Naylor among others.

transmitted, if current historical circumstances are taken into account and anterior models are re-shaped accordingly.

Linking her female characters to the world of African American music, Shange sets out to redefine the place of women in history, black women in particular. That they see themselves part of a cultural continuity both black and feminine Andrée Nicola Mclaughlin emphasizes in her depiction of current black women's writing; to her it is an intercontinental movement that deserves the label "Black women's literary renaissance." The idea of rebirth and change is explicit:

> Transforming political systems necessitates changing human consciousness and human behavior. Hence, Black women bear witness against domination based on nationality, race, gender, class, ethnicity, sexuality, and other indexes of difference. . . . Creating a new reality rooted in diversity and equality, women of the intercontinental Black women's literary renaissance are redefining themselves as well as language, images, ideas, forms of expression within frameworks of cultural continuity.[10]

As Mclaughlin makes clear, the desired change depends upon ideological, semantic, and aesthetic renewal To Shange, too, it is the ideological and cultural imperative behind the language that influences our thinking about black women which is at issue in the process of defining the role of women in history.[11]

Accordingly, Shange's blues women redefine their relations to time contradicting and subverting existing stereotypes about the black female. I want to refer here briefly to the standard images of black women in American writing before we explore the responses to and corrections of these images in contemporary writings by black women and in Shange's novel in particular. Barbara Christian points out four basic stereotypes of the black woman in nineteenth century literature: "the mammy", "the licentious, exotic black woman", "the tragic mulatta image", and "the conjure woman."[12] All these stereotypes bear traits of inferiority and continue especially to shape white conceptions of black womanhood. Taken together, they project an image that counterpoints the image of the delicate, pure, and chaste white lady of the South. Overall the above stereotypes suggest bondage, overt sensuality, and heathenism.

---

10   Andrée N. Mclaughlin, "A Renaissance of the Spirit: Black Women Remaking the Universe," *Wild Women in the Whirlwind: Afro-American Culture and the Contemporary Literary Renaissance*, eds. Joanne M. Braxton and Andrée N. Mclaughlin (New Brunswick: Rutgers UP, 1990) xxxi-xlix; xlvi.

11   See also Jerry D. Ward, "Bridges and Deep Water," *Sturdy Black Bridges: Visions of Black Women in Literature*, eds. Roseann P. Bell, Bettye J. Parker, and Beverly Guy-Sheftall (New York: Anchor Press, 1979) 184-90.

12   See Barbara Christian, *Black Women Novelists: The Development of a Tradition, 1892-1976* (Westport: Greenwood Press, 1980) 11-17.

Similarly, more recent stereotypes cultivated by African American males view the black woman as sexual object and traitor to the race. "Spaniards created whole nations with you / black queensilk snatch," Otis Goodwin-Smith—one of the few male characters present in the novel—assaults black women when he reads from his book *Ebony Cunt*.[13] When Shange's women cook, make music, sing or dance they counteract such acts of humiliation creating their own images and telling their own story.[14] Hence, Shange's as well as the works of twentieth century African American women writers in general remain rooted in their will to create and possess their images, to name themselves, and to establish their place in history.[15] The temporal complexity of these works emerges from their direct confrontation with the past and clear-eyed vision of the future. Shange's women are neither "licentious" nor "tragic." After a process of maturation, they all commit themselves to a social cause and express an affirmative spirit as concerns their role in the community. Moreover, Shange's women are neither "subservient" nor "devilish." They take their lives in their own hands and serve the needs of the black community socially through Indigo's midwifery, economically through Sassafrass' selling of weavings, and artistically as well as politically through Cypress' dance engagement in support of the Civil Rights Movement. Indeed, they take positions within the linear time of history at the same time, however, redefining this temporal pattern from a maternal or cyclical perspective.

Throughout *Sassafrass, Cypress & Indigo*, Shange underscores that her poetic message is more than simply a narrative of black female culture. It is a political narrative that nourishes both the dream of and the will for social change. In that regard, almost all her characters, despite their clearly visible personal identities, become poetic extensions of Shange's ideological aims. The major female characters not only form a family; as a whole they represent the totality of black womanhood and its cultural achievements. History and its potential transformation are believed to be shaped by means of the individual and the collective imagination: "Here Digo, Crunch, & Spats performed, mixing the skills of modern wayward children with the past-times of the more traditional cultural iconoclasts."[16]

The blues, in Shange's hands, becomes the medium to converse with the past. The blues expresses the continuity of the cultural heritage as well as the

---

[13]   Ntozake Shange, *Sassafrass, Cypress & Indigo* (New York: St. Martin's Press, 1982) 88.

[14]   Hence, the African American women writer shares the concern of the feminist historian who links the history of women's work closely to the women's private lives. Thus both are capable of avoiding male paradigms which prefer the discourse of public life over the discourse of private life. See also Kathryn Kish Sklar, "Engendering Women's History: New Paradigms and Interpretations in American History," *Amerikastudien / American Studies* 41.2 (1996): 207-15.

[15]   For a discussion of specifically feminine narrative voices in African American fiction see Jacqueline Bobo, *Black Women as Cultural Readers* (New York: Columbia UP, 1995) 203-05.

[16]   Shange, *Sassafrass, Cypress & Indigo* 41.

awareness of the historical pain—"the slave within us"—that are necessary for the political and aesthetic vision in Shange's novel. On a cultural level, the blues in *Sassafrass, Cypress & Indigo* takes on the role of the African drum. As Julio Finn writes,

> The drum plays a role in every facet of Africans' lives: in birth. initiation, puberty, marriage, hunting, pregnancy, war, death, and in the religious life of the community. Some countries possess 'royal' drums, instruments used only for the recounting of the history of the monarchs. As played by the court musicians, they relate the genealogy and auspicious events of the royal family's past.[17]

As the drum speaks of history to the African community, the blues tells Shange's characters of the past. All four female protagonists gain insight into the historical burden and creations of black women in the course of the novel. On the level of content, it is the artistic, the social, and the political achievements of African American women in the United States that permit a historical vision. Within this context Shange uses the blues chiefly as a means through which characters reach a heightened stage of racial and historical awareness. This is the case for both the blues performance and the blues reception. Playing the blues or listening to it, the characters in the novel encounter the memory of their private and social history.[18] While the blues mainly relates to memory in *Sassafrass, Cypress & Indigo*, jazz connotes historical renewal and the continuing search for formal openness. Within this dichotomy the blues embodies continuity. Jazz forms after bebop are the most influential, though. Their often abrupt changes of rhythm shine through in Shange's sudden shifts from prose to poetry, from narrative to dialogue. Hence, the novel's overall structure resembles a synthesis of various literary and extra-literary genres or modes. Poems, prose, letters, and dialogue together with folk ways, cartographies, journal entries, newspaper announcements, concert reviews, and recipes form the structural complexity of the novel.

The use of various genres creates a polyphonic effect so prevalent in African American music. Shange moves back and forth between these different modes of expression, as Shange uses musical techniques by John Coltrane for literary purposes. Changes such as the interpolation of concert reviews in the midst of a prose narrative resemble surprising turns in modern jazz solo improvisations. Interestingly, Shange relates the concert reviews of Leroy McCullough's Europe tour to two of the most important jazz musicians for the

---

17   Julio Finn, *The Bluesman: The Musical Heritage of Black Men and Women in the Americas* (London: Quartet Books, 1986) 83-84.

18   Shange resorts to a temporal function that anthropologists have located in the blues. William Ferris, for instance, claims that "through the blues, memories return as a message or truth about one's life." William Ferris, *Blues from the Delta* (New York: Anchor Press, Doubleday, 1979) 48. In *The Bluesman*, Julio Finn maintains that "the blues is a cultural memorial of slavery, a musical memoir commemorating the history of blacks in the United States" (230).

development of modern jazz: "Leroy McCullough's debut in Europe is the most startling event since John Coltrane worked with Miles Davis."[19] Within the jazz tradition the latter jazz musicians—along with Ornette Coleman—are famous for their solo improvisations and creation of free and idiosyncratic forms. Martin Williams, for instance, describes Miles Davis' chorus on "Move" as "a striking episode of meaningful assymmetry."[20] Commenting on Coltrane's solos with Davis, Williams refers to them as fragmentary. To the latter, Coltrane "seemed more interested in discovery than in making final statements."[21] Obviously, a tendency to explore and experience time in an experimental formal framework characterizes modern and free jazz pieces.

Especially Coltrane's innovations concerning rhythm and tempo seem to influence Shange's handling of form and spelling. Applying a fast-paced style in shifting genres, Shange creates a narrative progression recalling the fast tempo of John Coltrane's tenor sax playing, which apparently produces three notes simultaneously. Coltrane's way of speeding up sequences of notes has been referred to as "sheets of sound" in the history of jazz. John Litweiler describes Coltrane's sound sequences, discussing the latter's piece "Traneing In":

> "Traneing In" (August 1957) is a themeless blues-with-a-bridge, opening with Red Garland's long, lyrical piano solo. Then Coltrane begins improvising with the power of the great blues tenormen, establishing authority immediately with broad whole notes and riffing. After the first bridge he begins double-timing, and from this point on the development in his solo occurs in sixteenth notes. Here are his "sheets of sound"—broken scales or arpeggios played so fast that he seems to be trying to give the impression of chords. Again and again the top notes of these sound sheets escape the gravity of tonality, fluttering momentarily or, as "Traneing In" progresses, for a few bars at a time.[22]

The "sheets of sound" mark the early period of Coltrane's musical achievement. The arpeggios and broken scales in Coltrane's playing allow for new approaches to subsequent chords of the musical progression.[23] His rapid sound sequences result from the necessity to keep up with fast-paced chord changes and implied harmonies. The melodic lines of flowing eighth-notes in preceding jazz pieces give way to further polyrhythmic complexity.

Coltrane's contribution to jazz is important especially due to his experiments with musical time. "Traneing In" consistently changes patterns of temporality. Thus Coltrane shifts from whole notes to double-time and his arpeggios

---

19   Shange, *Sassafrass, Cypress & Indigo* 195.

20   Martin Williams, *The Jazz Tradition* (New York: Oxford UP, 1993) 200.

21   Williams 228.

22   John Litweiler, *The Freedom Principle* 86.

23   Cf. Gerd Filtgen and Michael Außerbauer, *John Coltrane* (Gauting: Oreos Collection Jazz, 1983) 50.

approaching a chord structure create the acoustic impression of simultaneity. No rhythmic frame remains consistent over a longer period of time; rather, as the fluttering top notes suggest, each moment within the improvisation requires a specific tonal and rhythmic expression.[24] What Shange refers to as Coltrane's highly idiosyncratic voice in *SeeNoEvil* (1984) finds further musical expression in Coltrane's late period as modal play turns into free play. Improvisations are no longer based on harmony, rhythm, or melody; instead they are inspired by mood and feeling. Sharp sounds in falsetto and constantly repeated rhythmical motifs—"riffs"—characterize his free play.[25]

A literary form of free play emerges from the interaction of sound and rhythm which underlies the intertextual dimension within Shange's novel. Her solo voices, dialogue, and omniscient narration change places rapidly and comment upon one another. A dialogue between personal time experience and the discourse of linear history results from this intertextual tension. Between the solo voices and the omniscient narration a call-and-response pattern emerges which implies communication between individual and community. On a temporal level, Shange's free play with voices creates the impression that all of them are simultaneously present. While the omniscient narrative expresses a diachronic view, interpolations such as recipes and cartographies stand for the eternal present. They, in particular, express a mythic sense of time whose magic ring results from verbal and syntactical repetition on a narrative level:[26]

> If there is a moon falling from her mouth, she is a woman who knows her
> magic, who can share or not share her powers. A woman with a moon

---

24   Rhythmic diversity in Coltrane's work always signalled a transcultural awareness of musical traditions which included those of India and Africa. See also Eric Nisenson, *Blue: The Murder of Jazz* (New York: St. Martin's Press, 1997) 197. Coltrane pieces such as "Kulu Se Mama, Africa" , for instance, are characterized by dense polyrhythms.

25   See Filtgen and Außerbauer, *John Coltrane* 56-57.

26   Shange's ability to constantly incorporate poetic and extra-literary forms into her prose underlines that she has no difficulties in crossing genres. Elements of the novel fuse seamlessly with elements of the romance. As Wellek and Warren explain: "The novel is realistic; the romance poetic or epic: we should now call it 'mythic'. . . . The two types which are polar, indicate the double descent of prose narrative: the novel develops from the lineage of non-fictitious narrative forms—the letter, the journal, the memoir or biography, the chronic or history; it develops, so to speak, out of documents; stylistically, it stresses representative detail, 'mimesis' in its narrow sense. The romance on the other hand, the continuator of the epic and the medieval romance, may neglect verisimilitude of detail [the reproduction of individuated speech in dialogue, for example], addressing itself to a higher reality, a deeper psycholoy." René Wellek and Austin Warren, *A Theory of Literature* (New York: Harcourt, Brace & World, Inc., 1956) 216. Shange probes both types in *Sassafrass, Cypress & Indigo*. The non-fictitious narrative forms are present in the letters, journal entries, recipes, and reviews. the "higher reality" and "deeper psychology" that Wellek and Warren address above are created by Shange's steady concern to maintain a mood in that her writing is dominated by tone and effect. This atmosphere is characterized by a sense of time which may be described as mythic, especially in the journal entries, cartographies, and dream passages.

> falling from her mouth, roses between her legs and tiaras of Spanish moss,
> this woman is a consort of the spirits.[27]

Frye's description of *melos*—"song"—seems useful to illustrate the effect of repetition: "The radical of *melos* is *charm*: the hypnotic incantation that, through its pulsing dance rhythm, appeals to involuntary physical response, and is hence not far from the sense of magic, or physically compelling power."[28] The use of repetition creates a temporal dimension that is intrinsically bound to the world of women and biological rhythms. And the incantatory nature of many poetic passages of Shange's prose underscores that her conception of time anchors itself in rhythms of nature before it seeks communication with other notions of temporality.

The individual stories of Sassafrass, Cypress, and Indigo in the novel are set against the historical background of the tumultuous 1960s, when the Civil Rights and the Black Power movements shook the foundations of white supremacy in the United States. The immediate historical circumstances only surface on the back-stage of this family history. Hence, the aforementioned movements make only brief appearances within the novel. Shange links the ideas of black nationalism with the "New Afrikans" of the Baton Rouge artist commune. And she regards Sassafrass' and Mitch's stay with them with ironic distance:

> The New World Found Collective where she & Mitch had been living for over a year offered spiritual redemption, if little else. The harvests had been meager so far. Everybody was from cities; never seen a hoe or hay before for that matter. Then, there were the problems of grinding grains, building homes, fetching water, so many things no nationalist dealt with in Newark or Los Angeles.[29]

Shange also uses irony to describe a commune of colored kids labelled "The Experiment in International Living," which is based upon socialist ideals. "Black kids Living in a socialist dream world that cost upwards of $4,000.00 a year."[30] Whereas Shange dismisses these innovative forms of living she views the political engagement of the Civil Rights Movement in a more favorable light. The historical presence of the Civil Rights Movement appears in the context of Cypress' dance tour with a ballet company in support of civil rights issues. This shows that Shange approaches the actual historical circumstances suggestively and indirectly. She does not focus on specific dates or events; rather, she emphasizes significant moments of the women's personal history.

---

27 Shange, *Sassafrass, Cypress & Indigo* 3.

28 Northrop Frye, *Anatomy of Criticism* (New York: Atheneum, 1966) 278.

29 Shange, *Sassafrass, Cypress & Indigo* 213.

30 Shange 186.

Within this feminine discourse, Shange's emphasis lies almost exclusively on black history and the African American community. Indigo's world in the mind of a child, then, stands *pars pro toto* for Shange's overall conception. As a socially and economically oppressive system, the white world hovers only marginally over the novel. Briefly, the white world becomes tangible in the shape of the art critic, the ballet teacher, the violin teacher, and the white sponsor, Miss Fitzhugh. But just as Miss Fitzhugh's Christmas visit at the Effania house is quickly ended—"Miz Fitzhugh couldn't keep her hat on. There was a wind justa pushing, blowing Miz Fitzhugh out the door"—the presence of white history evaporates almost immediately after its appearance.[31] Shange then places the text largely outside the linear time concepts advocated by Western culture, thus running the risk not be to able to subvert it from within. Still, as far as African American history is concerned, the hope for change underlies Shange's vision for the future. And she shares with her characters "the will to simply change the world," knowing that it is not all that simple.[32] In consideration of a long state of oppression the picture of female endurance and creativity that Shange draws is all the more affirmative. Although it is rather domestic than public it continuously breaks down the barrier between the family and the political world.

History in *Sassafrass, Cypress & Indigo* is presented through various female voices. Her novel, like Toni Morrison's *Song of Solomon* (1977), represents a *Bildungsroman* that goes beyond the individual life to comprehend the development and growth of a family and community. In choosing primarily female characters, Shange underscores that she sets out to subvert male conceptions of history. She does so by celebrating the traditional roles of black women in history: weaver, quilt-maker, midwife, mother, dancer, and musician. The awareness of the past and the continuity of past achievements is fused with a feminist consciousness of the need for change. This conception of history is portrayed by the survival and transformation of female creativity within the family itself. Throughout the novel Shange emphasizes that tradition and vision are equally important sources for a woman to define her place within history. Both are present in the characters of the novel. Traditional female values are chiefly embodied by the youngest child Indigo and the mother Hilda. The visionary desire for political change is mainly voiced through Sassafrass and Cypress. Nevertheless, these characters transcend simplifying categorizations. Sassafrass, for instance, combines the traditional role of weaver with the visionary role of writer.[33] And she turns to tradition before she sets out to create new positive images of African American womanhood.

---

31   Shange 71.

32   Shange 208.

33   This dialectic of tradition and innovation is again reminiscent of jazz. Repeatedly jazz
       musicians have returned to the blues to signify upon it. Many melodies of jazz employ the blues
       scale, for instance. See Marshall W. Stearns, *The Story of Jazz* (New York: Oxford UP, 1970)

The general setting of the novel is domestic, a setting that illustrates that Shange is not concerned with the history of battlefields and empires as represented in traditional history books; on the contrary, she withdraws from written history to give voice to female histories so long silenced and neglected. Although she announces that her novel "is dedicated to all women in struggle" it is obvious that she is primarily concerned with the life of black women in America. Gender and race rather than class differences shape Shange's conception of history. To her the history of women is a long story of suppression and for black women, as Shange views it, this discrimination is doubled because of black male supremacy. Hence, she considers it necessary for African American women to develop alternative visions.

Revising traditionally male views of history—black and white—, Shange subverts general criteria of discourse, too. What appears most provocative in relation to canonically accepted literary standards is her enhancement of recipes to a literary form of historical documentation. The recipes handed down and varied from generation to generation again signify a so-far-unrecorded history of female productivity in the field of literature. Shange moves, to borrow a title from Barbara Omolade, "toward a black woman's history through a language of her own."

The revision of history, to Shange, requires an alternative framework of mythical reference. As Northrop Frye has shown, "myth operates on the top level of human desire. . . ."[34] In male-centered Western mythology this longing divides women into groups of either innocent angels or sensuous monsters. Alicia Ostriker explains that

> at first thought, mythology seems an inhospitable terrain for a woman writer. There we find the conquering gods and heroes, the deities of pure thought and spirituality so superior to Mother Nature; there we find the sexually wicked Venus, Circe, Pandora, Helen, Medea, Eve, and the virtuously passive Iphigenia, Alcestis, Mary, Cinderella. It is thanks to myth we believe that woman must either be 'angel' or 'monster'.[35]

---

281. Almost all innovators in jazz—Louis Armstrong, Charlie Parker, Miles Davis and John Coltrane—have turned back to the blues for artistic inspiration. Thus Miles Davis' "Sippin at Bells" is a twelve bar blues. See Martin Williams, *The Jazz Tradition* 200. Williams points to two of Miles Davis' basic blues performances, "'Walkin'" and "Blue 'n' Boogie", that he considers essential to Davis' contribution to modern jazz: Like Louis Armstrong, Roy Eldridge, and Dizzy Gillespie in their early repertoires, Davis in effect reinterpreted in his own terms , the immediate past of jazz—and did it for much of the same reason as the others had, in order to move on." *The Jazz Tradition* 201.

34   Northrop Frye, *Anatomy of Criticism* (New York: Atheneum, 1966) 136.

35   Alicia Ostriker, "The Thieves of Language: Women Poets and Revisionist Mythmaking," *The New Feminist Criticism: Essays on Women, Literature and Theory*, ed. Elaine Showalter (London: Virago Press, 1986) 314-38; 316.

However, in the mythic background of the novel, thought and spirituality are reunited with Mother Nature. Shange associates all three daughters of the Effania family with female figures of mythic nature, partly derived from African American lore, partly derived from Western mythology. Blue Sunday, Erzulie, and the women of Thebes are, like the characters of Shange's fictitious world, women who are willing to take their stand, able to think, and capable of caring. They embody the spirit of love as well as that of rebellion. Accordingly, in her revision of history, myth, and literary conventions Shange displays a firm belief in the myth- and history-making power of language. The future course of history is determined by creation not destruction, Shange makes us believe. It is not surprising, then, that almost all her characters are engaged in acts of creation: cooking, weaving, writing, dancing, and fiddling.

Shange's historical vision becomes transcultural when she refers to the female contribution to music and dance within black cultures. Within the musical discourse, Shange sees a specifically black medium of articulating a feminine aesthetic which bears relevance for African, Caribbean, and African American cultural territories. Since black women have occupied a much more important role in the history of music than their counterparts of European or Western descent, music also provides a matrix to set African American women's concerns apart from white feminist thinking. Otto Werner charts the differences between European and African women in their relation to music, as follows:

> Unlike the music of Europe, where women played relatively small roles in music, the Africans gave the women in the villages major roles in producing the music for the various tribal functions or rituals. The European women were utilized in the choral area as either vocal soloists in songs, or as members of an opera cast, or as soloists in religious works such as masses and requiems. They were given very little consideration in the field of composition/orchestration or as instrumental specialists either as orchestra members or chamber musicians. In African music women were employed in virtually all the musical activities. As instrumentalists, they performed on the mallet instruments (xylophone), the thump piano, the aerophones (windblown instruments such as flutes) and the chordophones which were stringed instruments (fiddle types, harps, zithers and lyres). But perhaps the most important role of women was that of singers. The female voice when performing in a high range has much better projection power than that of men. Without any form of amplification or acoustical treatment, voices should have the capacity to project over distance as well as above any form of accompaniment. While the quality and musical development could not be compared to their European contemporaries, they did perform an important function for the tribe. Their roles in tribal dances were equally important to that of the males. There are instances where tribal women were also members of the drum ensemble, but these occasions were quite rare.[36]

---

[36]   Otto Werner, *The Origin and Development of Jazz* (Dubuque: Kendall/Hunt, 1984) 25-26.

In the female contribution to the development of blues and jazz Shange sees an extension of African female creativity. From these music forms she draws the inspiration for the struggle for an improved social status of black women in the United States as well as for aesthetic renewal. In particular she refers to blues singers such as Ma Rainey, Mamie Smith, Big Mama Thornton, Freddie Washington, Josephine Baker, and Victoria Spivey to emphasize the fact that African American women played a pivotal role in the process of turning blues and jazz into art forms thus bridging the gap between folklore and the fine arts, folk heritage and commerce.[37] Indeed, the classical blues signaled a new degree of professionalism.[38] Blues and jazz turned into art forms that could be used to entertain an audience formally. Hence, the blues singer turned into an artisan who could even make a living. While the country blues represented folklore, classic blues signified entertainment and the female classic blues singers established and dominated the main theatrical blues tradition in the 1920s. Despite the more sophisticated performances which characterized this tradition, singers such as Ma Rainey and Bessie Smith preserved the music's communal meaning from earlier historical epochs. Even if this communal function was deeply related to the world of entertainment, the music still conveyed psychological and social meaning. The classical blues singers responded to the needs of African Americans who often felt uprooted having moved from the country to the city.[39]

Beyond their general communal importance, the female blues artists represented an important alternative to the blues sung by males. The classical blues singers expressed the reality of their lives as African American women and through their style of performance they enhanced the aesthetic and emotional impact of their music. Not only melancholy but irony and satire, too, found their way into lyrics and performance styles of blues women such as Ida Cox and Ma Rainey. This elements functioned as major artistic devices for pronouncing the pain and sorrow of daily life. Besides a cathartic effect, their singing styles also expressed a will to protest. Especially the rap-like performances within the theatrical blues tradition underscored that the female blues singers drew upon their music as a strong means of retaliation. On the one hand, the female blues singers reversed the tradition of the male bragging blues.

---

[37]   Blues singers such as Mamie Smith produced records that remained close to the African American folk roots, whereas earlier records had been made to suit the European taste

[38]   Cf. LeRoi Jones, *Blues People: Negro Music in White America* (New York: William Morrow and Company, 1963) 82.

[39]   See also Lawrence Cohn, *Nothing But the Blues: The Music and the Musicians* (New York: Abbeville Press, 1993) 87. Cohn explains that during years of prosperity which followed after the war numerous vaudeville shows took place in houses like the Pekin and Vendome in Chicago and the Lincoln and Lafayette in New York. Female blues singers commanded center stage in those urban clubs and houses in particular. See also Houston A. Baker, Jr., *Modernism and the Harlem Renaissance* (Chicago: U of Chicago P, 1987) 92.

In some of their songs they boasted about their tremendous erotic appeal and sexual ability; thus they celebrated the power of female attraction.[40] On the other hand, they resorted to practices developed by African and African Caribbean women to embarrass male members of their community who had abused, mistreated, or neglected them. On this level, the blues gave voice to a specific female community that expressed a sense of belonging and solidarity.[41]

Economically, too, the female blues tradition turned into a success story. Most of the early ethnic records were aimed at immigrant groups. For those who attempted to break into the recording industry, race records symbolized a triumph. For instance, Mamie Smith's "Crazy Blues" sold at an impressive rate, making recording history. As a result all major record companies started to record the classical blues singers. As Kathy J. Ogren mentions, "classic blues recordings helped pull record companies out of the early twenties slump produced by radio competition."[42] Indeed, classical blues enjoyed a tremendous popularity, especially within the black communities. African American consumers bought blues records in great number even if they suffered from low family income.[43] Hence, the female blues singers made the blues popular; at the same time they advocated race pride. Shange, therefore, presents them as ideal role models for black women writers in their efforts to establish their own literary tradition. The blues performed by women becomes the matrix for a female black aesthetic and political stance against male oppression, black or white.

Yet, the historical consciousness and the folk spirit musically and lyrically expressed in the blues need constant revision. Shange makes clear that there is a difference between tradition and conformity. In "takin a solo" she poetically voices her belief that art should not be trapped by ideology. As an example of a vital art form that keeps its ability to change she gives jazz, and modern jazz in particular. To her, African American writers should develop their own voices, following the example of John Coltrane and other black jazz musicians:

> That's the division of a realm bordered by bebop & one sunk syllable /
> where only the language defines reality. / we have poets who speak to you of
> elephants & avenues / we have others who address themselves to worlds
> having no existence beyond the word. that's fine. we live in all those places.

40   See Paul Garon, *Blues and the Poetic Spirit* (New York: Da Capo Press, 1979) 104-09. As
      Garon points out, images of male and female worlds turned into metaphors which linked foods,
      animals, automobiles, trains, and weapons with the sex act or genitals. Within this context
      Garon discusses blues lyrics by Ida Cox, Memphis Minnie, and Mandy Lee among others.

41   See also Daphne Duval Harrison, *Black Pearls: Blues Queens of the 1920s* (Brunswick:
      Rutgers UP, 1988) 89, 20-21. Harrison's study on the classical blues singers is the most
      comprehensive analysis of the female blues tradition during the 1920s.

42   Kathy J. Ogren, *The Jazz Revolution: Twenties and the Meaning of Jazz* (New York: Oxford
      UP, 1989) 91.

43   Ogren 92.

> but, if we don't know the voice of a writer / the way we know 'oh . . . that's
> trane' / then something is very wrong. we are unfortunately / selling
> ourselves down the river again. & we awready know abt that. if we go down
> river again / just cuz we don't know or care to recognize our particularities /
> won't nobody come / cuz dont nobody care / if you don't know yr poets as
> well as yr tenor horns.[44]

Shange then urges black women writers in particular to use their individual
voices for re-writing the history of African Americans. And she asks them to be
courageous enough to turn female realms into aesthetic and political spaces for
experimentation and innovation. History in *Sassafrass, Cypress & Indigo* is
primarily presented in terms of domestic labor and art, accordingly.

Shange is certainly not concerned with a chronological sense of time, as can
be illustrated by the overall structure of the novel.[45] From the very beginning
Shange subverts a linear progression opening the novel with the story of Indigo,
the youngest child of the family. The tradition of black culture, especially blues
and jazz, comes to her naturally in her fiddling. The fiddle becomes a substitute
for dolls as a medium to converse with a spiritual world, as she grows up:
"Whenever she wanted to pray, she let her fiddle talk. Whenever she was angry,
here came the fiddle."[46] Indigo carries "the South in her." She plays the fiddle
to soothe the pain of her dolls as well as her own; moreover the fiddle gives
voice to her anger and rebellious spirit. Thus the instrument expresses Indigo's
moods and establishes a rapport with a larger spiritual world full of myth and
magic. Whenever she is displeased with her mother, whenever she feels under
attack from the outside, she takes the fiddle. Whereas her sisters at first need to
explore the possibilities of imagination to finally tap into its power, Indigo lives
by it from childhood onward. Shange, then, places her story first. Indigo lives
closest to the African and African American heritage. Her relationship to the
imagination is the most intense and intuitive.

The opening of the novel shows that Shange subverts a chronological set-up
in favor of intensity. Time in *Sassafrass,Cypress & Indigo*, it seems to me, is
psychic, affective. A sense of time passages is conveyed through memories
called forth when characters experience the intensity of the moment.
Introspection marks most of the scenes evoking images of the past. The
characters live through moments of pain or joy when they start thinking about
history on a larger scale. The journal entries, for example, expose the psyche of
the women and how they grow into an understanding of their role in history.
This indicates as well how they define their social and political roles. History is

---

44   Ntozake Shane, *SeeNoEvil: Prefaces, Essays & Accounts 1976-1983* (San Francisco: Momo's
     Press, 1984) 27-28.

45   Shange's first novel was preceded by her novella *Sassafrass*, first published in 1976, and the
     structure of the novella anticipates many structural devices prominent within the novel. Just
     like the novella, the novel comprises a multiplicity of forms and genres.

46   Shange, *Sassafrass, Cypress & Indigo* 33.

internalized in the minds of the female protagonists and closely related to a sense of place and culture. "The South in her" are the words the mother uses to describe Indigo's otherness compared to the rest of the community. Indigo's temporal journey back to the world of ancestry takes place in her mind and is spatially static, since she remains in the South all the time. Baker points out that "the time of *Sassafrass, Cypress & Indigo* is, finally, not so much the space-time of theories of relativity as the place-time in Bantu."[47] A conception of time then is intricately connected with an experience of place. What Baker suggests here is that time is not measured out as a linear progression but reflected in the intensity of the instant.

What is true for Bantu philosophy is true for jazz, too. The emphasis on intensity and immediacy in jazz has repeatedly been pointed out. Shange applies this focus on the moment in the development of her characters. She concentrates upon important instants in their lives and intensifies them into moments of epiphany. Indigo's cavern experience, Sassafrass' encounter with Mamie Smith, and Cypress' dream of matriarchal terror epitomize such experiences of growing consciousness. Consequently, the characters mature and change. Time is not at a stand-still in the novel. Yet, the psychological changes and geographical moves are counterpointed by the steady voice and local stability of the mother. Hilda Effania's home in Charleston remains an ever-present center of home and comfort in the lives of her daughters. With symbolic references they all gather at home toward the end of the novel to celebrate Christmas together.

It is obvious that the rural South lies at the heart of Shange's historical imagination since the region remains connected with the East and the West coast through Hilda Effania's letters throughout the novel. Again Shange resorts to a technique of call-and-response which functions on a structural level to give her novel coherence despite its multiplicity of forms and genres. Hilda, as a representative of black Southern culture, transmits rural values in the letters to her daughters. In her literary adaptation of the call-and-response pattern Shange repeatedly interpolates letters by the mother within the stories of the three sisters. The written mode of interaction is the chief form of communication during times of absence in the Effania family. They represent responses to the calling of the three sisters in that they give maternal advice and provide comment on their different ways of living. Shange thus uses the mother figure—"Mama was there"—for fusion on a thematic, formal, and temporal level.[48] She stands for continuity and stability. Her voice signifies an ever-ready response to the yearnings and problems of her daughters. The calls, so to speak, are variations of growing up and maturing, as each of the daughters undergoes an individual process of learning her own social and historical role.

---

47   Houston A. Baker, *The Workings of the Spirit: The Poetics of Afro-American Women's Writing* (Chicago: U of Chicago P, 1991) 199.

48   Shange, *Sassafrass, Cypress & Indigo* 225.

Throughout the novel Shange constantly shifts between three major time levels—past, present, and future. Syntactically, she associates the shift of time with a change of rhythm or beat in the novel. After a fight with her lover Mitch, Sassafrass visits her sister Cypress in San Francisco. The main plot narrated in the past tense describes them while they are getting ready for one of Cypress' dance rehearsals:

> Cypress had a two-hour rehearsal and then a show, and Sassafrass was going to help dress the women dancers in their elaborate costumes and fix anything looking like it might fall down in the middle of a running jump. Sassafrass got up out of her chair and startedsinging "Tonight' The Night," with all the swivelling of hips and arms beckoning whatever lovers.[49]

The state of trance that Sassafrass reaches while dancing introduces a new time level. She starts on an imaginary journey to the Caribbean and ancient black cultures, re-constructing her dead father's life as a seaman. Shange resorts to italics and poetic breaks to indicate the new time level visually and acoustically:

> Down to the wharf, there was always sailors / shippers from all over the world / daddy was a seaman / a ship's carpenter. he was always goin' round the world / that's what mama said / & he died in the ocean offa zanzibar.[50]

Unlike the first passage, the second is marked by abrupt transition. The rhythm appears jerky.[51] Shange thus mimics the polyrhythmical progression of jazz as an expression of a specific sense of time. The constant shifts produce an effect of simultaneity. Since time passages move back and forth in a fast tempo frequently Shange achieves the effect of temporal fusion. Past and present have lost a chronological order or linear significance. Future, as Shange designs history in her novel, is not merely a follow-up to the present; instead it always constitutes a call back on the past as well. It is in the experience of the single moment that characters reach an awareness of time going beyond the here-and-now.

On the level of language, Shange's imagistic diction underlines the temporal intensity she is looking for. The short phrases, the clear and concise images that

---

49   Shange 107.

50   Shange 108.

51   As I have mentioned in chapter I, the association of time and beat is also crucial to jazz performances during funeral ceremonies. A slow beat is associated with the grief of the mourners on the way to the graveyard. It is related to the past and transitoriness. The fast beat played after the funeral, however, expresses the return to the present and the hope for the time to come. Bohlaender, for instance, describes a funeral ceremony in New Orleans to present the interrelation of time and musical beat in African American culture. A slow and solemn version of "When The Saints Go Marchin' In" is superseded by a fast and joyful one. The musicians resort to double time. The music starts swinging, and the choruses are improvised freely. See Carlo Bohlaender, *Die Anatomie des swing* (Frankfurt/Main: Jas publication 1986) 47.

give her prose a sense of poetry underscore the importance of the here-and-now. She obviously aims at adapting the intensity of the improvisational moment in blues and jazz to her literary rendering of time in *Sassafrass, Cypress & Indigo*. Her concern with the single sound present in each letter or word underscores that acoustic elements are inseparable from Shange's narrative discourse. In an interview with Claudia Tate she reveals how closely she sees her syntactical devices related to speech: "Basically, the spellings reflect language as I hear it. I write this way because I hear the words."[52] Just as many jazz musicians elicit voice-like sounds from their instruments, Shange uses idiosyncratic ways of spelling—"& thru me / i am dazzled by yr beneficence i shall create new altars"—to come closer to the spoken word.[53]

Shange then plays with both Coltrane's jazz and Black English in the novel when she experiments with spelling. The reduction in spelling—"yr, thru"— parallels reductionist tendencies in the grammatical signs of Black English. Dwight Bolinger points to the frequent omission of the copula "to be" and the short clause groups within sentences to illustrate the reduction principle in Black English. He gives examples such as "they singing", "they sick", "he be here."[54] Shange uses these shortened spellings not only to express the black aspects of the English spoken in the South but also to produce the effect of a fast-paced sound sequence reminiscent of Coltrane's "sheets of sound."

Like John Coltrane's tenor horn performances Shange's prose addresses ear, eye, and intellect simultaneously. Many passages of the novel reveal their true beauty when read aloud. Reading, to Shange, is more than a removed intellectual activity. She pulls the reader acoustically into her novel:

> The South in her, the land and salt-winds, moved her through Charleston's streets as if she were a mobile sapling, with the gait of a well-loved colored woman whose lover was the horizon in any direction. Indigo imagined tough winding branches growing from her braids, deep green leaves rustling by her ears, doves and macaws flirting above the nests they'd fashioned in the secret, protected niches way high up in her headdress.[55]

Via alliteration, assonance, and a smoothly expanding prose, Shange achieves here the effect of incantation. Enchanting the reader on a narrative level, she thus approaches the act of negotiation between the musicians' and the listeners' sense of time in blues and jazz. What she brings to the novel is a jazz musician's ear and a poet's sense of concrete diction. With fast-paced shifts in form, spelling, and visual arrangement she demands an intense participation on the part of the reader in the act of reception. It is almost as if she wants the reader to relive the experience of a blues or jazz performance while reading.

---

52   Claudia Tate, ed. *Black Women Writers at Work* (New York: Continuum, 1983) 163.

53   Shange, *Sassafrass, Cypress & Indigo* 110.

54   Dwight Bolinger, *Aspects of Language* (New York: Harcourt Brace Jovanovich, 1975) 338-39.

55   Shange, *Sassafrass, Cypress & Indigo* 4.

Just like a blues or jazz musician Shange searches for direct contact to the audience.[56] And rhythm and sound become equally important in this process of mediating time levels between author and recipient, as the subsequent textual passages illustrate:

> She desperately wanted <u>to</u> make Ochá. <u>To</u> wear white with her élèkes. <u>To</u> keep the company of the priests & priestesses. . . . Then there were the problems of <u>grinding</u> grains, <u>building</u> homes, <u>fetching</u> water. . . . He wandered from the collective frequently, returning <u>incoherent</u>, <u>dirty</u>, <u>unacceptable</u>. . . . She made cloth for all the collective, <u>for</u> feasts, <u>for</u> rituals, <u>for</u> sale to tourists. . . .[57]

This excerpt—only a few lines have been left out—displays the highly rhythmic quality of Shange's prose. Read aloud, these lines reveal a repetition-variation pattern. The stringing together in syntax and diction creates a rhythmic continuity based on three beats, as the underlined words in the quotation demonstrate. Thus these sections are reminiscent of triplets in jazz's shuffle rhythm (and other music forms). According to Bohlaender and Holler, dotted eighth notes reminiscent of triplets create a swing-style basic tempo here.[58] In Shange's literary discourse the variations result from the shift in diction, as the excerpt shows. She uses particles, adjectives, and participles to create 'triplets'.

While the above passage contains a varied though continuous beat, other passages underscore the polyphonic quality of *Sassafrass, Cypress & Indigo* through counterrhythmic effects thus expressing various individual experiences of time syntactically. In her description of a dance performance, for instance, Shange juxtaposes two different rhythms in her narrative:

> Black men <u>and</u> women in miniskirts <u>and</u> wigs, dashikis <u>and</u> flowing robes, rub tootsies <u>and</u> exchange greetings through the dark.

> Deep drumming is heard from the street; folks turn their heads backwards. The Kushites Returned leap, sweep down the aisles, silk cloth flies in the air gleaming with silver threads, the painted dancers burst through the darkness.

> Spotlights follow the sounds of the bells on their wrists <u>and</u> ankles; they scream <u>and</u> sigh <u>and</u> all is joy, mighty <u>and</u> profound.[59]

For matter of textual scrutiny I have divided the excerpt into three fragments that expose the shift in syntactic rhythm within the passage. As the repetitive

---

[56]   As Ferris elucidates, this contact involves music as well as talk. "Within the blues performance the distinction between music and talk disappears as performer and audience respond to each other. Blues talk complements verses and at times becomes the most important part of the performance." William Ferris, *Blues from the Delta* 107.

[57]   Shange, *Sassafrass, Cypress & Indigo* 214 (underlining mine).

[58]   Carlo Bohlaender and Karl Heinz Holler, *Reclam Jazzführer* (Stuttgart: Reclam Verlag, 1970) 786.

[59]   Shange, *Sassafrass, Cypress & Indigo* 113-14 (underlining mine).

use of 'and' in the first fragment shows, Shange is obviously concerned with producing a smooth rhythm. The middle fragment differs succinctly and creates a counterrhythmic effect since the flow of the words in the first fragment is replaced by an almost staccato beat. The connection 'and' is superseded by punctuation. In the third fragment, finally, Shange returns to the smooth-flowing prose of the beginning. The flow here comes from more than just syntactical parallelism: sound itself flows via alliteration and assonance in particular.

Syntax and sound translate Shange's understanding of temporal movements verbally. Structurally, the novel keeps moving like a pendulum; time appears to swing back and forth. The story of Indigo, the youngest of the family, opens the novel, as we have seen. The major narration of the past, then, moves from Sassafrass to Cypress. Toward the end of the novel, Shange first shifts back to Sassafrass and finally returns to Indigo. The circle is completed when all three reunite at home to bear witness to the birth of Sassafrass' child. The structural cycle as well as the thematic cycle closes at this point. In the beginning and in the end the celebration of creativity stands forth, and it comes full circle when creation moves from the realm of the imagination to the matrix of nature. Indigo's imaginative power gives way to Sassafrass' biological strength—the birth of her child. Thus Shange links her circular structure to a feminine consciousness which is embedded in what Kristeva labels "monumental time":

> There was nothing straight at Ovary Studio. Everything was round, curving, textured, and dense. No sense of the possibility of masculinity existed. The ceiling was covered with moss, like pubic hair. The aisles of the theatre arena moved like errant streams. Everywhere there was flow.[60]

Natural images intermingle with an artistic setting in the description of the dance studio and both dimensions deny any form of stasis. Flux is ever-present and becomes inseparably connected with the female body and psyche, as Shange develops feminine conceptions of time.

In order to live and express these temporal alternatives to the male-centered linear discourse, acts of liberation are necessary in a male-dominated world.[61] As Shange puts it, it also requires an individual sense of time through which one discerns "woman" as multiplicity and a collective sense of history through which one is capable of perceiving "women" as equally exposed to forms of oppression. All daughters of the Effania family have to struggle on their way to identity. When the reader encounters the three female characters for the first

---

60   Shange 141.

61   Shange demonstrates, though, that there are more than male restrictions to the historical opportunities for women. Matriarchy, as soon as it assumes a totalitarian power structure, is as repressive as its patriarchal counterpart. The vision of a society solely inhabited and guided by women turns into a nightmare in Cypress' dream (203-207). The change, then, that Shange projects upon the acts of liberation for her female characters is not a simple matter of turning the tables. Rather, it is a complex historical process invoking preservation and renewal alike.

time, each of them sees herself confronted with a time of change or crisis. Their worlds differ, though. While Indigo lives through the crucial transition from girlhood to adolescence and wanders in the zone between Christian belief and Southern magic, Sassfrass struggles in a male-female partnership. Cypress, finally, faces being torn between white and black traditions artistically, between male and female attraction sexually. Starting from these moments of crisis, each of them sets out, guided by female perceptions of time, to find her place within an alternative discourse to purely teleological conceptions of history.

To free herself from societal gender expectations, Indigo withdraws at first into the realm of the imagination.In Shange's rendering, she embodies the magic and the myth of the South—"the South in her."[62] She makes dolls and lives and talks with them in the universe of her own mind. In Indigo's childhood imagination her dolls inhabit a black world that is cross-cultural and cross-continental[63]:

> Indigo had made every kind of friend she wanted. African dolls filled with cotton root bark, so they'd have no more slave children. Jamaican dolls in red turbans, bodies formed with comfrey leaves because they'd had to work on Caribbean and American plantations and their bodies ache and be sore. Then there were the mammy dolls that Indigo labored over for months. They were almost four feet high, with big gold earrings made from dried sunflowers, and tits of uncleaned cotton. They smelled of fennel, pead leaves, wild ginger, wild yams.[64]

Indigo's imaginary world is always related to the needs of the black community: "Black people needed so many things."[65] When she meets only white folks she conjures them into black folks. "Indigo only had colored dolls and only visited colored ladies."[66] Her imagination is further intrigued by the

---

[62]   Shange 4.

[63]   To Indigo her intense relation to African American folklore comes naturally. In her imaginative conversations with her dolls and her intuitive violin playing she expresses the true folk spirit. As the novel progresses to the stories of Sassafrass and Cypress, the reader experiences a gradually growing detachment from the African American oral tradition. Euro-American written or notated tradition surfaces in Sassafrass' poems and even more so in Cypress' frequent use of French expressions and her endeavor to imitate French ballet. With an increasing awareness of their own rootedness in African American folk culture, however, Sassafrass and Cypress develop their own authentic forms of artistic expression. Sassafrass creates a poetic voice rooted in the rhythm of the black speech idiom and black music. Cypress, on her part, liberates herself from the dance conventions of European ballet. Pursuing the inner struggles for artistic expression of the two older sisters, the reader, finally returns to the powerful presence of folk culture in the figure of Indigo towards the end of the novel. See also my discussion of the three sisters' development in the final parts of this chapter.

[64]   Shange 6.

[65]   Shange 4.

[66]   Shange 7.

storytelling of the older black women in Charleston: Mrs Yancey, the old lady who gets all she wants from white folks, and Sister Mary Louise, who wants her to be a good Christian girl. Especially in her talks with them her growing awareness of what it means to be a black woman in the South takes shape. "Folks in these parts got sucha low idea of the women of the race," Mrs Yancey tells Indigo.[67] As Mrs Yancey describes the history of black people, "the white folks drove down the Colored, drove the Colored to drink and evil ways, drove decent young girls into lives of sin. . . ."[68] Sister Mary explains to Indigo that the black woman's role is to tend "to beauty and children."[69] She continues to educate Indigo through the teachings of the Bible: "'And your sons will become shepherds in the wilderness' Numbers 14:33."[70] Hearing this passage from the Bible, Indigo becomes angry. She clearly senses the exclusion of women from history: "But that doesn't have anything to do with me, Sister Mary Louise! . . . I'm a girl that's all. I want to know what I'm supposed to do."[71] Detecting male supremacy in Christian faith, Indigo chooses the haints of African American folk belief over Christian spirits. She feels closely related to "the heathenish folks, pagans out there on those islands," which clearly signal a different time frame.[72]

African American music supersedes the role of the dolls in Indigo's imaginary world, as she enters puberty. Uncle John's definition of the blues as "talkin' wit the unreal" is central to Indigo's imaginative power and Shange's use of the blues in *Sassafrass, Cypress & Indigo*:

> 'Listen now, girl. I'ma tell ya some matters of the reality of the unreal. In times blacker than these,' Uncle John waved the violin & the bow toward the deepening night, 'when them slaves was ourselves & we couldn't talk free, or walk free, who ya think be doin' our talkin' for us? . . . The fiddle be callin' our gods what left us/be given' back some devilment & hope in our bodies worn down & lonely over these fields & kitchens. . . . What ya think music is, whatchu think the blues be . . . but talkin wit the unreal what's mo real than most folks ever gonna know.'[73]

Historically, Uncle John refers back to times when African Americans had to develop secret codes for communication. During the years of slavery the white slave owners deprived the black slaves of their instruments, the drum particularly, to uproot them from their African heritage and to prevent rebellion.

---

67   Shange 10.

68   Shange 10.

69   Shange 19.

70   Shange 19.

71   Shange 16.

72   Shange 17.

73   Shange 26-27.

Nevertheless music continued to be the major communicative medium for black people; through music they kept on conversing with each other and their gods, with the real and the supernatural. As Uncle John's explanation—"the fiddle be callin' our gods"—underscores, Voodoo beliefs and rites have lived on in the folk-music of African Americans and in the blues, specifically. And "the reality of the unreal" paradoxically circumscribes the subjective experience of time on the part of Indigo. In her imaginative world she creates her private history which, from the rational historical perspective, is illusionary. Yet, to Indigo, this imagined world takes a concrete shape when she joins the people on the islands of the Carolinas.[74] Time envisioned and real time overlap. Whereas the dolls represent the medium for the articulation of visionary thinking in her early years, the fiddle becomes a new medium of communication. When Uncle John presents Indigo with his fiddle as a gift she stands at a point in her life where she fears to be silenced –her mother wants her to put the dolls away. Shange obviously draws parallels between Indigo's growing up and early African American history. But Indigo breaks through the imposed silence since her music conjures up the sounds of nature—"The crescendoes of the cicadas, swamp rushes in light winds, thunder at high tide, & her mother's laughter down the hall."[75] Indigo's fiddle playing –like the guitar in blues and the saxophone in jazz—mimics the sound of the human voice. Symbolically, the instrument voices Indigo's awareness of self and her awakening female ethics. But it also bears the potential for social protection and change. She successfully defends herself against the pubescent sexual advances of the two Geechee Capitans, who move a twig up and down her legs. The magic spell cast by her fiddle playing defeats the boys' roughness and paves Indigo's ritualistic admission to the Geechee motorcycle gang. Thus Indigo manages to infiltrate this all-male group with a respect for nature and social behavior.

Indigo, still, has to learn that the cultural power of her fiddle playing can cut both ways. While she finds herself a place as violinist in Pretty Man's social room she gradually undermines Mabel's role at Sneeds. Mabel, Pretty Man's girlfriend, "a simple sweet woman who helped out in the social room", sees her social and private standing jeopardized through Indigo's performances of "Blues in C" or "Arabian Song, No. 42."[76] In an act of jealousy she throws out Indigo and her fiddle. Pretty Man, in return, loses control and assaults Mabel physically. Indigo's revelation regarding common black and female suffering in the Caverns is reminiscent of epiphanies in the subterranean worlds of Richard

---

[74] See Samuel Charters, *The Bluesmen: The Story and the Music of the Men Who made the Blues* (New York: Oak Publications, 1967) 27. In isolated areas such as the sea islands of Georgia and the Carolinas African cultural concepts could persist for a long time.

[75] Shange 36.

[76] Shange 46.

Wright and Ralph Ellison.[77] Shange links Indigo's epiphany in the Caverns with blues and slave songs:

> The slaves who were ourselves had known terror intimately, confused sunrise with pain, & accepted indifference as kindness. Now they sang out from the walls, pulling Indigo toward them. Indigo ran her hands along the walls, to get the song, getta hold to the voices. Instead her fingers grazed cold, hard metal rings. Chains. Leg irons. The Caverns revealed the plight of her people, but kept on singing. The tighter Indigo held the chains in her hands, the less shame was her familiar. Mabel's tiny woeful voice hovered over the blood thick chorus of The Caverns. Indigo knew her calling.[78]

After the intense experience of this instant, Indigo leaves behind the historical role of female blues entertainer. Although she continues to work on her violin—she even studies violin with a teacher—she chooses a more ancient, traditional role for a living. She follows in the footsteps of Aunt Haydee, healer and midwife, when she moves in at Aunt Haydee's hut in Difuskie. The "rough blues" she plays at Aunt Haydee's death bed symbolizes the return of art to social functioning.[79] In combining the role of midwife and healer with that of musician, Indigo roots her life in the traditions of ancient Africa. When Indigo soothes the women in labor, she revives African tribal functions on American soil: "Well versed in songs for every occasion, African tribes had used music as a practical art which reflected all facets of everyday living," Hilda Roach elucidates.[80] Thus she also enters an African time zone turning her back on linearity completely. This new temporal orientation suggests resistance and rebellion alike. Toward the end of the novel, Indigo is transformed into a woman warrior, to borrow a title from Maxine Hong Kingston. She is compared to a mythic female figure of African American lore who "turned into a crocodile. As a crocodile, Blue Sunday was benign. Her only struggle was to remain unconquered."[81]

Similar to Indigo's coming of age, Shange portrays Sassafrass' movement from victimization to consciousness. Like Indigo she has to learn to take her stand against male dominance. Mitch, Sassafrass' life companion, embodies male aggression. Celebrating Otis Goodwin-Smith's new book, *Ebony Cunt*, Mitch and his male artist friends trigger a chauvinist assault on the status of

---

[77]   In Richard Wright's *The Outsider* (1950), the protagonist Damon temporarily assumes a new identity after the subway incident in which he is believed to have been killed. Ellison's protagonist in *Invisible Man* (1952) comprehends the invisibility of blackness only in his black hole in the underground.

[78]   Shange, *Sassafrass, Cypress & Indigo* 49.

[79]   Shange 221.

[80]   Hilda Roach, *Black American Music: Past and Present* vol I (Malabar: Krieger Publishing Company Inc., 1985) 17.

[81]   Shange, *Sassafrass, Cypress & Indigo* 223.

black women. The language used by Otis in his new book is explicitly sexist. According to the historical image of women presented by Mitch and his friends, black women occupy the very bottom of social hierarchy:

> The white man want you/ the Indian run off with / You / Spaniards created whole nations with you / black / queensilk snatch / / I wander all in your wombs & make babies in the Bronx when I come / you screammmmmmm / jesus / my blk man / ebony cunt is worth all the gold in the world / 15 millions of your shinin' blk bodies crossed the sea / to bring all that good slick pussy to me.... [82]

Black women are portrayed as purely passive and they are reduced to sexual objects and child-bearing creatures. Otis' text signifies a sexist parody on the ancient mother of earth myth. In his rendering of history he puts black women down, paralyzing them into will-less instruments of an historical process exclusively controlled by males. Otis' text can be compared with the kind of bragging song in the male blues tradition. Bo Diddley's version of E. McDaniel's "I'm a Man" (1955) and Muddy Waters' version of W. Dixon's "I'm Your Hoochie Coochie Man"(1954) are just two examples. As Paul Garon explains, many references to women in the male blues are of a demeaning nature.[83] Male supremacy can even take the form of outward aggression , as in Georgia Tom's Six Shooter Blues:

> Now, the blues don't mean nothing when you got your six-shooter on your side. (x2) / If your women mistreats you, shoot her and grab / a train and ride.[84]

When Sassafrass dares to defy this male version of history—"don't you ever sit in my house and ask me to celebrate my inherited right to be raped"—she encounters physical violence; Mitch beats her.[85]

To overcome male dominion Sassafrass gathers strength in her imaginary conversations with Miss Brown Blues, the lady who "knows all about the blues."[86] Personifying the rich variety of female blues singers, Miss Brown Blues signals creativity and endurance in the face of oppression: "I gotta sing this low; I gotta share this burden; I gotta pay the Devil his due."[87] Sassafrass' secret communication with the blues lady parallels Indigo's experience in the Caverns and that of her violin-playing. It signifies a psychic journey back to the

---

[82]   Shange 80.

[83]   Paul Garon, *Blues and the Poetic Spirit* 100.

[84]   Garon 101·

[85]   Shange, *Sassafrass, Cypress & Indigo* 89.

[86]   Shange 81. For further analysis of references to social injustice in the female blues tradition see Angela Y. Davis, *Blues Legacies and Black Feminism: Gertrude "Ma" Rainey, Bessie Smith, and Billie Holiday* (New York: Pantheon Books, 1998) 113-15.

[87]   Shange 127.

past. And Sassafrass goes on to plunge even deeper into history: "*& she layed up nights readin' histories of ancient civilizations. . . .*"[88] Her journey through time takes place in her mind; it is not spatial. In the blues she finds a force that makes her dance and fall "back to the South."[89]

Parallel to Indigo's growth Sassafrass gains a larger historical consciousness in the intense experience of the moment. Introspection characterizes her talks with the blues lady, yet Sassafrass seeks to break through her own silence. Drawing strength from her heritage and talent—"making cloth was the only tradition Sassafrass inherited that gave her a sense of womanhood that was rich and sensuous"—, she gradually finds her own voice as woman and poet.[90] Like Indigo she manages to synthesize the spiritual with the practical for she creates with needle and pen. Her poems express a sense of selfhood rooted in tradition and display the visionary role Sassafrass has taken on in her creation of positive images of women in history:

> i am sassafrass / a weaver's daughter / from charleston / i'm a woman makin cloth like all good women do / . . . / i am the maker of warmth & emblems of good spirit.[91]

The expression of her personal identity changes into an assertion of collective identity among women in general.

> I'm a weaver with my sistahs from any earth & fields / we always make cloth / love our children / honor our men / . . . / we proffer hope / & food to eat / clothes to wear / wombs to fill.[92]

Thus Sassafrass reverses the naming motif of the male blues tradition. The aggressive and derogatory mood of the male blues is replaced by a creative spirit in the female blues. That Sassafrass sees herself as " a river gatherin space" earlier on in the poem implies that she is willing and capable of turning her pride as a woman into a political message.[93] She takes womanhood out of her domestic scenery onto a platform of public history. As Sassafrass' poem illustrates, the act of weaving permits time to contemplate and to create. In her rendering of the myth of the Theban women she asserts the active part of women in history. "When women make cloth, they have time to think, and Theban women stopped thinking, and the town fell."[94]

---

[88]   Shange 109.

[89]   Shange 129.

[90]   Shange 92.

[91]   Shange 91.

[92]   Shange 91.

[93]   Shange 90.

[94]   Shange 92.

Her stay with Mitch in the artists' commune in Louisiana turns out a failure; Shange thus seems to mock black nationalists' endeavors to occupy a separate black territory in the United States. As Hilda's letter implies, Sassafrass will return home, perhaps to go into business to sell her weavings in Charleston. Different from Indigo, Sassafrass' mythic sense of time does not separate her from linear progression as such. Rather she is willing to fuse the memory of the past with the necessity to produce for the future. Tradition is important to Shange but it must be adapted to the changes time brings.

Cypress' process of defining her role represents the third and final variation of the theme of growing up. She is the furthest detached from her African American roots when the reader meets her for the first time. Even more than Sassafrass she is given to experimental ways of living that involve drugs as well as constantly changing sexual partners. Being the only woman with Ariel's ballet troup on tour along the East coast, she experiences growing dissatisfaction, though:

> Men talking to men about being men who like men and occasionally take a woman. Cypress tweezed her eyebrows, pushed cuticles, braided her hair, slept, stared out of windows, kept quiet, and remembered too many men. Long men standing by trees in parks. Smart men being glib. Men taking off her clothes. Men flirting with each other when they danced with her. Men eating her food; men in her bed. Men holding her, leaving her wet and lonely.[95]

Her sexual wanderings introduce her to heterosexual as well as lesbian love until she decides to marry the jazz musician McCullough. Artistically, she is at first ambitious to imitate and master the European ballet tradition. Shange underscores Cypress' initial preference in that she frequently infiltrates Cypress' speech with French expressions: "rond de jambe en l'air; gargouillade; cabriole, brisé."[96] But, similar to the development of Indigo and Sassafrass, Cypress has to revive the memory of her own cultural past to find the strength to discover her own historical role. She finally dismisses the idea of exile in France and embraces African American dance expression.

Again, it is through music that the link between America and Africa is established. On the tour through the South the dancers of Ariel's company introduce the black communities to "the brazen mystical motions of black Nile dance".[97] The dances include "modern black American contractions," "belly dance" by "hootchy coo carnie girls" from the 1920s, and acrobatic movements of ancient African dances.[98] The music underlying the various dance sections range from African drumming—"deep drumming is heard from the street"—to

---

[95]   Shange 137.

[96]   Shange 56.

[97]   Shange 136.

[98]   Shange 114.

jazz from the 1920s.[99] To Cypress, dance assumes political and historical implications. Like the dances in ancient Egypt, Ariel's dance tour has social and political meaning. Whereas dance represented a medium between ruler and subjects in Egypt—through the performance both assured mutual solidarity and confirmed political continuity—the act of dancing, to Cypress, signifies black affirmation in the face of white dominion.[100] And dancing becomes suggestive of freedom, at least in private, psychological terms. "Her dance took on the essence of the struggle of colored Americans to survive their enslavement . . . when she danced she was alive; when she danced, she was free."[101] Like her sisters she learns to draw on the memory of African American culture to define a historical role for herself.

Repeatedly Shange compares her to the Voodoo fetish Erzulie. As Reginald Martin explains, "Erzulie is known as a love/romance/sexual fetish in Hoodoo; her United States version would be W.C. Handy's 'woman with the red dress on' or Josephine Baker."[102] Clearly Shange envisions a subversive role for Cypress when she relates her to Erzulie. And the fusion of artistic and political engagement links Cypress to Josephine Baker who became famous through her performances with the dance group "Black birds" in Paris in the 1920s. As Ishmael Reed puts it, "when jazz and Josephine Baker entered Europe, Europe went out of its mind."[103] Indeed Josephine Baker took European metropols such Paris and Berlin by storm. Her dance performances—frequently she was topless—embraced sensuality, unbound vitality, and comic effects alike.[104] Dancing to the music of Sidney Bechett in the Revue Nègre in Paris in 1925, Baker's dance performances included acrobatic expressions of the whole body, hips and bottom being the most involved.[105]

For Shange's historical imagination, it is important that, like Baker, Cypress becomes politically active in the Civil Rights Movement.[106] Art and political engagement coincide, when Cypress picks a career as a dancer. She chooses to be "the original aboriginal dancin' girl" in the "Soil and Soul" dance company

---

99   Shange 114.

100   See for the role of dance in Egypt Giovanni Calendoli, *Tanz: Kult-Rhythmus-Kunst*, trans. Johannes Werres (Braunschweig: Westermann, 1986) 19.

101   Shange, *Sassafrass, Cypress & Indigo* 136.

102   Reginald Martin, *Ishmael Reed and the New Black Aesthetic Critics* (New York: St. Martin's Press, 1988) 91.

103   Ishmael Reed, *Shrovetide in Old New Orleans* (New York: Doubleday & Company, 1978) 286.

104   See Phyllis Rose, *Josephine Baker*, trans. Liselotte Julius (Wien: Paul Zsolnay Verlag, 1990) 160-61·

105   Cf. Phyllis Rose, *Josephine Baker* 38-43.

106   See Phyllis Rose, *Josephine Baker* 359.

supporting the Civil Rights Movement.[107] While she joins the struggle for changing history , in her private life, she quits shifting partners to turn to the traditional institution of marriage. Cypress' return home to marry reflects Shange's general tendency to place rebellion inside traditional patterns. To her, change must come from within.

Cultural tradition, family values, and modern forms of art as a new way of expressing female solidarity coexist in *Sassafrass, Cypress & Indigo*. Blues and jazz in particular shape the affirmative spirit which advocates a belief in continuity and renewal, when Shange, as a symbol of female communion and power, reunites her characters at the end. After all their solo performances, they return home to take their stand within familial and communal structures. They have gained access to their African American cultural heritage and learned to use it in order to survive spiritually, artistically, and economically. Their music, art, and personal commitments express a historical vision, embracing individuality and creativity in a communal framework which is governed by complex and differing feminine conceptions of time.

---

[107]   Shange, *Sassafrass, Cypress & Indigo* 158.

Afterword

More than any other mode of expression, music has struck a keynote in the development of African American culture from slavery to the contemporary period. From spirituals and blues via jazz to rap, black musical expression has continuously expressed cultural affirmation for African Americans in the United States. For most of them, music not only calls forth aesthetic pleasure; it also provides them with an African American sense of time and a cultural matrix for an orientation in history. Rewriting history from the novelist's point of view, African American writers, on their part, have established a tradition of reference to and borrowings from music in the course of the 20th century. The authors chosen, I hope, represent a fair sample of African American novelists whose historical imagination has been thoroughly influenced by blues and jazz from the Harlem Renaiisance to the present.

Obviously, this study has not been an attempt to chart through all of African American novels displaying the influence of blues and jazz in one way or the other. Rather, it has intended to show a certain movement from modernist to postmodernist forms of writing in the African American novel. As the pattern of influence illustrates, the impact of temporal elements related to music represents a basic guidance for the rendering of history within the literary genre. And it continues to do so, as publications in the late 80s and the 90s document. Among those Xam Cartiér *Be-Bop, Re-Bop* (1987) and *Muse-Echo Blues* (1991), Toni Morrison's *Jazz* (1992), Bebe Moore Campbell's *Your Blues Ain't like Mine* (1992), Djbot Baghostus' *Run* (1993), and Wesley Brown's *Darktown Strutters* (1994) stand forth as significant extensions of the musical paradigm in African American fiction.

According to my analysis of time in music and fiction, two major modes of change accompany the continuous influence of blues and jazz on the novel. Overall there is a movement from the primarily concrete presence of music—on the level of content and character—in early African American modernism to highly abstract adaptations—both formal and cultural—in Ellison's *Invisible Man* and its postmodern successors. The novelists' use of musical time clearly responds to the changes in blues and jazz as musical forms on the one hand; thus they pay tribute to the constant search for renewal in the jazz tradition and the music's concurrency with temporal changes. On the other hand, the writers connect innovations in music with social and cultural concepts effecting and reflecting the role of African Americans within the United States. Hence, aspects of crosscultural phenomena, class, gender, and race shape the way musical elements are appropriated in the novelistic discourse, in the postmodern era in particular. Musical time then interacts with new understandings of temporal processes within the novelists' contribution to the cultural discourse.

For future studies investigating the interrelation of time in music and the African American novel, it should be of interest to explore if blues and jazz will be replaced by more recent expressions of African American music or other musical modes. The traditional forms still exert a very powerful influence upon the African American literary discourse for the time being. Yet, the role of jazz within American culture has entered a new era, so it seems. Although it is not the first time that a revival in jazz takes place, the return of many jazz musicians to the hard bop of the 1950s at present is different from earlier revival movements in the history of blues and jazz. Today a neoclassical style of jazz insisting that genuine jazz must be based upon blues or swing calls forth a canonization and reduction of jazz forms unparalleled before in the history of jazz music. And it is backed up by the music industry. According to Eric Nisenson,

> it is not a crime to revive the hard bop of the 1950s, any more than there was
> anything wrong with reviving New Orleans jazz. But what is wrong is the
> insistence that this music was simply a continuation of the "true" jazz
> tradition. By conceptualizing that tradition as the kind of limiting
> straightjacket against which—as we have seen—jazz musicians have
> rebelled since the very birth of jazz, the neoclassicists are killing the living
> spirit that made jazz so unique, so vital in the creation of a truly American
> culture.[1]

Since a strong backward orientation underlies the current dominance of neoclassical jazz on the music market—Wynton Marsalis being one of the revival's most outspoken supporters—, the question arises if the rediscovery of hard bop can adequately respond to the temporal changes of today's society. The answer is "No!" indeed. With its canonization of past forms neoclassical jazz does not keep up with societal developments at the core of contemporary American culture.

Not surprisingly, then, critical voices have multiplied announcing that jazz may have run its course at the end of the millenium. Outside mainstream neoclassical jazz, though, experiments with musical form and concepts of time continue. Musical innovators from America, Europe, Asia, and Africa expand the African American musical and cultural context in a process of increasing globalization. Accordingly, jazz elements fuse with other forms of folk music such as in the work of Jan Garbarek from Norway. His music—"Twelve Moons", for instance—is frequently a fusion of free jazz, John Coltrane, East Indian and Brazilian rhythms and his native Norwegian folk heritage. Or think of the Lebanese oud player Rabih-Abou Khalil who has produced innovative musical fusions of East and West in his cooperation with Indian musicians and American jazzmen.[2] Clearly, jazz continues to be a vital part of intercultural processes which already marked its very beginnings in the United States. American and African American culture, however, are no longer the only

---

[1] Eric Nisenson, *Blue: The Murder of Jazz* (New York: St. Martin's Press 1997) 242.

[2] Cf. Nisenson, 243-45.

cultural frame for jazz's new developments and its effects upon other art forms. Increasingly, jazz has become an important aspect of musical traditions outside the United States. For the field of American studies and beyond, it is of interest to see if the music's complex rendering of time will also find access to the representation of flux and history in the literary discourse of cultures which do not share the historical background of African Americans.

Bibliography

Achtner, Wolfgang, Stefan Kunz, and Thomas Walter. *Dimensionen* der Zeit: *Die Zeitstrukturen Gottes, der Welt und des Menschen*. Darmstadt: Primus Verlag, 1998.

Andrews, Dwight. "From Black to Blues." *Sacred Music of the Secular City / A Special Issue of Black Sacred Music: A Journal of Theomusicology* (Spring 1992): 45-54.

Baker, Houston A., Jr. *Long Black Song: Essays in Black American Literature and Culture*. Charlottesville: UP of Virginia, 1972.

---, "To Move Without Moving: Creativitiy and Commerce in Ralph Ellison's Trueblood Episode." *Black Literature and Theory*. Ed Henry L. Gates, Jr.. New York: Methuen, 1984. 221-48.

---. *Modernism and the Harlem Renaissance*. Chicago: U of Chicago P, 1987.

---. *The Workings of the Spirit: The Poetics of Afro-American Women's Writing*. Chicago: U of Chicago P, 1991.

Bachtin, Michail M. *Literatur und Karneval: Zur Romantheorie und Lachkultur*. Trans. Alexander Kaempfe. Frankfurt/Main: Fischer Taschenbuch Verlag, 1990.

Bakhtin, M. M. *The Dialogic Imagination: Four Essays by M. M. Bakhtin*. Trans. Caryl Emerson and Michael Holquist. Austin: The U of Texas P, 1994 [1981].

Baraka, Amiri and Amina Baraka. *The Music: Reflections on Jazz and Blues*. New York: William Morrow, 1987.

Beardsley, Monroe C, ed. *The European Philosophers: From Descartes to Nietzsche*. New York: The Modern Library, 1960.

Bell, Roseann P., Bettye J. Parker, and Beverly Guy-Sheftall, eds. *Sturdy Black Bridges: Visions of Black Women in Literature*. New York: Anchor Press, 1979.

Bellamy, Joe David, ed. *The New Fiction: Interviews with Innovative American Writers*. Urbana: U of Illinois P, 1974.

Bender John and David E. Wellbery, eds. *Chronotypes: The Construction of Time*. Stanford: Stanford UP, 1991.

Benston, Kimberley W., ed. *Speaking for You: The Vision of Ralph Ellison.* Washington, D.C.: Howard UP, 1987.

Berendt, Joachim-Ernst. *Das Jazzbuch* Frankfurt/Main: Fischer Verlag, 1991 [1953].

---. *Die Story des Jazz: Vom New Orleans zum Rock Jazz*. Stuttgart: Deutsche Verlagsanstalt, 1975.

---. *Ein Fenster aus Jazz: Essays, Portraits, Reflexionen*. Frankfurt/Main: Fischer Verlag, 1977.

Bhabha, Homi K.. "'Race,' Time and the Revision of Modernity." *Oxford Literary Review* 13.1-2 (1991): 193-219.

---. *The Location of Culture*. London: Routledge, 1994

Bigsby, C. W. E. "Improvising America: Ralph Ellison and the Paradox of Form." *Speaking For You: The Vision of Ellison*. Ed. Kimberly W. Benston. Washington D.C.: Howard UP, 1987. 173-83.

Bjork, Patrick. *The Novels of Toni Morrison: The Search for Self and Place Within the Community*. New York: Lang, 1992.

Blake, Susan L. "Ritual and Rationalization: Black Folklore in the Works of Ralph Ellison." *Ralph Ellison*. Ed. Harold Bloom. New York: Chelsea House Publishers, 1986. 77-99.

Bloom, Harold, ed. *Ralph Ellison*. New York: Chelsea House Publishers, 1986.

. ---. , ed. *Toni Morrison*. New York: Chelsea House Publishers, 1989.

Bobo, Jacqueline. *Black Women as Cultural Readers*. New York: Columbia UP, 1995.

Bock Hedwig, and Albert Weinheim, eds. *Essays on The Contemporary American Novel*. München: Max Hueber Verlag, 1986.

Bohlaender, Carlo. *Die Anatomie des swing*. Frankfurt/Main: Jas publikation, 1986.

Bohlaender, Carlo, and Karl Heinz Holler. *Reclam Jazzfuehrer*. Stuttgart: Reclam Verlag, 1970.

Bolinger, Dwight. *Aspects of Language*. New York: Harcourt Brace Jovanovich, 1975.

Bone, Robert. "Ralph Ellison and the Uses of the Imagination." *Ralph Ellison: A Collection of Critical Essays*. Ed. John Hersey. Englewood Cliffs: Prentice Hall, 1974. 95-114.

Bontemps, Arna. *The Harlem Renaissance Remembered*. New York. Dodd, Mead & Company, 1972.

Bradbury, Malcolm. *The Modern American Novel*. Oxford: Oxford UP, 1983.

---. , ed. *Contemporary American Fiction*. London: Edward Arnold, 1987.

Braxton, Joanne M., and Andrée N. McLaughlin, eds. *Wild Women in the Whirlwind: Afro-American Culture and the Contemporary Literary Renaissance*. New Brunswick: Rutgers UP, 1990.

Bröck, Susanne. "Postmodern Mediations and Beloved's Testimony: Memory Is Not Innocent." *Amerikastudien / American Studies* 43.1 (1998): 33-49.

Bruhn, Herbert and Helmut Rösing. *Musikwissenschaft: Ein Grundkurs*. Reinbek: rowohlts enzyklopädie, 1998.

Byerman, Keith E. *Fingering the Jagged Grain: Form and Tradition in Recent Black Fiction*. Athens, Ga: U of Georgia P, 1986.

---, "Beyond Realism: The Fictions of Toni Morrison." *Toni Morrison*. Ed. Harold Bloom. New York: Chelsea House Publishers, 1989. 52-62.

Calendoli, Giovanni. *Tanz: Kult-Rhythmus-Kunst*. Trans. Johannes Werres. Braunschweig: Westermann, 1986.

Calvino, Italo. *Kybernetik und Gespenster: Überlegungen zu Literatur und Gesellschaft*. Trans. Susanne Schoop. München: Carl Hanser Verlag, 1984.

Campbell, Jane. *Mythic Black Fiction: The Transformation of History*. Knoxville: U of Tennessee P, 1986.

Cataliotti, Robert H. *The Music in African American Fiction*. New York: Garland Publishing, 1995.

Charters, Samuel. *The Bluesmen: The Story and the Music of the Men Who made the Blues*. New York: Oak Publications, 1967.

--- *The Roots of the Blues: An African Search*. New York: Da Capo Press, 1981.

Christensen, A. M. H. *Afro-American Folk Lore*. New York: Negro UP, 1969 [1892].

Christian, Barbara. *Black Women Novelists: The Development of a Tradition, 1892-1976*. Westport, Conn.: Greenwood Press, 1980.

Clark, Vèvè A., Ruth Ellen B. Joeres and Madelon Sprengnether, eds. *Revising the Word and the World: Essays in Feminist Literary Criticism*. Chicago: U of Chicago P, 1993.

Cohn, Lawrence. *Nothing But the Blues: The Music and the Musicians*. New York: Abbeville Press, 1993.

Cooke, Michael G. *Afro-American Literature in the 20th Century: The Achievement of Intimacy*. New Haven: Yale UP, 1984.

Courlander, Harold. *Negro Folk Music U.S.A.*. New York: Columbia UP, 1963.

Danuser, Hermann, Dietrich Kämper, and Paul Terse, eds. *Amerikanische Musik seit Charles Ives: Interpretationen, Quellentexte, Komponistenmonographien*. Laaber: Laaber-Verlag, 1987.

Dauer, Alfons. *Jazz: Die Magische Musik*. Bremen: Carl Schuenemann Verlag, 1961.

Davies, Carole B. *Black Women, Writing and Identity: Migrations of the Subject*. London: Routledge, 1994.

Davis, Angela Y. *Blues Legacies and Black Feminism: Gertrude "Ma" Rainey, Bessie Smith, and Billie Holiday*. New York: Pantheon Books, 1998.

Davis, Francis. *The History of the Blues*. New York: Hyperion, 1995.

Davis, Miles, and Quincy Troupe. *Miles Davis: Die Autobiographie*. Trans. Brigitte Jakobeit. Hamburg: Hoffman und Campe, 1990.

Dawson, Alan, and Don DeMichael. *A Manual for the Modern Drummer*. Boston: Berklee Press, 1962.

Derrida, Jacques. *Of Grammatology*. Trans. Gayatri Spivak.
Baltimore: John Hopkins UP, 1976.

DeVeaux, Scott. *The Birth of Bebop: A Social and Musical History*. Berkeley: U of California P, 1997.

Digel, Werner, and Gerhard Kwiatkowski. *Meyers Grosses Taschenlexikon*. 24 vols. Mannheim: Bibliographisches Institut, 1983.

Dixon, Melvin. *Ride Out the Wilderness: Geography and Identity in Afro-American Literature*. Urbana: U of Illinois P, 1987.

Drake, Clair St., and Horace R. Cayton. *Black Metroplis: A Study of Negro Life in a Modern Community*. New York: Harcourt, Brace & World, Inc., 1945.

Drewry, Henry N., and Drewry Cecelia H., eds. *Afro-American History: Past to Present*. New York: Charles Scribner's Sons, 1971.

DuBois, William E. B.. *Souls of Black Folk,1903: Essays and Sketches*. New York: NAL, 1969.

---. *Souls of Black Folk*. New York: Fawcett Premier Books, 1916.

Ellison, Ralph W. *Invisible Man*. New York: Vintage Books, 1972.

---. *Shadow and Act*. New York: Random House, 1964.

Ellman, Richard, and Robert O'Clair, eds. *The Norton Anthology of Modern Poetry*. New York: W. W. Norton & Company, 1973.

Ensslen, Klaus. *Einführung in die schwarzamerikanische Literatur*. Stuttgart: W. Kohlhammer, 1982.

Erenberg, Lewis A. *Swingin' the Dream: Big Band Jazz and the Rebirth of American Culture*. Chicago: U of Chicago P, 1998.

Erzgräber, Willi. *Utopie und Antiutopie in der englischen Literatur: Morus Morris Wells Huxley Orwell*. München: Wilhelm Fink, 1980.

Faber, Anne. *Louis Armstrong*. Hamburg: Cecilie Dressler Verlag, 1977.

Finn, Julio. *The Bluesman: The Musical Heritage of Black Men and Women in the Americas*. London: Quartet Books, 1986.

Fitzgerald, Ella. *New York: Recordings 1943-50*. Delta Music GmbH 57 554-8, 1991.

Ferris, William. *Blues from the Delta*. Garden City, New York: Anchor Press / Doubleday, 1979

Ferstl, Erich. *Die Schule des Jazz mit 104 Notenbeispielen*. München: Nymphenburger Verlagshandlung, 1963.

Filtgen, Gerd, and Michael Außerbauer. *John Coltrane*. Gauting: Oreos Collection Jazz, 1983.

Fisher, Dexter and Robert B. Stepto, eds. *Afro-American Literature: The Reconstruction of Instruction*. New York: The Modern Language Association, 1979.

Frankenberg, Ruth. *White Women, Racial Matters: The Social Construction of Whiteness*. Minneapolis: U of Minnesota P, 1993.

Frye, Northrop. *Anatomy of Criticism*. New York: Atheneum, 1966.

Furman, Jan. *Toni Morrison's Fiction*. Columbia: U of South Carolina P, 1996.

Gabbard, Krin, ed. *Representing Jazz*. Durham: Duke UP, 1995.

Garon, Paul. *Blues and the Poetic Spirit*. New York: A Da Capo Paperback Press, 1979.

Gates, Henry L., Jr., ed. *Black Literature and Literary Theory*. New York: Methuen, 1984.

---. *The Signifying Monkey: A Theory of African-American Literary Criticism*. New York: Oxford UP, 1988.

Gates, Henry L., Jr., and K. A. Appiah, eds. *Langston Hughes: Critical Perspectives Past and Present*. New York: Amistad, 1993.

Gayle, Addison, Jr., ed. *The Black Aesthetic*. New York: Anchor Books, 1972.

Gioia, Ted. *The Imperfect Art: Reflections on Jazz and Modern Culture*. New York: Oxford UP, 1988.

Gillespie, Dizzy. *Paris Concert*. GNP Cresecendo Records 9006, 1972.

Gover, Robert. "An Interview with Ishmael Reed." *Black American Literature Forum* 12/1 (1978): 12-19.

Grahl, Helmut. *Die Folkblues Gitarre*. Frankfurt/Main: Tenuto-Musik-Edition, 1976.

Harper, Michael S., and Robert B. Stepto, eds. *Chant of Saints: A Gathering of Afro-American Literature, Art, and Scholarship*. Urbana: U of Illinois P, 1979.

Harris, Norman. "Politics as an Innovative Aspect of Literary Folklore: A Study of Ishmael Reed." *Obsidian* 5 (1979): 41-50.

Harrison, Daphne D. *Black Pearls: Blues Queens of the 1920s*. Brunswick: Rutgers UP, 1988.

Hegel, G. W. F. "Introduction to the Philosophy of History." *The European Philosophers: From Descartes to Nietzsche*. Ed. Monroe C. Beardsley. New York: The Modern Library, 1960. 537-608.

Heinz, Denis. The Dilemma of "Double-Consciousness": *Toni Morrison's Novels*. Athens: U of Georgia P, 1993.

Hellhund, Herbert. "Jazz: Traditionslinien zwischen Folklore, Kommerz und Kunst." *Amerikanische Musik seit Charles Ives: Interpretatationen, Quellentexte, Komponistenmonographien*. Eds. Herman Danuser, Dietrich Kämper, and Paul Terse. Laaber: Laaber-Verlag, 1987. 39-49.

Hersey, John, ed. *Ralph Ellison: A Collection of Critical Essays*. Englewood Cliffs: Prentice-Hall, Inc., 1974.

Hoffmann, Gerhard. *Raum, Situation, erzählte Wirklichkeit: Poetologische und historische Studien zum englischen und amerikanischen Roman*. Stuttgart Metzler, 1978.

Holloway, Karla F.C., and Stephanie A. Demetrakopoulos. *New Dimensions Of Spirituality: A Biracial and Bicultural Reading of the Novels of Toni Morrison*. New York: Greenwood Press, 1987.

Hornung, Alfred. "Postmoderne bis zur Gegenwart." *Amerikanische Literaturgeschichte*. Ed. Hubert Zapf. Stuttgart: Metzler, 1997. 257-304.

Hornung-Fischer, Dorothea. *Folklore and Myth in Ralph Ellison's Early Works*. Diss., U Heidelberg, 1979. Stuttgart: Hochschulverlag, 1979.

Hughes, Langston. *Not Without Laughter*. New York: Macmillan Publishing Company, 1967.

Huke, Thomas. *Jazz und Blues im afroamerikanischen Roman*. Erlangen: Hochschulverlag, 1990.

Hunter-Lattany, Kristin. "The Girl With the Red Dress On." *Langston Hughes: The Man, His Art and His Continuing Influence*. Ed. C. James Trotman. New York: Garland Publishing, 1995. 141-48.

Hurston, Zora Neale. *Mules and Men*. Bloomington: Indiana UP, 1963 [1935].

---. *Their Eyes Were Watching God*. Urbana: U of Illinois P, 1978 [1937].

Hyme, Kathryn. "Ishmael Reed and the Problematics of Control" *PMLA* 108 (1993): 506-18.

Isaacs, Harold R. *The New World of Negro Americans*. New York: The John Day Company, Inc., 1963.

Jones Bessie W., and Bess Lomax Hawes. *Step It Down: Games, Plays, Songs, and Stories from the Afro-American Heritage*. Athens: U of Georgia P, 1972.

Jones, Bessie W., and Audrey L. Vinson. *The World of Toni Morrison: Explorations in Literary Criticism*. Dubuque, Iowa: Kendall/Hunt Publishing Company, 1985.

Jones, Gayl. *Liberating Voices: Oral Tradition in African-American Literature*. Cambridge: Harvard UP, 1991.

Jones, LeRoi. *Blues People: Negro Music in White America*. New York: Morrow & Company, 1968.

Jones, Max, and John Chilton. *Die Louis Armstrong Story*. Trans. Karl Ludwig Nicol. Freiburg: Herder, 1972.

Jongh, James D. *Vicious Modernism: Black Harlem and the Literary Imagination*. New York: Cambridge UP, 1990.

Jost, Ekkehart. *Sozialgeschichte des Jazz in den USA*. Frankfurt/Main: Fischer Verlag, 1982.

Kammen, Michael. *Meadows of Memory: Images of Time and Tradition in American Art and Culture*. Austin: U of Texas P, 1992.

Kant, Immanuel. *Observations on the Feelings of the Beautiful and the Sublime*. Trans. John T. Goldthwait. Berkeley: U of California P, 1960.

Keil, Charles. *Urban Blues*. Chicago: U of Chicago P, 1991 [1966].

Klostermann, Berthold. *Blue Notes-Black Fiction: Schwarze Musik in der afroamerikanischen Erzählliteratur der zwanziger und dreißiger Jahre*. Trier: Wissenschaftlicher Verlag Trier, 1993.

Kristeva, Julia. "Women's Time." *The Kristeva Reader*. Trans. Alice Jardine and Harry Blake. Ed. Toril Moi. Oxford: Blackwell Publishers, 1992. 188-213.

---. "Word, Dialogue and Novel." *The Kristeva Reader*. 34-61.

Kubitschek Missy D. *Toni Morrison: A Critical Companion*. Westport: Greenwood Press, 1998.

Lee, Valerie. *Granny Midwives & Black Women Writers. Double-Dutched Readings*. New York: Routledge, 1996.

Leitch, Vincent B. *Deconstructive Criticism*. New York: Columbia UP, 1983.

Lenz, Günter H. "Ishmael Reed." *Essays on the Contemporary American Novel*. Eds. Hedwig Bock and Albert Weinheim. München: Max Hueber Verlag, 1986. 305-34.

Levine, Lawrence W. *Black Culture and Consciousness: Afro-American Folk Thought from Slavery to Freedom*. New York: Oxford UP, 1977.

Lewis, David Levering. *When Harlem Was in Vogue*. New York: Vintage 1982.

Litweiler, John. *The Freedom Principle: Jazz after 1958*. New York: William Morrow & Company, Inc., 1984.

Lomax, Alan. *The Land Where the Blues Began*. London: Minerva, 1995 [1993].

Lovell, John, Jr. *Black Song: The Forge and the Flame*. New York: The Macmillan Company, 1972.

Major, Clarence, ed. *The New Black Poetry*. New York: International Publications, 1969.

Martin, Reginald. *Ishmael Reed and the New Black Aesthetic Critics*. New York: St. Martin's Press, 1988.

Mbalia, Doroeatha. *Toni Morrison's Developing Class Consciousness*. Selingsgrove: Susquehanna UP, 1991.

McKay, Nellie. "Toni Morrison: Interview." *Contemporary Literature* 24 (Winter 1983): 413-29.

McSweeney, Kerry. *Invisible Man: Race and Identity*. Boston: Twayne Publishers, 1988.

Mezzrow, Mezz, and Bernard Wolfe. *Really the Blues*. New York: Random House, 1946.

Migner, Karl. *Theorie des modernen Romans*. Stuttgart: Alfred Kröner Verlag, 1970.

Miller, Nancy K., ed. *The Poetics of Gender*. New York: Columbia UP, 1986.

Miller, R. Baxter. *The Art and the Imagination of Langston Hughes*. Lexington: The U of Kentucky P, 1989.

Moeckel-Rieke, Hannah. "Introduction: Media and Cultural Memory." *Amerikastudien / American Studies* 43.1 (1998): 5-17.

Moi, Toril, ed. *The Kristeva Reader*. Oxford: Blackwell Publishers, 1986.

Morrison, Toni. *Song of Solomon*. New York: Signet Books, 1977.

Naylor, Gloria. "A Conversation, Gloria Naylor and Toni Morrison." *Southern Review* 21 (1985): 567-593.

Nisenson, Eric. *Blue: The Murder of Jazz*. New York: St. Martin's Press, 1997.

Oakley, Giles. *The Devil's Music: A History of the Blues*. New York: Harcourt Brace Jovanovich Inc., 1976.

Obrecht, Jas, ed. *Blues Guitar: The Men Who Made the Music*. San Francisco: Miller Freeman Books, 1993.

Ogren, Kathy. *The Jazz Revolution: Twenties America & the Meaning of Jazz*. New York: Oxford UP, 1989.

---, "Controversial Sounds: Jazz Performance as Theme and Language in the Harlem Renaissance." *The Harlem Renaissance: Revaluations*. Eds. Amritjit Singh, William S. Shiver, Stanley Brodwin. New York: Garland Publishing, 1995. 159-84.

Oliver, Paul. *Screening the Blues: Aspects of the Blues Tradition*. New York: Da Capo Press, 1968.

---. *Blues Fell This Morning: Meaning in the Blues*. Cambridge: Cambridge UP, 1993 [1960].

O'Meally, Robert, ed. *New Essays on Invisible Man*. New York: Cambridge UP, 1988.

---, ed. *The Jazz Cadence of American Culture*. New York: Columbia UP, 1998.

Ostendorf, Berndt. "Ralph Waldo Ellison: Anthropology, Modernism, and Jazz." *New Essays on Invisible Man*. Ed. Robert Meally. Cambridge: Cambridge UP, 1988. 95-121.

---, ed. *Multikulturelle Gesellschaft: Modell Amerika?*. München: Wilhelm Fink Verlag, 1994.

Ostriker, Alicia. "The Thieves of Language: Women Poets and Revisionist Mythmaking." *The New Feminist Criticism: Essays on Women, Literature and Theory*. Ed. Elaine Showalter. London: Virago Press, 1986. 314-38.

Owens, Thomas. *Bebop: The Music and Its Players*. New York: Oxford UP, 1995.

Oxford Advanced Learner's Dictionary of Current English. London: Oxford UP, 1974.

Palmer, Robert. *Deep Blues*. London: Penguin Books, 1981.

Panassie, Hugues. *The Real Jazz*. New York: Smith and Durrel, 1942.

Panish, Jon. *The Color of Jazz: Race and Representation in Postwar American Culture*. Jackson: UP of Mississippi, 1997.

Parsons, Elsie C. *Folk-Lore of the Sea Islands, South Carolina*. New York: The American Folk-Lore Society, 1923.

Peterson, Nancy J. *Toni Morrison: Critical and Theoretical Approaches*. Baltimore: The John Hopkins UP, 1997.

Plessen, Elisabeth. *Fakten und Erfindungen*. Frankfurt am Main: Ullstein Materialien, 1981.

Polillo, Arrigo. *Jazz: Geschichte und Persönlichkeiten*. Trans. Egino Biagoni. München: F.A. Herbig, 1991 [1975].

Rampersad, Arnold. "Langston Hughes and Approaches to Modernism in the Harlem Renaissance." *The Harlem Renaissance: Revaluations*. Eds. Amritjit Singh, William S. Shiver and Stanley Brodwin. New York: Garland. 49-72.

Rawick, George P. *From Sundown to Sunup: The Making of the Black Community*. Westport: Greenwood Publishing, 1972.

Record, Wilson. "The NAACP and the Communist Party." *Afro-American History: Past to Present*. Eds. Henry Drewry and Cecelia Drewry. New York: Charles Scribner's Sons, 1971. 414-20.

Reed, Ishmael. *Conjure*. Amherst: U of Massachusetts P, 1972.

---. *Mumbo Jumbo*. New York: Avon Books, 1972.

---. *The Last Days of Louisiana Red*. New York: Avon Books, 1976.

---. *Yellow-Back Radio Broke-Down*. New York: Doubleday, 1969.

---. *Shrovetide in New Orleans*. New York: Doubleday, 1978.

Reilly, John M., ed. *Twentieth Century Interpretations of* Invisible Man: *A Collection of Critical Essays*. Englewood Cliffs, New Jersey: Prentice Hall, 1970.

Richter, Stephan. *Zu einer Ästhetik des Jazz*. Frankfurt/Main: Peter Lang Europäische Hochschulschriften, 1995.

Roach, Hilda. *Black American Music: Past and Present Vol I*. Malabar: Krieger Publishing Company, Inc., 1985.

Rodgers Lawrence R. *Canaan Bound: The African-American Great Migration Novel*. Urbana: U of Illinois P, 1997.

Roesing, Helmut. "Interkultureller Musikaustausch." *Musikwissenschaft: Ein Grundkurs*. Eds. Herbert Bruhn and Helmut Roesing. Reinbek: rowohlts enzyklopädie, 1998. 289-310.

Rose, Phyllis. *Josephine Baker*. Trans. Liselotte Julius. Wien: Paul Zsolnay Verlag. 1990.

Rosenberg, Christina. *Handbuch für Jazz Dance*. Aachen: Meyer und Meyer, 1995.

Ruland, Hans. *Duke Ellington*. Gauting-Buchendorf: Oreos Verlag, 1983.

Russel, Ross. *Jazz Style in Kansas City and the Southwest*. Berkeley: U of California P, 1971.

Russel, Sandi. *Render Me My Song: African-American Women Writers from Slavery to the Present*. New York: St. Martin's Press, 1990.

Samuels, Wilfred D., and Clenora Hudson-Weems, *Toni Morrison*. Boston: Twayne Publishers, 1990.

Schultz, Elisabeth. "The Novels of Toni Morrison: Studies of the Individual and the Neighborhood." *Essays on the Contemporary American Novel*. Eds. Hedwig Bock, and Albert Weinheim. München: Max Hueber Verlag, 1986. 281-304.

Schwerfel, Peter. "Mister Multikult." *Zeitmagazin* 17 (1992): 61-64.

Sekoni, Ropo. "Africanisms and Postmodernist Imagination in the Popular Fiction of Langston Hughes." *Langston Hughes: The Man, His Art, and His Continuing Influence*. Ed. C. James Trotman. New York: Garland Publishing, 1995. 63-73.

Shange, Ntozake. *Sassafrass, Cypress & Indigo*. New York: St. Martin's Press, 1982.

---. *SeeNoEvil. Prefaces, Essays & Accounts 1976-83*. San Francisco: Momo's Press, 1984.

Shaw, Arnold. *Black Popular Music in America*. New York: Macmillan, 1986.

Showalter, Elaine, ed. *The New Feminist Critcism: Essays on Women, Literature and Theory*. London: Virago Press, 1986.

Singh, Amritjit, William S. Shiver, and Stanley Brodwin, eds. *The Harlem Renaissance: Revaluations*. New York: Garland Publishing, 1989.

Snead, James A. "Repetition as a Figure of Black Culture." *Black Literature and Literary Theory*, Ed. Henry L. Gates, Jr. New York: Methuen, 1984. 59-79.

Spencer, Jon M. *Blues and Evil*. Knoxville: The U of Tennessee P, 1993.

Spillers, Hortense. "Ellison's Usable Past: Toward a Theory of Myth." *Speaking For You: The Vision of Ralph Ellison*. Ed. Kimberly W. Benston. Washington D.C.: Howard UP, 1987. 144-158.

Stearns, Marshall W. *The Story of Jazz*. New York: Oxford UP, 1970 [1956].

Stepto, Robert B. *From Behind the Veil: A Study of Afro- American Narrative*. Urbana: U of Illinois P, 1979.

Stepto Robert, and Michael Harper, eds. *Chant of Saints: A Gathering of Afro-American Literature, Art, and Scholarship* (Urbana: U of Illinois P, 1979.

Tanner, Tony. "The Music of Invisibility." *Ralph Ellison*. Ed. Harold Bloom. New York: Chelsea House Publishers, 1986. 37-50.

Tate, Claudia, ed. *Black Women Writers At Work*. New York: Continuum, 1983.

Terdiman, Richard. *Present Past: Modernity and the Memory Crisis*. Ithaka: Cornell UP, 1993.

Tracy, Steven C. *Langston Hughes & The Blues*. Urbana: U of Illinois P, 1988

---, "To the Tune of Those Weary Blues." *Langston Hughes: Critical Perspectives Past and Present*. Eds. Henry L. Gates Jr. And K. A. Appiah. New York: Amistad, 1993. 69-93.

---, "Langston Hughes: Poetry, Blues, and Gospel—Somewhere to Stand." *Langston Hughes: The Man, His Art, and His Continuing Influence*. Ed. C. James Trotman. New York. Garland Publishing, 1995. 51-61.

Trotman, James C. *Langston Hughes: The Man, His Art, and his Continuing Influence*. New York: Garland Publishing, 1995.

Viera, Joe. *Jazz: Musik unserer Zeit*. Schaftlach: Oreos Collection Jazz, 1992.

Von Schiers, Mattias Ludwig. *Concrete Language: Intercultural Communication and Identity in Maxine Hong Kingston's The Woman Warrior and Ishmael Reed's Mumbo Jumbo*. Diss. Universität Bern, 1994.

Wall, Cheryl. "Whose Sweet Angel Child? Blues Women, Langston Hughes, and Writing During the Harlem Renaissance." *Langston Hughes: The Man, His Art, and His Continuing Influence*. Ed. C. James Trotman. New York: Garland Publishing, 1995. 37-50.

Walser, Robert, ed. *Keeping Time: Readings in Jazz History*. New York: Oxford UP, 1999.

Ward, Jerry D. "Bridges and Deep Water." *Sturdy Black Bridges: Visions of Black Women in Literature*. Eds. Roseann P. Bell, Bettye J. Parker, and Beverly Guy-Sheftall. New York: Anchor Press, 1979. 184-90.

Washington, Booker T. *Up from Slavery: An Autobiography*. New York: Doubleday & Company, Inc., 1933.

Wegs, Joyce. "Toni Morrison's Song of Solomon: A Blues Song." *Essays in Literature 9*, no. 2 (Fall 1982): 211-23.

Wellek, René, and Austin Warren. *A Theory of Literature*. New York: Harcourt, Brace & World, Inc., 1956.

Werner, Craig. "The Insurrection of Subjugated Knowledge: Poe and Ishmael Reed." *Poe and Our Times: Influences and Affinities*. Ed. Benjamin Franklin Fisher IV. Baltimore: The Edgar Allan Poe Society, 1986. 144-56.

---. "Recent Books on Modern Black Fiction: An Essay-Review." *Modern Fiction Studies*, Vol 34, Number 1, Spring 1988, 125-35.

---. *Playing the Changes: From Afro-Modernism to the Jazz Impulse*. Urbana: U of Illinois P, 1994.

Werner, Otto. *The Origin and Development of Jazz*. Dubuque: Kendall/Hunt, 1984.

Werther, Iron. *Bebop*. Frankfurt/Main: Fischer Verlag, 1988.

Wicke, Peter, and Wieland Ziegenruecker. *Sachlexikon Populaermusik*. Leipzig: Deutsche
    Verlagsgesellschaft, 1987.

Williams, Martin. *The Jazz Tradition*. New York: Oxford UP, 1993 [1970].

Willis Susan A. "Eruptions of funk: historicizing Toni Morrison." *Black Literature and Theory*. Ed.
    Henry L. Gates, Jr. New York: Methuen, 1984. 263-83.

Wilson, Peter N. and Ulfert Goeman. *Charlie Parker*. Schaftlach: Oreos Verlag, 1988.

Young, Robert. *Intercultural Communication: Pragmatics, Genealogy, Deconstruction.* Clevedon:
    Multilingual Matters LTD, 1996.

Zagarell, Sandra A. "Narrative of Community: The Identification of a Genre." *Revising the Word and
    the World: Essays in Feminist Literary Criticism*. Eds. Vèvè A. Clark, Ruth-Ellen B. Joeres,
    and Madelon Sprengnether. Chicago: U of Chicago P, 1993. 249-278.